Ida Pfeiffer, Henry William Dulcken

The Last Travels of Ida Pfeiffer

Inclusive of a Visit to Madagascar

Ida Pfeiffer, Henry William Dulcken

The Last Travels of Ida Pfeiffer
Inclusive of a Visit to Madagascar

ISBN/EAN: 9783337112028

Printed in Europe, USA, Canada, Australia, Japan

Cover: Foto ©Andreas Hilbeck / pixelio.de

More available books at **www.hansebooks.com**

THE

LAST TRAVELS

OF

IDA PFEIFFER:

INCLUSIVE OF A VISIT TO MADAGASCAR.

WITH

An Autobiographical Memoir of the Author.

TRANSLATED BY H. W. DULCKEN.

NEW YORK:

HARPER & BROTHERS, PUBLISHERS,

FRANKLIN SQUARE.

1861.

PREFACE.

It was at Buenos Ayres that I received the intelligence of the death of my beloved mother. Shortly before her decease she had expressed the wish that I should arrange and prepare for publication the papers she left concerning her last voyage to Madagascar. The dangerous illness which befell her in the Mauritius immediately after she had left Madagascar, and which, in spite of the most careful medical attention, and the kindest nursing on the part of her friends, proved fatal, prevented her from doing this herself.

When, after a few months, I returned from Buenos Ayres to Rio de Janeiro, I found my mother's papers waiting for me there; but the loss was too recent, and my grief too violent, to allow me to read them then, much less to peruse them with the care and attention which must necessarily precede their publication.

At length I made up my mind to the task. I was obliged to go through it, for it was my mother's last wish. Filial duty induced me to leave my dear mother's journal as little altered as possible. In thus giving this last work of my mother to the world, I trust that our kind readers will receive it with the indulgence they have so frequently extended to the other works of the late enterprising traveler.

OSCAR PFEIFFER.

Rio de Janeiro, July 8th, 1860.

CONTENTS.

CHAPTER VII.

CHAPTER VIII.

CHAPTER IX.

CHAPTER X.

CHAPTER XI.

CHAPTER XII.

CHAPTER XIII.

CHAPTER XIV.

CHAPTER XV.

CHAPTER XVI.

A BIOGRAPHY OF IDA PFEIFFER

(COMPILED FROM NOTES LEFT BY HERSELF).

SEVERAL biographies of Ida Pfeiffer are already scattered through various encyclopædias and periodicals. These
are based partly on oral communications made by the deceased lady, partly on particulars collected from her friends.
No authentic sketch of her life has, however, yet been published, though many whose sympathy has accompanied the
dauntless voyager on her dangerous way will doubtless be
glad to hear something of the earlier life of Ida Pfeiffer.
In remarkable people, the germs of extraordinary faculties
are generally recognizable in early youth; and those readers who have followed the course of a remarkable life from
its meridian to its close will doubtless be gratified by the
opportunity of casting a glance backward to its early years,
when the seeds of future distinction were sown.

This consideration will probably be thought a sufficient
justification for publishing the following pages; the more
so as the facts given in this biographical sketch rest exclusively on the authority of the heroine herself. Madame
Ida Pfeiffer left behind her a short outline of her life written by her own hand, and her family very courteously permitted this manuscript to be used. It is to be followed by
a summary of her travels, and by her diary in Madagascar,
to which her son, Mr. Oscar Pfeiffer, has added the narrative
of her sufferings and death. Thus the whole career of the
late adventurous pilgrim, with particular reference to the
latest circumstances of her checkered life, namely, her in-

A 2

teresting and eventful voyage to Madagascar, will be placed before the reader.

Our traveler was born in Vienna on the **14th of** October, 1797. She was the third child of **the** wealthy merchant Reyer, and at her baptism received the name Ida Laura. Till she was nine years old, all the family in her parents' house, except herself, **were** boys, so that she was the only girl among a party of six children. Through continual intercourse with her brothers, **a** great predilection for **the games and pursuits** of **boys** was developed in her. "I was **not shy,**" she says of herself, "but wild as a boy, and bolder **and** more forward than my elder brothers;" and she adds **that it** was her **greatest pleasure** to romp with the boys, to **dress in** their **clothes, and to take** part in all their mad pranks. The parents **not only** abstained from putting any check on this tendency, **but** even allowed the **girl to wear** boy's clothes, so that little **Ida** looked with sovereign contempt upon dolls and **toy** saucepans, and would only **play** with drums, swords, guns, and similar playthings. Her father seems to have looked with complacency upon **this** anomaly **in** her character. He jestingly promised **the girl** that he would have her educated for an officer in a military school, thus indirectly encouraging the child to a display **of** courage, resolution, and contempt of danger. Ida did **not fail** to cultivate these qualities, and her most ardent **wish was** to carve her own way through the world, sword **in** hand. Even **in** her early childhood she gave many proofs of fearlessness and self-command.

Mr. Reyer had peculiar ideas on the subject of education, and carried out these notions strictly in his family circle. He was a very honest, and, moreover, strict man, holding the opinion that youth should be carefully guarded against excess, and taught to moderate its desires and wishes; consequently, his children were fed on simple, almost a parsimonious diet, and were taught to sit quietly at table, and see their elders enjoy the various dishes that were served up, without receiving a share of those dainties. The little people were, moreover, forbidden to express their wish for any much-coveted plaything by repeated requests. The father's strictness of discipline went so far as to induce him to refuse many of the children's reasonable requests, in order, as he said, to accustom them to disappointments. Opposition of any kind he would never allow, and even remonstrances against a discipline that bordered on harshness were always unavailing.

There is no doubt that the old gentleman carried his system to excess, but it is equally certain that, but for this Spartan education, little Ida would never have ripened into the fearless traveler, able to bear the heaviest fatigue for months together, living meanwhile on the most miserable food. The chief characteristics of Ida Pfeiffer's courage, endurance, and indifference to pain and hardship became developed by an eccentric course of education, which would hardly find a defender at a time like the present, when every thing peculiar is hastily condemned. The unusual, with its sharp outlines and deep shadows, disappears more and more in the light of common-sense mediocrity, and the characteristic heads that we remember in our youth gradually disappear, and are succeeded by very rational, but somewhat tedious and commonplace figures.

Ida's father died in the year 1806, leaving a widow and seven children. The boys were in an educational institution, and the mother undertook the education of the girl, who was now nearly nine years old. Though the father had appeared formidable to the children by his strictness, his rule appeared to the girl far preferable to the melancholy *régime* of her mother, who watched the child's every movement with suspicion and alarm, and caused her daughter to spend many a bitter hour, merely from an exaggerated notion of duty.

A few months after her father's death the first attempt was made to deprive the girl of the attire she had hitherto worn, and substituted petticoats for their masculine equivalents. Little Ida, then ten years old, was so indignant at this measure that she absolutely fell ill from grief and indignation. By the doctor's advice her former costume was restored to her, and it was resolved that the girl's obstinacy must gradually be **subdued** by remonstrance.

The boy's **garments were** received by Ida with a burst **of** enthusiasm, **her health** returned, and she behaved more like **a** boy than ever. **She** learned every thing that she **thought** a boy **should** know with industry and zeal, and, **on the** other hand, looked with the greatest contempt on every female occupation. Piano-forte playing, for instance, she despised as a feminine accomplishment, and would actually cut her fingers, or **burn** them with sealing-wax, **to** escape the hated task **of** practicing. For playing **the violin,** on the contrary, she showed a great predilection. But her mother **would not** allow her to have her way in this **matter,** and the piano-forte was formally subsidized and **maintained** at its post by maternal authority.

When the year 1809 came, a most eventful period for Austria, Ida was twelve years old. **From** what has been said of her ideas and inclinations, it will readily be believed **that** she took great interest in the fortunes of the war. She **read** the newspaper eagerly, and often traced out on the map the relative positions of the two armies. She danced and shouted with glee, like a good patriot, when the Austrians conquered, and wept bitter tears when the fortune of war brought victory to the enemy's standard. Her mother's house was situated in one of **the** busiest streets of the capital; and the frequent marching past of troops caused many interruptions to study, and gave many opportunities for the expression of ardent wishes that the Austrian banners might triumph. When Ida, looking from the window, saw her fellow-countrymen march past to battle, she would vehemently deplore her youth that prevented her from taking part in the impending struggle. She considered her youth the only obstacle that prevented her from going to war.

Unhappily, the French were victorious; the enemy entered the capital, and the affairs of Austria were in a very bad way. The little patriot had the mortification of seeing a number of the hated conquerors quartered in her mother's house, and evidently considering themselves masters of the situation—dining at the table with the family, and expecting to be treated with the most anxious civility. The members of the household generally thought it best to keep up an appearance of friendship toward the conquerors, but nothing could induce the girl to look at the Frenchmen with favor; on the contrary, she showed her feelings by obstinacy and silence; and when requested by the Frenchmen to express her sentiments, she broke out in words of passionate anger and dislike. She herself has said on this subject, "My hatred to Napoleon was so great, that I looked upon the attempt of the notorious Staps to assassinate him at Schönbrunn as a highly meritorious action, and considered the perpetrator, who was tried by a court-martial and shot, in the light of a martyr. I thought if I myself could murder Napoleon, I should not hesitate one instant to do so."

It is related that Ida was compelled to be present at a review of his troops held by Napoleon in Schönbrunn. When the hated emperor rode past, the girl turned her back, and received a box on the ear for her demonstrativeness from her mother, who then held her by the shoulders lest she should repeat the trick. But nothing was gained by this manœuvre, for when the emperor came riding back with his glittering staff of marshals around him, Miss Ida resolutely closed her eyes.

At the age of thirteen she again dressed in female attire, and this time the change was persevered in. She had indeed become sensible enough to acknowledge the necessity of the measure, but still it cost her many tears, and made her very unhappy. With the garb of her sex, she was also obliged to adopt different manners and occupations, and a new system of life. "How awkward and clumsy I was at first!" she exclaims, in her diary; "how ridiculous I must have looked in my long skirts, jumping and racing about, and behaving generally like a wild, restless boy!"

"Fortunately, a young man came to us at that time as tutor, who took particular pains with me. I afterward heard that my mother had given him secret directions to treat me with especial indulgence, as a child whose earliest impulses had received a wrong bias. He certainly behaved to me with great kindness and delicacy, and showed great patience and perseverance in combating my overstrained and misdirected notions. As I had learned rather to fear my parents than to love them, and he was, so to speak, the first human being who had displayed affection and sympathy toward me, I clung to him, in return, with enthusiastic attachment, seeking to fulfill his every wish, and never so happy as when he appeared satisfied with my endeavors. He conducted my entire education; and though it cost me some tears to give up my youthful visions, and busy myself with pursuits I had looked upon with contempt, I did it out of affection for him. I even learned many female occupations, such as sewing, knitting, and cookery. I owe to him the insight I received in three or four years into the duties of my sex; and he it was who changed me from a wild hoydenish creature into a modest girl."

At the period when Ida was compelled to give up her boyish character, there arose in her the first wish to see the world. She turned her thoughts from war and soldiering to fix them upon travel; descriptions of voyages excited her warmest interest, and literature of this kind occupied in her mind the place that, in the majority of young girls' heads, is filled with thoughts of dress, balls, theatres, and amusements generally. When she heard of any one who had attained celebrity by travel, she would grieve to think that she was debarred by her sex from the happiness of ever crossing the sea and exploring strange lands. Often she felt an inclination to occupy herself with scientific studies; but she always suppressed it, seeming to recognize therein a relapse into the "extravagant ideas" of earlier days. It must be remembered that at the beginning of the present century the daughters of middle-class families did not enjoy the education they receive now.

An important passage in the life of Ida Pfeiffer shall be related in her own words. She tells us:

"In my seventeenth year a wealthy Greek proposed for my hand. My mother declined to entertain his offer because he was not a Catholic, and she thought me too young for such a step. According to her ideas, it was indecorous for a girl under twenty years of age to marry.

"A great change now took place in my character. I had hitherto had no idea of the powerful passion which makes mortals the happiest or the most miserable of beings. When my mother told me of the proposal made to her, feelings of which till then I had been unconscious became clearly defined within me, and I felt that I could love no one but T——, the guide of my youth.

"I was not aware that T—— was attached to me with his whole soul. I scarcely knew my own feelings, and far less was I capable of guessing those of another person. When, however, T—— heard of the proposal that had been made for me, and when the possibility of losing me arose before him, he confessed his love to me, and determined to urge his suit to my mother.

"T—— had devoted himself to the Civil Service, and

had for some years occupied a post, with a salary on which
he could live very **well.** He had long given up the profession **of a** tutor, though he continued **to** visit our house as
frequently **as** ever, passing all his leisure hours with us, as
if he belonged to the family. My five brothers were **his**
friends, and my mother was so fond of him that she often
called him ' her dear sixth son.' He was at every party
in our house, and went with us wherever we accepted an
invitation; **always** accompanying us to theatres, in our
walks, and **so on.** **What** was more natural than that we
should both **persuade** ourselves that my mother had intend-
ed us for each other, and would perhaps only stipulate for
our waiting till **I** had attained my twentieth year, and T——
had a better appointment?

" Accordingly he proposed for **my hand.**

" But who **can** paint our grievous surprise **when my**
mother not only **entirely** refused her consent, but from **this**
moment detested T—— just as much as she had **before**
liked him. There could be no other objection **to T——**
except that I could look forward to having **a tolerable for-**
tune, while T—— had at present nothing but his modest
salary. **If my** mother could have imagined what was one
day **to** become of my fortune, how very different my fate
would be from what she had sketched out for me in her
mind, what deep sorrow and endless grief might she not
have spared me!

" After T——'s proposal, my mother wished to get me
married as quickly as possible. I declared resolutely that
I would become T——'s wife, or remain unmarried. T——
was, of course, forbidden to come to our house, and as my
mother knew how obstinately I adhered to my resolutions
when I was in earnest about a matter, she took **me** to a
priest, who was enjoined to explain to me the duty of children toward **their** parents, and particularly the obedience
the latter are authorized to exact. They wanted to bind

me by a solemn oath, **sworn on** the crucifix, that **I would** not see T—— secretly, nor correspond with **him.** I refused to take the oath, but gave the required promise, stipulating, however, that I should be allowed to inform T—— of every thing. My mother at last made this concession, and I wrote a long letter to T——, acquainting him with every thing, and begging him not to believe any thing he heard concerning me from other people. I added that it **was out** of my power either to see him or to write to him **again,** but that if another suitor presented himself and was accepted by my mother, I would at once inform T—— of the circumstance.

"T——'s reply was short, and full of bitter sorrow. He seemed to understand that, under the circumstances, there was no hope for us, and that nothing remained but to obey my mother's commands. He declared positively, however, that he would never marry.

"And thus our correspondence closed. **Three long, sor**rowful years passed away without my seeing him, and without any change in my feelings or position.

"Walking one day with a friend of my mother's, I met T—— by chance. We both stopped involuntarily, but for a long time neither he nor I could utter a word. At last **he conquered** his emotion, and asked after my health. I **was too** deeply moved **to be** able **to reply.** My knees trembled, and I felt ready to sink into the earth. I seized my companion by the arm and drew her away with me, and rushed home, scarcely conscious of what I was doing. Two days afterward I was stretched on my couch in a burning fever.

"The physician who was called in seemed to have a suspicion of the cause of my illness, and declared to my mother, as I **afterward** heard, that the source of evil was mental, **not bodily; that** medicines would be of little avail in my **case, and that every** effort must be directed . . . . .

But my mother persisted in following her own course, and told the physician she could not alter any **thing about** me."

The patient's life **hung** for a long **time in the** balance, and in her fevered state of mind **she** wished ardently for **death.** When by chance she heard **from** an indiscreetly-communicative nurse that her dissolution **was** daily expected, this intelligence produced **such a** quieting effect that she sank into a deep **slumber, and the** crisis of her **disease was** happily passed.

Ida's father had left a considerable **fortune,** and there was **no** lack of suitors **for her hand.** She refused every offer, however, and thereby increased **the** discomfort of her position at home, for her mother **insisted more** and more strongly upon Ida's making her choice. **These domestic** broils **at** length broke the girl's spirit, and any **fate seemed to** her preferable to the continuance of such a state of **things. She accordingly** declared **herself ready to** accept **the next** proposal **that** should be made, provided the suitor was **of** advanced age. She wished to convince T—— that moral co**e**rcion, **and not** her own inclination, had impelled **her to** take this course.

In the year 1819, when Ida **was** twenty-two **years old,** Doctor Pfeiffer, **one of the** most distinguished advocates in Lemberg, and a widower, moreover, with a grown-up son, was introduced to the Reyers. He staid in Vienna a few days for professional purposes, and at his departure recommended his son, who was studying law at the University of Vienna, to the notice of the family.

About four weeks afterward came **a** letter from Dr. Pfeiffer, containing a formal proposal for Ida's hand. As he had only exchanged **a** few words with her on totally **unimportant** subjects, she had not the least anticipation **of an offer** in that direction; but her mother did not fail to remind her of the promise she had made to accept the next suitor who came forward.

"I promised to consider the matter," she says in her diary. "Dr. Pfeiffer seemed to me a very intelligent, well-educated man; but a circumstance that told far more in his favor in my estimation was that he lived a hundred miles from Vienna, and was twenty-four years older than I."

A week afterward she consented to the marriage on the condition that she should be allowed to acquaint Dr. Pfeiffer with the real state of her affections. This she did in a long letter, in which she concealed nothing from her suitor, evidently indulging the hope that he would abandon his pursuit of her; but Dr. Pfeiffer at once replied, expressing himself not in the least surprised to hear that a maiden of twenty-two years had already loved. The honest, candid avowal of this passage in her life made Ida appear in his eyes all the more worthy of respect; and he avowed his intention of persisting in his suit, feeling assured that he should never have cause to regret it.

The difficult duty of acquainting T—— with this change in her destiny now devolved upon Ida. This duty she fulfilled by means of a few lines, and it will readily be imagined that they were painful ones. The answer was conceived in the manliest spirit, full of self-abnegation and nobility of mind. T—— repeatedly declared that he would never forget her, and would never marry. He kept his word.

The marriage with Dr. Pfeiffer was celebrated on the 1st of May, 1820, and a week afterward the newly-wedded couple departed for Lemberg. The journey brought relief by reviving in the young wife the old predilection for traveling, and allowing the pair an opportunity of becoming better acquainted. Ida found that her husband possessed high principle, candor, and intelligence; and if it was beyond her power to love him, she could not withhold from him respect and hearty appreciation, especially as he showed as much affection as delicacy in his conduct toward her. She was resolved to fulfill her duties honorably, and looked forward with a certain amount of tranquillity to the future.

Dr. Pfeiffer was one of those straightforward, independent-spirited men who attack and expose wrong wherever they find it, and make no secret of their sentiments.

In the official routine in Galicia in those days there were many weak points, and the number of dishonest and venal employés was not small. In an important lawsuit which he brought to a triumphant conclusion, Dr. Pfeiffer discovered peculation of the gravest kind. This he fearlessly and unflinchingly denounced to the highest authorities in Vienna. An investigation was ordered; Dr. Pfeiffer's accusations were found to be well-grounded, and several officials were dismissed, and others moved.

Very disagreeable results, however, accrued to Dr. Pfeiffer himself. By his report of these delinquencies he had drawn down upon himself the enmity of the majority of official personages; and this enmity was so frequently and so openly manifested, that Dr. Pfeiffer found himself compelled to resign his appointment as councilor, for he found that his advocacy, so far from benefiting his clients, became absolutely prejudicial to their interests.

"My husband," writes Ida Pfeiffer, "had foreseen all this; but it went against his nature to shut his eyes to flagrant injustice. In the same year he resigned his office, and, after he had arranged his private affairs, we removed, in 1821, to Vienna, where, trusting to his skill and knowledge, he hoped to have no difficulty in obtaining employment. But his reputation had preceded him: his sentiments and his mode of action were as well known in Vienna as at Lemberg, and he was looked upon with suspicion as a restless character and an enemy of existing institutions. All his applications for employment in agencies, etc., were consequently unavailing. Posts which he had solicited in vain were continually given away to the most insignificant and least talented of the profession."

All this had naturally a very disastrous effect on Pfeiffer's mind. He saw himself **every** where crossed and hampered in **his** work and in his efforts; and labors which he **had** formerly performed with zeal and pleasure now fretted and annoyed him. At length he lost a portion of his energy, and what he did brought him little or no advantage.

Thus the social position of the Pfeiffers became more and more critical from day to day. As a skillful lawyer, Dr. Pfeiffer had earned **a** considerable income at Lemberg; but he **had** liked to live **in** good style, kept carriages and horses, **and a good** table, and had not thought of providing for the **future.** Many people who knew his generosity made use **of him, and** borrowed his money. Thus Ida's paternal inheritance vanished also, being lent to **a** friend of Pfeiffer's, whom it was to help out of his embarrassments. The man failed in spite of the loan, and thus the whole fortune **was** lost.

After vainly seeking employment in Vienna, Dr. Pfeiffer returned, with his wife, to Lemberg, but afterward **came** back again to Vienna, and at length even tried his fortune in Switzerland, his native country, where he had, however, only passed the earliest years of his life. But fortune would nowhere smile upon him, and bitter poverty knocked at the door **of** the family.

"**Heaven** only knows what I suffered during eighteen years of my married life!" exclaims Ida Pfeiffer; "not, indeed, from any ill treatment on my husband's part, but from poverty and want. I came of a wealthy family, and had been accustomed from my earliest youth to order and comfort; and now I frequently knew not where I should lay my head, or **find** a little money to buy the commonest necessaries. I performed household drudgery, and bore cold and hunger; I worked secretly for money, and gave lessons in drawing and music; and yet, in spite of all my exertions, there were many days when I could hardly put any thing but dry bread before my poor children for their dinner.

"I might certainly have applied to my mother or my brothers for relief, but my pride revolted against such a course. For years I fought with **poverty** and concealed my real position, often brought so near to despair that the thought **of** my children alone prevented me from giving way. At last the urgency of my necessities broke my spirit, and **several times I had** recourse to my brothers for **assistance.**"

Ida Pfeiffer had **two sons.** A daughter was born to her, **but** only lived a few days. The education of the children devolved entirely upon the mother; and as the younger showed a great appreciation for music, she took great pains to cultivate his talents.

In the year 1831 old Madame Reyer died. During the long illness which preceded **her death** she was tended **by** her daughter with **the most** affectionate care. **After her** mother's death **Ida betook herself again to** Lemberg, **from** whence Dr. Pfeiffer **had** again written, announcing that **he** had a sure prospect of employment. He was now **sixty** years old, and lived in a state of constant illusion; a mere promise was sufficient to inspire him with the greatest confidence in the future. After experiencing a series of hopes and disappointments during a period of two years, she returned to Vienna, where she could at least obtain for her sons a better education.

At her mother's death she had not, indeed, come into a great property, but she inherited enough to keep her in a respectable style, and to provide good teachers for her children. In 1835 she settled definitely in Vienna. Dr. Pfeiffer remained in Lemberg, where he was kept by force of habit, and by his affection for his son by his first marriage. From time to time, however, he visited Vienna to see his wife and children.

During a journey to Trieste which Ida Pfeiffer **undertook** with her youngest **son,** in order **that** he might have **sea-**baths, she enjoyed her first sight of the ocean. The impression made upon **her** by the sea was overpowering. The dreams of her youth came back, with visions of distant unexplored climes, teeming with strange, luxuriant vegetation; an almost irresistible impulse for travel arose in her, and she would gladly have embarked in the first ship to sail away into the great, mysterious, boundless ocean. Her duty toward her children alone restrained her; and she felt happy **when** she had quitted Trieste, and miles of mountain and **plain** intervened between the sea and herself, for the **longing** to **see** the world had weighed like a mountain on **her spirit** in the maritime city.

Returning to the routine of every-day life in Vienna, she still secretly nourished the wish that her health and strength might be spared until her sons **should** have been **established** in life, and she should be enabled **to go out into the world** depending on her own resources alone. This **wish of hers** was to be fulfilled. Her sons grew and throve, **and** became prosperous, successful men in their profession.

The completion of their education and the establishment of each **in** his vocation gave Ida Pfeiffer leisure to mature **her plans** of travel. The old project of seeing the world **arose anew, and now** no obstacle existed in the calls of duty **and common sense.** She began to mature a plan for a long journey, **to be undertaken** alone; **for** she must journey by herself, as her husband's advanced age prevented him from participating in the toil and fatigue of such an undertaking, and her sons could not be spared from their professional duties. The financial aspect of the question required much consideration. In the countries she wished to visit railways and hotels were unknown institutions, and travelers in those regions would be necessarily subjected to the expense of carrying with them all they required during the journey;

and after she had devoted part of her maternal inheritance to the education of her sons, the funds at Ida Pfeiffer's disposal were limited indeed.

"But I soon settled these **weighty points** to my satisfaction," **she** writes in her diary. "Respecting the first, namely, the design that I, a woman, should venture into the world alone, I trusted to my years (I was already forty-five), to my courage, and to the habit of self-reliance I had acquired in the hard school of life, during the time when I was obliged to provide, **not** only for my children, but sometimes for my husband **also**. As regarded money, I was determined **to practice the most** rigid economy. Privation and discomfort had no terrors for **me**. **I had** endured them long enough by compulsion, and considered that they would be much easier to bear if I encountered them voluntarily with a fixed object in view."

Another question, namely, whither she should **bend her** steps, was quickly **answered**. **Two** projects had occupied her mind **for** many years—a voyage to the North, **and a** journey to the Holy Land. When, however, she imparted to her friends her intention of visiting Jerusalem, she was looked upon simply as a crazy, enthusiastic person, and **no-**body thought her in earnest in the **matter**.

Nevertheless, she kept to her resolution, **but** concealed the real goal of her journey, declaring that her intention was to visit a friend at Constantinople, with whom she had for a long time kept up an active correspondence. She kept her passport concealed, and no one of those from whom she parted had any idea of her destination. Very painful was the parting from her sons, to whom she was tenderly attached; but she fought bravely against her softer **emo-**tions, consoled her friends with the prospect of soon meeting them again, and on the 22d of March, 1842, embarked on the steamer that was to convey her down the Danube to the Black Sea and the City of the Crescent. She visited

Brussa, Beyrout, Jaffa, Jerusalem, the Dead Sea, Nazareth, Damascus, Baalbek, the Lebanon, Alexandria, and Cairo, and traveled across the Desert to the Isthmus of Suez and the Red Sea. From Egypt she returned by way of Sicily and the whole of Italy to her home, arriving in Vienna in December, 1842.

As she had carefully kept a diary of her journey, from which she frequently read extracts to friends and acquaintances, she was often requested to print her experiences. The thought of becoming an authoress was repugnant to her modesty, and it was only when a publisher made her a direct offer that she consented to trust her first book to the press. It bore the title, "Journey of a Viennese Lady to the Holy Land." The first edition appeared in two volumes in 1843, the fourth in 1856; and though the authoress neither had much that was new to tell, nor rode her Pegasus in the approved style of the traveled ladies of the period, her little book was still successful, as the four editions sufficiently prove. The very simplicity of the narration, and its appearance of unvarnished truth, at once gained numerous readers for the book.

The good result of this first journey, which gave the pilgrim fresh funds in the form of copyright money, awakened within her fresh plans; and this time she felt impelled toward the far north, where she expected to see majestic sights, and to behold nature exhibited in new and startling forms.

After various preparations, among which may be mentioned the study of the English and Danish languages, and of the art of taking Daguerreotypes, and after obtaining accurate information concerning the countries she purposed visiting, she began her journey to the north on the 10th of April, 1845. On the 16th of May she landed on the coast of Iceland, and proceeded to traverse that interesting island in every direction, visiting the Geysers and other hot springs, and ascending Hecla, which shortly after her departure began to vomit flame, after remaining for seventy years in a quiescent state.   At the end of June she sailed back to Copenhagen, and from thence journeyed to Christiania, Thelemark, across the Swedish lakes to Stockholm, and over Upsala to the iron mines of Danemora.   She returned to her native city by way of Travemünde, Hamburg, and Berlin, arriving in Vienna on the 4th of October, 1845, after an absence of six months.

The journal of this second voyage appeared under the title, "Voyage to the Scandinavian North and the Island of Iceland," in two volumes, at Pesth, and was much read. The money realized by a sale of the geological and botanical specimens collected during this tour, together with the sum paid for the copyright of her book, were put aside by Ida Pfeiffer as the nucleus of a fund for a new undertaking, and one of a more ambitious character.   A voyage round the world now occupied the thoughts of this brave woman ; and when once she had conceived the idea, she could not rest until it was put in execution.

"Greater privations and fatigue than I had endured in Syria and Iceland," she writes, "I could scarcely have to encounter.   The expense did not frighten me, for I knew by experience how little is required if the traveler will but practice the strictest economy, and be content to forego all comforts and superfluities.   My savings accumulated to a sum barely sufficient perhaps to serve such travelers as Prince Pückler-Muskau, Chateaubriand, or Lamartine for a fortnight's excursion, but which seemed enough for me during a journey of two or three years, and the event proved that I had calculated rightly."

Again concealing the whole extent of her undertaking from her relations, and especially from her sons, and naming Brazil as her destination, our traveler bade adieu to Vienna on the 1st of May, 1846, and betook herself to Hamburg, where she was compelled to wait till the 28th of June before a suitable opportunity for proceeding to the Brazils offered itself in the shape of a little Danish brig.

Retarded by contrary winds and calms, the ship was a full month in making its way from Hamburg through the English Channel—as long a time as it required to get from thence to the equator. On the 16th of September the harbor of Rio Janeiro was reached. From that port Ida Pfeiffer made several excursions into the interior of the country. On one of these expeditions she was attacked by a runaway negro slave, whose purpose appeared to be robbery and murder. The miscreant was armed with a knife; she received more than one wound, and only owed her life to casual help which arrived at the critical moment.

At the beginning of December she left Rio Janeiro, sailed round Cape Horn on the 3d of February, 1847, and landed at Valparaiso on the 2d of March. The aspect of tropical scenery, particularly in Brazil, made a vivid impression upon her; but she was greatly disgusted at the state of things in what had been Spanish America. Quickly re-embarking, she traversed the Pacific Ocean, and landed at the island of Otaheite at the end of April. She was presented to Queen Pomare, of whose court she afterward published a sufficiently spirited account, which was read with much interest. The state of Europe at that period was one of such tranquillity that, for mere want of matter, the papers were often full of Queen Pomare for weeks together. Her Otaheitan majesty has now gone considerably out of fashion, inasmuch as Europe has enough to do with its own concerns, and has neither time nor inclination to patronize happy islands in the far Pacific.

From Otaheite the enterprising voyager proceeded to China, arriving at Macao in the beginning of July. She afterward visited Hong Kong and the city of Canton, in which she would gladly have spent more time, had not the

appearance of a European woman been too much for the
weak nerves of the natives of the Celestial Empire. The
visitor found herself in danger of being insulted by the
mob, and accordingly turned her back on the fortunate
country, paid a short visit to Singapore, and proceeded to
Ceylon, landing there in the middle of October. She traversed this beautiful island in various directions, and saw
Colombo, Candy, and the famous temple of Dagona. At
the end of October she landed on the continent of India, at
Madras, remained for some time at Calcutta, proceeded up
the Ganges to Benares, admired the ruins of Saranath, and
visited Cawnpoor, Delhi, Indore, and Bombay. She also
had an opportunity of seeing the celebrated rock temples
of Adjunta and Ellora, and the islands of Elephanta and
Salsette. The houses of many Indians of rank were thrown
open to her, and she showed herself every where a close observer of foreign manners, customs, and peculiarities. **At**
more than one tiger-hunt she was also present, and **at a sut-**
tee. The position and proceedings of the English **mission-**
aries also excited her especial attention.

At the end of April, 1848, we find Ida Pfeiffer again **at**
sea, bearing her pilgrim's staff toward Persia. From Bushire
she intended to proceed to Shiraz, Ispahan, and Teheran,
but was deterred from this project by disturbances in the
interior of the country, and turned her footsteps toward
Mesopotamia. Through the bay Shat-el-Arab she betook
herself to Bassora, and afterward to Bagdad. After an excursion to the ruins of Ctesiphon and Babylon, she traveled
with a caravan through the Desert to Mosul and the neighboring ruins of Nineveh, and afterward to Urumia and Tebris. This expedition through Mesopotamia and Persia
may be reckoned among the most daring exploits of this
courageous woman. A large amount of mental energy, as
well as of physical stamina, was required, to enable her to
endure without fainting the many hardships of the under-

taking—the burning heat by day, discomfort of every kind at night, miserable fare, an unclean couch, and constant apprehension of attack by robber bands. When she introduced herself at Tebris to the English consul, he would not believe that a woman could have achieved such a feat.

At Tebris our traveler was introduced to the vice-king Vali-Ahd, and received permission to visit his harem. On the 11th of August, 1848, she resumed her journey through Armenia, Georgia, Mingrelia, by Eriwan, Tiflis, and Kutais to Redutkale; she touched at Anapa, Kertch, and Sebastopol, landed at Odessa, and returned home by Constantinople, Greece, the Ionian Islands, and Trieste to Vienna, where she arrived on the 4th of November, 1848, just after the taking of the city by the troops of Prince Windischgrätz. It seemed that even in her fatherland, distracted as it was by faction, she was to find no rest.

Ida Pfeiffer's fame spread more and more after this journey round the world; for a woman who, trusting to herself alone for protection, could travel 2800 miles by land and 35,000 by sea, was looked upon, not unnaturally, as a remarkable character. Her third work, which appeared in Vienna in 1850, under the title "A Woman's Journey round the World," was well received. It was translated twice into English, and afterward appeared in a French garb.

It was now for some time Ida Pfeiffer's purpose to consider her traveling days as over, and to settle down in repose. But this resigned frame of mind did not last long. When, after selling her collections, and preparing and publishing her journal, she found herself in the enjoyment of undiminished health and strength, she gradually began to entertain the idea of a second voyage round the world. Her slender traveling fund was this time increased by a grant of 1500 florins from the Austrian government; and on the 18th of March, 1851, she left Vienna, betaking herself first to London, as she had no fixed goal in view, and intended to wait till an occasion offered for traveling farther. Even **when** she had left London, and arrived in Cape Town **on** the 11th **of** August, she had come **to no** definite determination. For a long time her mind wavered between the intention of visiting the interior of Africa and that of proceeding to Australia, till at last she sailed to Singapore, and decided to visit the Sunda Islands. Landing on the west coast of Borneo, at Sarawak, she received a hospitable welcome and energetic assistance from Sir James Brooke, who has established an independent principality in these **regions.** During an excursion she made among the savage, independent Dyaks, she **was** not only spared by the " head hunters," but was even received with great cordiality. Proceeding to Sinting, she continued her journey westward to Pontianak and the diamond mines of Landak. Every where the Dutch officials, civil and military, **offered her the** readiest assistance, without which she would have found **it** impossible to extend her travels so **far as she** did in the Indian Archipelago. Ida Pfeiffer's design **was to** push on from Pontianak directly through the interior of the island, a region never yet traversed by Europeans; but **she** could endure **no** one to be her guide or companion on so dangerous an expedition. **She** therefore cast her eyes on Java, and landed at Batavia **at the** end of May, 1852. Here, likewise, she received every assistance and support **from** the Dutch authorities, and, in consequence of their example, from the native grandees also. This she often afterward publicly acknowledged, with the warmest thanks.

On the 8th of July, 1852, her journey to Sumatra began; and this she has declared to be the most interesting of all her undertakings. From Padang she proceeded to trust herself among the Battas, who are cannibals, and have never suffered any European to come among them. Though the savages opposed her farther advance, she passed forward through the primeval forest, among a population of man-eaters, almost as far as the Lake Eier-Tau. **But** here she was compelled by threatening spears to retreat, **after having** been repeatedly assured that **she** should be killed and **eaten.** On the 7th of October she got back to Padang. **In** Sumatra she was twice attacked **by** the malignant intermittent fever of the country.

Returning to Java, she made excursions to the principalities of Djokdjokarta and Surakarta, to the temple **Boro** Budoo, and to Surabaga. From thence she sailed to several of the smaller Sunda Islands, and to the Moluccas, Banda, **Amboyna,** Saparna, Ceram, and Ternate; remained for **a few months among** the wild Alfores, and closed her rambles among the Sunda Islands by a visit to Celebes.

Again she traversed the Pacific to a distance of 10,150 **miles to** visit California. For two months she saw nothing but sea and sky. On the 27th of September, 1853, she landed at San Francisco, visited the gold-washing districts on the Sacramento and the Yuba, and slept in the wigwams **of** the red-skins of Rogue River.

At the end of 1853 Ida Pfeiffer sailed to Panama, and from thence to the Peruvian coast. From Callao she betook herself to Lima, with the intention of crossing the Cordilleras, and proceeding to Loretto, on the Amazon, and thus gaining the eastern coast of South America. The revolution, however, which had just broken out in Peru, made **the** land unsafe, and compelled our traveler to try and cross the Cordilleras at another point. She returned, accordingly, to Ecuador, and in March, 1854, began her toilsome passage across the mountains. She crossed the chain in the immediate neighborhood of Chimborazo, **came to the elevated** plateau of Ambato **and** Tacunga, and witnessed **the** rare spectacle of an eruption of the volcano Cotopaxi—a sight for which she was afterward envied by Alexander von Humboldt. On reaching Quito on the 4th of April, she did not, unfortunately, find the assistance she had expected in the shape of several trustworthy guides to the Amazon. She therefore gave up her plan of embarking on that river, and had to repeat her wearisome march across the Cordilleras. In the neighborhood of Guayaquil she twice stood in imminent danger of being killed—first by a fall from her mule, and then from an immersion in the River Guaya, which abounds in caymans. Her companions wished her to perish, and did not render the slightest assistance. Deeply disgusted at their inhumanity, she turned her back upon Spanish South America, betook herself by sea to Panama, and at the end of May crossed the Isthmus.

From Aspinwall she sailed to New Orleans, remaining there till the 30th of June; then she ascended the Mississippi to Napoleon, and the Arkansas as far as Fort Smith. Her projected visit to the Cherokee Indians had to be abandoned, on account of a renewed and violent attack of the Sumatra fever. Returning to the Mississippi, she reached St. Louis on the 14th of July, and paid a visit to the Baden democrat Hecker, who had established himself in the neighborhood of Lebanon. Then she turned northward toward St. Paul and the Falls of St. Anthony, proceeded to Chicago, and thus came to the great lakes and to the Falls of Niagara. After an excursion into Canada, she staid for some time in New York, Boston, and other cities, then went on board a steamer, and, after a passage of ten days, landed in England, at Liverpool, on the 21st of November, 1854.

To this great voyage round the world she added a little supplement, by paying a visit to her son, who was residing at San Miguel, in the Azores. It was not until May, 1855, that she returned to Vienna, by way of Lisbon, Southampton, and London.

The specimens and the ethnographical objects collected by Ida Pfeiffer were for the most part deposited in the British Museum and in the Imperial Cabinets in Vienna. Alexander von Humboldt and Carl Ritter, in Berlin, took great interest in the efforts of Ida Pfeiffer, and Humboldt especially rewarded her with the warmest praise for her energy and perseverance. At the request of these two eminent men, the Geographical Society of Berlin elected Ida Pfeiffer an honorary member, and the King of Prussia awarded her the gold medal for arts and sciences. In Vienna the expressions of approval were much more sparing, probably according to the old rule that no prophet is regarded in his own country.

The brave traveler's journal again appeared in Vienna in 1856, under the title, "My Second Journey round the World."

After each of her former voyages, Ida Pfeiffer had for a time cherished the idea of retiring from future enterprises, and living in the memory of the past. But after the second journey round the world, which resulted entirely to her satisfaction, no such ideas seem to have troubled her. Before she had even finished arranging her cabinet of specimens and superintending the publication of her book, she already conceived the plan of exploring Madagascar, and was not to be dissuaded from her purpose even by the representations of Alexander von Humboldt, who proposed various other plans for her consideration.

The farther fortunes of Ida Pfeiffer will be found chronicled in the accompanying journal of her voyage to Madagascar, and, with the communication of her son, Mr. Oscar Pfeiffer, tell the story of her sufferings and death. But, before we enter upon the last act of her toilsome and instructive career, it will be well to say a few words concerning the character of our traveler.

Ida Pfeiffer did not give those who saw her the impression of an emancipated, strong-minded, or masculine woman. On the contrary, she was so simple and downright in word and thought, that those who did not know her had some difficulty in getting at the depth of her knowledge and experience. In her whole appearance and manners there was a quiet staidness that seemed to indicate a practical housewife, with no enthusiastic thought beyond her domestic concerns. Many people were accordingly premature in their judgment concerning Ida Pfeiffer, and felt inclined to ascribe her passion for traveling to mere inquisitive restlessness. This supposition was, however, completely negatived by a leading trait in Ida Pfeiffer's character, namely, a total absence of any thing like prying curiosity. In proportion as her whole existence had been troubled, was her appearance quiet and sedate.

The sharpest observer would fail to detect in her any tendency to push herself forward, or to interfere in matters not within her sphere. Serious, silent, and reserved, she presented few of the agreeable features of her mind to people with whom she was imperfectly acquainted.

But those who succeeded in gaining her intimacy could not fail to recognize under this unpretending exterior the qualities which make a remarkable woman. Strength of purpose, firmness of character, sometimes amounting almost to obstinacy, were quickly discernible in certain favorite expressions of hers. If we add to these gifts an amount of personal courage rarely found in a woman, indifference to physical pain and to the ordinary conveniences of life, and, moreover, the never-ceasing desire to add something to the stock of human knowledge, it will be allowed that she possessed the qualities with which success is achieved in the world. The value of these gifts was heightened in Ida Pfeiffer by a strict regard for truth and strong sense of conscientious responsibility, and a love of right and justice. She never told any thing that had not happened exactly as she chronicled it, and never made a promise which she did not keep. She had what, in common life, we emphatically term *character*.

That her communications derive an additional value from

her well-known truthfulness is self-evident; **and** as she was **free from sectarian and** other prejudices, her judgments **were** always based upon a solid foundation. Had she in her youthful days employed herself more than she did in scientific **study, and** gained positive knowledge in that direction, her travels would doubtless have been more useful; but at the commencement of our century even men **were** seldom found who would employ themselves in scientific pursuits that had no immediate bearing upon their professions, **and** learned women were rarer still. Ida Pfeiffer **was** conscious of **this** defect in her education, and in her **mature years** often thought of remedying it, but she lacked **both the** necessary time and patience.

To divest her efforts of all scientific value would, however, be unjust, for the most competent men have given a different verdict. She pressed forward into many regions never before trodden by European foot; and **the** very fact of her being a woman was her protection **in her most dangerous** undertakings. She was allowed to pursue her journey where a man would assuredly not have been suffered to advance. Her communications, consequently, have often the merit of containing entirely new facts in geography **and** ethnology, or of correcting the exaggerations and errors of previous accounts. Science was likewise benefited by the valuable collections **she made** of plants, animals, and **minerals.** Frequently **she did not** herself know the value of what **she** had brought together; but, nevertheless, she brought **many** important specimens; and the sciences of conchology and entomology are indebted **to her for the** discovery of several new genera.

If we compare the results of Ida Pfeiffer's undertakings with the limited means at her disposal for carrying out her plans, her achievements become **marvelous.** She traversed nearly 150,000 miles of sea and 20,000 miles of land; and the funds for these travels were gained entirely by wise

economy, and by the energy with which she kept the goal
continually before her eyes. If her passion for traveling
was great, her talents as a traveler were far greater. Without sacrificing her dignity or becoming importunate, she
had the art of first arousing and then benefiting by the interest and sympathy of people in all parts of the world.
At last she became quite accustomed to see her plan fur-
thered in every possible way, and though she never failed
to express her thanks, she seemed at last to receive the
good offices of foreigners in all quarters of the globe as almost a matter of course. She even had to fight against little outbursts of wrath when she missed the sympathy for
her efforts and herself to which she had become so accustomed. In later years especially, she was fully conscious
of her own value, and showed it when people attempted to
behave in a condescending or patronizing way to her.
Persons of higher rank than herself were obliged to be very
careful in their intercourse with her; but with plain, unpretending people she never uttered a word that could hurt or
offend. Hating all pretension, and all boastful self-assertion,
she showed herself obstinate and self-willed wherever she
met with such qualities. Antipathy or sympathy were
quickly evoked in her, and it was not easy to make her
swerve from an opinion she had once formed. Even when
she appeared to give way, it generally happened that she
returned by some circuitous route or other to her old start-
ing-point.

For every kind of knowledge she showed the most profound respect, but particularly for the acquirements of people who had distinguished themselves in the domain of
science. For Alexander von Humboldt her admiration
amounted to perfect enthusiasm, and she never mentioned
the great philosopher's name without testifying the respect
she felt toward him. Nothing, perhaps, gave her so much

pleasure in her later years as the appreciation for, and sympathy with her efforts manifested by Humboldt.

Ida Pfeiffer was of short stature, thin, and slightly bent. Her movements were deliberate and measured, but she could walk at a very quick pace for her years. When she returned from one of her journeys, her complexion used to give strong evidence of the power of the tropical sun. Beyond this there was nothing in her features to tell of her remarkable trials and adventures; a quieter countenance could not readily be found. But when she became animated in conversation, and spoke of things which strongly awakened her interest, her whole face lighted up, and its expression became exceedingly engaging.

In all that related to the toilet, a matter of importance to most women, Ida Pfeiffer confined her wants within the smallest limits. She was never seen to wear trinkets or jewels; and none of the lady readers who honor these pages with their perusal can show more simplicity in the adornment of her beauty, or greater indifference to the requirements of custom, than were displayed by this voyager round the world.

Straightforward, of high principle, with a promptitude and wisdom in action rarely equaled among her sex, Ida Pfeiffer may justly be classed among those women who richly compensate for the absence of outward charms by the remarkable energy and rare qualities of their minds.

IDA PFEIFFER'S LAST TRAVELS.

IDA PFEIFFER'S LAST TRAVELS.

CHAPTER I.

Departure from Vienna.—Linz.—Salzburg.—Munich.—The Artists' Festival.—The King of Bavaria.—Berlin.—Alexander von Humboldt.—Hamburg.

ON the 21st of May, 1856, I left Vienna, and set forth on another of my long journeys. At Nussdorf, near Vienna, I embarked on board the fine steamer "Austria," bound up the river for Linz. The steam-boat company was not only so obliging as to give me a free pass, but even placed a cabin at my disposal, and provided board and every comfort for me.

The short distance (about thirty German miles) from Vienna to Linz can be accomplished in twenty-one hours, and a beautiful trip it is. Few rivers can boast such an endless variety of scenery as greets the eye of the traveler on the Danube. Hill and valley, city and hamlet, magnificent convents and elegant villas glide past in endless succession, nor lacketh there the knightly castle, or the half-decayed ruin with its appropriate legend of romance. Favored by the Fates with the finest possible weather, and surrounded by agreeable company, I could only wish that my journey might continue to present the auspicious appearance under which it had begun.

I made acquaintance with several passengers on board, and among the rest with the wife of the respected physician, Dr. Pleninger, of Linz. This amiable lady insisted upon my taking up my quarters in her house. Unfortunately, I

had but a short time to stay at Linz, as I purposed proceeding to Lambach the same day. But kind Dr. Pleninger arranged a little pleasure party for the morning to the
neighboring " Freudenberg" (Mountain of Joy), on which a
great Jesuit convent is built. Besides its clerical occupants,
this establishment numbers more than a hundred and fifty
pupils, who, for the sum of only twelve florins* per month,
are boarded and lodged, and get their education into the
bargain. The institution appears to be conducted with
care and with notable order. It already possesses a little
collection of ethnographical objects and a botanic garden,
the latter under the superintendence of Herr Hintereker, a
very eminent botanist. The view from the Freudenberg
is very charming, and I herewith recommend this walk to
all future tourists, including those who are unable to see
the convent.

I remained at Dr. Pleninger's till the afternoon, and then
proceeded by rail to Lambach, a distance of eight German
miles, which it required full three hours to accomplish.

At Lambach I took the Salzburg omnibus. Unfortunately, this vehicle was not managed on English principles.
It was a true, genuine, and unadulterated German omnibus,
drawn by German horses, who tramped stolidly along at
the rate, as I judged, of a German mile an hour. The distance is twelve German miles, and in just twelve hours we
got to our destination, so that my calculation was quite correct.

At Salzburg it was pouring wet weather, of course: my
countrymen do not call this town the "rainy corner" without reason.

They tell a story of an Englishman who once came to
Salzburg at midsummer, and found town, valley, and hills
alike shrouded in mist and rain. He had read so much of
the charming situation of Salzburg that he lingered there a

---

* A florin, of sixty kreutzers, is worth about 2s. English money.

few days, but, as the **sky showed no token of** clearing **up,**
this son of Albion **at** length **lost** patience **and decamped.**
Two years afterward, on his journey **home** from Italy, he
took the route by this town, in the hope of being more fortunate this time; but, behold, it was raining as it had rained two years ago. " By Jove!" exclaimed the Briton, in
astonishment, " hasn't it *left off* yet?"

I might have made the same observation; for, although
in my journeys I had several times passed through Salzburg, I had not once had the good luck to see this beautiful region smiling in the sunshine. And beautiful it is—
wonderfully beautiful. It would be difficult to find a pret-
tier little town, or one situate in so fertile **a** valley, and sur-
rounded by such majestic masses **of** mountains. One of
these, the Watzmann, is nearly 9000 feet high.

I had only half a day to spend in Salzburg, **and had just**
time to **look at** the statue of Mozart, set up **here** since **my**
last visit. Mozart, as is well known, **was born** in this **town**
in the year 1756.

From Salzburg I took the stage-coach (stellwagen) **to**
Munich. This kind of conveyance could never be classed
among the most agreeable methods of traveling, but since
the invention of railways it has become intolerable. Crowded together like negroes in a slave-ship, we loitered for two
whole days in accomplishing this little distance of nineteen
German miles. The rain fortunately ceased **a** few miles
from Salzburg, **and,** moreover, the scenery is very fine to
within four miles of Munich. The Bavarian frontier is
crossed within the first mile. To my great surprise, the inspection of passports and of luggage was speedily accomplished.

Toward evening we came to the Chiem Lake, also called
the "Bavarian Sea." This beautiful sheet of water is two
German miles in length, **and one and** a half in breadth.
On three **sides** it is shut **in by high** mountains, while on

the fourth it is bordered **by a plain of** seemingly unlimited extent.

Not far from **Traunstein we** struck **into** a by-road toward Sekon, a pretty seat belonging to the widowed Empress of Brazil, who was by birth a princess of Leuchtenberg. Sekon is situate on a tiny lake, whose waters are said to possess **mineral** properties. The empress has caused a large building, originally a convent, on the banks of the lake, to be converted into a bathing hotel, with fifty rooms, **and** it has **been** very tastefully arranged. A neat garden surrounds the building, the kitchen is well supplied, and conveyances can be had, and every thing is marvelously cheap. A very good room, for instance, costs only three florins per **week**; the *table d'hôte*, twenty-four kreutzers; a one-horse **carriage** can be had for **two florins a day, and** other expenses are in proportion. This pleasant bathing-place, when its existence becomes more widely known, can not fail to attract a multitude of guests, and then, of course, **the** prices will rise.

From Sekon we went on to Wasserburg. **This little** town is wonderfully placed as regards situation. It lies in a perfect basin, shut in at almost every point by steep walls of rock and sandstone. When I came to the edge a giant crater seemed to open suddenly at my feet, but, instead of fire and flames, this crater contained a charming rural scene. The little houses lay there hidden and secluded as if they belonged to another world. The Inn flowed between them, its yellow waters covered with signs of a busy life; for hundreds of rafts, built of **the** trunks of trees and **planks,** float down hence to distant harbors. Taking a wide circuit, **we** drove **down** into this crater; and then **I** became aware **that** the basin was much wider **than it** had appeared from above, and that it afforded space **for** numerous hop-gardens. This region might not inaptly be called the Vineyard of Bavaria.

On the **26th of May** I arrived in Munich. The **portion** of Bavaria with which I became acquainted on this little journey pleased me greatly. The scenery is splendid, the towns and villages look pretty and prosperous, and the fields are well cultivated. The scattered farms in particular **bear** a certain impress of prosperity, cleanliness, and order. The buildings are of stone, are sufficiently roomy, and generally have an upper story; the roof is constructed in **the** Swiss manner, almost flat, and weighted with heavy stones, as a protection against the violent storms which prevail here. Exception might be taken to the fact that dwelling-house, barn, and stable are all under the same roof; for, **in** the event of a fire, the farmer would most probably lose all his property at once.

No **one** who looks at these teeming fields and valleys (and when I saw them the crops were waving in rich abundance), the smiling villages, the well-built farms, would suppose that poverty could lurk here, and that many of **the inhabitants** are forced to emigrate, to seek beyond the sea a country that will better repay their toil.

And yet it is so. The chief reason is perhaps to be found in the fact that in Bavaria, and particularly in Upper **and** Lower Bavaria and the Upper Palatinate, farms are not divided, but given to one of the children, who is chosen **by** the father from among his family. The fortunate individual thus selected has certainly the responsibility of " paying out" his brothers, as it is called; but they never receive much, as the estate is always appraised considerably below its value, and the chief heir, moreover, receives a considerable sum under the name of " Mannslehen." The rest have naturally no course left but to seek a service, to learn a trade, or to emigrate. Even in the other provinces, where the estates are divided, there is a great deal of poverty, and emigration is always going on. Why this should be so I can not pretend to determine.

The costume of the peasant women in these regions is very peculiar. They wear short **but** very full skirts, with double bodices, the one with long sleeves, **the** other sleeveless. **This** second jacket, generally of dark-colored velvet, **is** put on over the other, and laced with silver tags. The wealthier peasant women adorn their necks with eight or ten strings of little **real** pearls, with great clasps in front. The poorer ones are fain to content themselves with imitation **pearls,** of silver.

Munich seemed to me a very quiet city. There is little traffic, **and none but** the principal streets show any signs **of life.**

I only remained in this city six days, but in that short time I made the acquaintance of several families. So far as I could judge, domestic life appears to be simple and social here, and the fair sex seemed to care less for outward show than the ladies of other capitals. I must confess that **the** mode of life in Munich pleased me much.

Through a fortunate chance I became acquainted with many distinguished men here, principally artists. The **Artists'** Festival was being celebrated, and I received a polite **invitation** to take part in it. Were I to chronicle the names **of all** the eminent people to whom I had the honor of an introduction on this occasion, I should perhaps tire my readers; but in my memory those names will always be impressed.

I must devote a few words, however, to the festival, which is celebrated every **year on a fine** day in May.

It was held at Schwanegg **and** Pullach, in **a** beautiful meadow surrounded by forests. **At** Schwanegg, a chateau built in the Gothic style by Herr von Schwanthaler, a comic interlude was represented, a parody on Schiller's "Fight with the Dragon." The fortress of Schwanegg is supposed to have been besieged for a whole year by a dragon, in such wise that no man could go out or in. A knight comes riding past by chance; he is seen from **the watch-tower,** and the inmates of the castle straightway assemble on the threshold, and in **very** comic verses implore the knight to deliver them from their enemy. Then follows the combat, with discomfiture of the dragon, etc.

After the dragon had been satisfactorily slain, we **had** another scenic **show in** the little wood near Pullach—*Spring expelling Winter.* Then we had **a** series of funny processions. Bacchus **appeared** seated on a wine-cask, drawn by gigantic cockchafers (each represented by a man), with similar **insects sporting** round him. Apollo came next, on a **triumphal car, with** Pegasus **as** his horse, and surrounded **by** butterflies, flowers, and beetles, from one **to** two feet in height, cut out of card-board, tastefully colored, and mounted on lofty poles. In short, one frolic succeeded another, and the appreciating public enjoyed the sight **most** unequivocally; it was a thorough " people's festival." **There** must have been nearly ten thousand people assembled, **all** passing the day in hearty enjoyment, and seeming to belong to a single family. Some found places at long tables under the trees, others simply threw themselves on the grass; but all seemed equally devoted to the national beverage of **the** country, the beer, without which a true Bavarian would scarcely be able to enjoy himself thoroughly. In **spite of** this bibulous propensity, every **thing** went off peaceably and well, and it was not **until the** evening that one or **two** of the company showed signs **of** having overdone the **thing a little.** Luckily, the Spirit of the Hop seems to be a good-natured **sort** of spirit, only promoting hilarity, for I did not hear of **a** single quarrel.

The first representation had been honored by **the** presence of King Max, who came in the dress of a plain **citizen.** Afterward in the theatre **I** saw the king **and the whole court in** private dress. It is a long time since I have seen **a monarch** in the garb of a civilian; crowned heads wear uniforms, and nothing but uniforms, as if they belonged exclusively to the military class. There **is** some fitness in that; for what would the majority of them be without soldiers?

King Max seems to take a different view of things. He honors the citizens, and does not scruple to associate with them. He marched along with the great crowd, with no followers to accompany **or** police to escort him. He cleared a path for himself, and the people passed to and fro around him quite unceremoniously.

The king was told that my insignificant self was among the audience at the feast, and I was speedily presented to him among thousands of spectators. His majesty conversed with me for some time in the most gracious manner.

To describe the "lions" of Munich and its Art treasures is no fit task for a journal like mine. Any of my readers who may wish for information on the subject will find it amply detailed in one or other of the capital hand-books which have been published concerning this city of Art.

Two amiable ladies, the Baronesses Du Prel and Bissing, were obliging enough to lead me from gallery to gallery, and from church to church. But nothing is more tiring, or more exhausting to the mind and body, than crowding a large amount of sight-seeing into a limited time. These six days tried me more than a sojourn of double that time in the virgin forests of the tropics, where I had to walk on the most tiring paths all day long, with the damp earth for my resting-place at night, and rice parboiled in water for my daily food.

Before I take leave of Munich I must relate a funny incident that occurred one evening on my leaving the theatre. I did not know my way well, and begged a good dame, who came walking past with a gentleman, to set me right. As they were walking in the same direction, they invited me to go with them. On the way she inquired if I had been to the Artists' Festival, and if I had seen the "great traveler," Ida Pfeiffer, there. My questioner added that **she had** been with her husband, but only in the evening, and had not seen the person in question. I replied that the "great traveler" was a quiet little woman, and that I knew her well enough; if I wanted to see her I had only to look in a glass. The good people seemed very glad to see me, and insisted on accompanying me to my door.

On the 1st of June I proceeded, by way of Hof, to Berlin (ninety-five miles), **and,** arriving on the following day, was received with their wonted hearty kindness by my dear friends, Professor Weisz and his wife.

The journey from Munich to Berlin offers few points of **interest:** the views are sometimes pretty, but nowhere striking; the country around Plauen is the most agreeable. Before we got to Hof, the **last** Bavarian station, **something** broke down in the engine; we thus lost **a** whole **hour, and** missed the corresponding train. At the Prussian **frontier** my passport was demanded, but the official scarcely **glanced** at it, and the inspection of my luggage was also entirely formal; in a few moments the whole ceremony was over.

In Berlin a great and joyful surprise awaited me. I received from Alexander von Humboldt an open letter of recommendation to **all** his friends in the wide world.

The celebrated geographer, **Carl** Ritter, also did me a great honor by inviting me to **a sitting of** the Geographical Society. In March last I had **been received** as an honorary member **of** that **body,** and **was** the first woman to whom such a distinction had been accorded.

I only staid **a** week in Berlin, and proceeded **thence to** Hamburg (a distance of thirty-eight German miles), taking up my quarters again with the worthy Schulz family. **But** in Hamburg also there **was no** long tarrying for me. I wanted **to** husband my **time for** Holland, a country **with** which I was unacquainted, and accordingly, on the 14th of

C

June, I embarked on board the steamer "Stoomward," Captain C. Bruns, for **Amsterdam,** distant **three** hundred- and
twelve sea-miles from this port.

This **was the first** passage I made in Europe on a Dutch
steamer, and here I experienced the same kindness I had
met **with** from the proprietors **of** Dutch steamers in India
during my second journey round **the** world; not only did
they give me a free passage, but refused to accept payment
for table **expenses,** etc. How much more easily would my
journeys **have been** accomplished **had I met** with similar
consideration from English steam-boat companies! but **un-**
fortunately, **till now,** such has **not** been my good fortune.
The English directors, agents, and managers have shown
far greater appreciation for my dollars than for my journeyings, and always made me pay my passage, alike for long
and short distances.

CHAPTER II.

Arrival in Holland.—Amsterdam.—Dutch Architecture.—Picture Galleries.—Mr. Costa's Diamond-cutting Works.—The Haarlem Lake.—A Dutch Cattle-stable.—Utrecht.—The Students' Festival.

I ARRIVED in Amsterdam at midday on the 16th of June. My worthy friend, Colonel Steuerwald, was waiting for me in the harbor. This gentleman is one of my oldest traveling acquaintances. I first met him on my journey from Gothenburg to Stockholm, afterward encountered him again at Batavia, and here again in his own native land, where he welcomed me in the heartiest manner, and introduced me at once to his family circle.

I staid in Holland till the 2d of July, and had an opportunity of traveling through the greater part of this interesting country; but I will merely indicate what I saw in as few words as possible, for it does not come within the scope of my book to give detailed accounts of well-known lands and cities.

The thing that struck me most in Amsterdam was the architecture of the houses, which I can best liken to the old German style, as seen, for instance, in Magdeburg. The houses, inhabited generally by a single family, are very narrow, from two to four stories high, terminating in fronted or rounded gable roofs. They are built of brick stained with a dark brown tint, and in some instances ornamented with arabesques. The streets have a singular appearance. The houses stand in straight rows, but do not by any means rise in a perpendicular line. In some the under, in others the upper, and in others, again, the middle story, bulges out beyond the rest, the deviation from the perpendicular fre-

quently exceeding a foot. It would seem that such houses
were peculiarly liable to fall in; but, from the dates over
the doors, I found that the majority had stood for one, and
not a few for two centuries. The narrow steep staircase is
a great drawback in Dutch houses. One ought to be a
born Hollander, and accustomed from childhood to the task
of climbing these stairs, to look upon them with equanimi-
ty, especially as in any of these lofty narrow houses one
seems to be mounting and descending the stairs all day
long. I need scarcely say that the houses of the rich, the
hotels, and similar buildings, are free from this inconvenience.

Equally surprised was I to notice that in houses where
the ground floor is arranged as a shop, the whole width of
the front is thus occupied, and no room left for a private
door. The cook with her market-basket, the water-carrier
with his pails, the housewife and the visitors, have all to go
through warehouses sometimes filled with costly wares arranged to the best advantage. Of course, too, the shop-door
must be left open on Sundays and holidays as on ordinary
occasions.

These inconveniences are all caused by the high price of
the ground. Every one knows with what labor the greater part of the Dutch soil was won from the sea, and how
expensive it is to build on ground where the foundation
must be almost *created*, so to speak, by driving heavy piles.
Generally the building *below* the ground costs quite as much
as all the rest of the structure.

Amsterdam is intersected by numerous canals, all sufficiently broad, and crossed by 250 bridges. This town
might indeed be called the Venice of the North, but that
the marble palaces, the bustle and life of the southern people, the crowd of passing gondolas, and the melodious songs
of the boatmen, are all wanting. Amsterdam has, however,
one advantage over Venice in possessing fine broad streets

running parallel with the canals, so that carriages can be used in traversing the city. Many of the streets are adorned with tall stately trees, which make the town look very fresh and pleasant.

There are some handsome buildings, but none of remarkable appearance except the royal palace—the council-house of old times. This is built in a grand style, and beautified with excellent sculpture.

I must farther mention a few peculiarities of Amsterdam which greatly surprised me. The first was, that in this great city of 200,000 inhabitants there are no stands for hired carriages; whoever wants to drive out must send to the stable-keeper's house, and wait until the horses are harnessed. Another peculiarity struck me as very original: in the middle of summer people may be seen traversing the paved streets in sledges. These sledges—low carriage bodies mounted on frames of wood and iron without wheels—are called "steepkoets," and are used chiefly by old people. The pace is very slow, but the traveling comfortable enough.

The Zoological Garden, adjoining the town, is spacious and tastefully laid out. The number of foreign animals is considerable, and had just been increased by the arrival of several giraffes. The classes of birds and reptiles were very fully represented.

The Museum contains a valuable collection of sea-shells and land-snails.

I visited two picture galleries, the Trippenhuis collection and that of Herr van der Hoop. The word *van*, by the way, unlike the German *von*, is not an indication of nobility; every Hollander may prefix it to his name. The principal pictures I saw were "The Watchmen and ———," by Rembrandt; Van der Helst's "Meal;" Steen's "Feast of St. Nicholas;" and the "School by Moonlight" of Dow. The two galleries can boast of many masterpieces by the above-mentioned artists and by various others, as Ruysdael, Wouvermans, Ostade, etc.

The Van der Hoop gallery is in the Academy, and was a bequest from the proprietor. The Academy hesitated long before accepting the valuable present, the institution then lacking funds to pay the high legacy-duty.

I was much interested during my visit to the diamond-cutting works of Herr Costa, reputed to be the chief establishment of the kind in existence. The Dutch enjoy an acknowledged pre-eminence over all the nations of Europe in the art of cutting diamonds; but in India they have found their masters, as is proved by the great diamond in the possession of the sultan, which was cut in Upper India. This diamond, the largest known to exist, though convex on the under side, has been cut in facets of uniform size, with an amount of skill which even the Hollanders are unable to emulate.

The size of the manufactory is very striking when one considers the smallness of the objects manipulated; the building is more than a hundred feet long and three stories high.

The various operations are conducted in the following way: the rough diamond passes first into the hands of the planer, then into those of the cutter, and finally is handed to the grinder. The first of these operators removes any defects that may be in the stone with a sharp diamond, wherewith he files the gem, and then chips off the faulty piece. The cutter gives the stone its proper shape by getting rid of the corners and inequalities in the same way. The dust obtained by these operations is carefully collected and husbanded, for the use of it is indispensable in grinding the diamond. The grinder uses a leaden bullet inclosed in wood, with the upper portion softened in the fire, so that the stone may be pressed into it as far as necessary. The diamond is then ground on a steel plate, on which a little diamond-dust has been strewn. The great art consists in making the facets and corners perfectly even, whereby the fire and beauty of the diamond are greatly increased.

The turning of the grinding machine (by steam power) is so rapid that the steel disk does not seem to move at all; it makes two thousand revolutions per minute.

A great deal is lost by this grinding; thus the English crown diamond Kôh-i-Noor was reduced one fourth in size on being cut the second time. The first cutting of this beautiful diamond had proved a failure, and in 1852 the English government sent for a Dutch workman from Herr Costa's establishment to cut the stone artistically. The work occupied the lapidary for six months, and the mere working expenses, apart from any profit, which indeed the proprietor of the factory, Herr Costa, would not accept, amounted to four thousand Dutch guilders, or something more than £330 sterling. In Herr Costa's works, of which he is sole owner, 125 workmen are employed, of whom five are planers, thirty cutters, and ninety grinders. These men earn each from thirty to seventy and eighty Dutch guilders per week.

In Amsterdam I saw also the sugar-refining works of Messrs. Spakler, Neoten, and Fetterode. The sugar is refined by means of steam-engines. I have seen the same thing done in other countries. This manufactory turns out about 5,000,000 kilos (about 4885 tons, English weight) of sugar every year. The greatest establishment of the kind in Holland manufactures 16,000,000 kilos, and the entire produce amounts to 80,000,000.

Very near Amsterdam lies the famous Haarlem Lake, the draining of which may be certainly reckoned among the most gigantic undertakings of the present century. Where a few years ago great ships sailed, and where the fisherman spread his nets, thousands of cows now graze, and beauteous fields and meadows smile with verdure; nay, scattered houses, already fast increasing, will soon probably expand into towns and villages.

The pumping out of this lake, which was about thirteen feet deep, was begun in February, 1849, and the whole great work was completed in four years. Engines of 400-horse power were set up in three different places; each of these engines raised the pistons of eight pumps six times a minute, and poured out the water into the canals leading to the sea. The twenty-four pumps of the three engines discharged 20,340 kilderkins of water per minute.

The area of land thus gained amounts to no less than 60,000 English acres. The cultivation of this great tract was begun as early as 1853.

Herr Muyskens, who had the kindness to show me this new wonder of the world, is the owner of a fair tract of the land, from which he carried the first harvest last year. His house, too, was finished, and had been built with much taste. Here I first saw how far the Hollanders' predilection for cattle-breeding leads them; the cow-stable was indisputably the handsomest part of the house. It must be borne in mind, however, that the greater part of the Dutch soil consists of rich pastures and meadows, and that stock-breeding is the chief source of the Dutchman's wealth; it is thus reasonable enough that every possible effort should be made to develop this branch of farming. But I had scarcely expected that their anxiety should go so far as to procure for the cows cleaner and more comfortable dwellings than many well-to-do people can boast in the less civilized countries of Europe, to say nothing of other quarters of the world. The cow-house monopolized the greater part of the building: its windows, of a handsome oval form, were absolutely festooned with white curtains, looped up with gay ribbons. The entrance door, of which the upper part was glazed, also boasted of a curtain of dazzling whiteness. The interior of this establishment was in the form of a lofty spacious

hall. The stalls were just broad enough to allow the hind
feet of the cows to rest on the edge of a canal or gutter a
foot in depth, so that the straw might be kept perfectly
clean. Just over this gutter, and parallel with it, a rope
had been stretched, and to this rope the tails of the cows
were tied, to prevent them from whisking their sides and
raising a dust. All these arrangements were pleasing enough
to the eye; but I fancy, if the poor animals had been consulted, they would have voted for a little more freedom, although **at some sacrifice** of neatness.

One compartment of the stable was partitioned off by a
wall **of** planks three feet high: it had a boarded floor, and
formed quite a neat little room, for the use of the farm attendants. The store-houses for milk, **cheese,** and similar
farm produce were as scrupulously clean as the stable itself. The walls of the entrance halls, staircases, kitchen,
store-rooms, etc., in almost every house, are covered, to **the**
height of three or four feet from the ground, with **tiles of**
white porcelain or green clay, which are not so difficult **to**
keep clean as whitewashed walls.

It was at Herr Muysken's house that, after a long absti-
nence, I enjoyed the luxury of good milk to my coffee;
milk pure and fresh as it comes from the cow. One would
think that in a country like Holland, where there are so
many cows, good milk could be had in abundance; but it
is not so; for the Hollander is such an enthusiast in making
butter and cheese, that, like the Swiss, he scarcely allows
himself enough good milk for domestic purposes. Almost
every where, **even** in the wealthiest families, the coffee was
very indifferent.

While I am speaking of coffee-drinking, that most important subject for us women, I can not help mentioning a
custom prevalent throughout Holland, which, in my humble opinion, is not very seemly or worthy of imitation. As
soon as the coffee or tea-drinking is over, the lady or daugh-

ter of the house, or one of the female authorities, *washes* the
tea-service at the table, in presence of the company. She
pours a little hot water in each of the cups, rinses them
out, wipes them on a cloth, and the business is done.

Herr Muyskens was kind enough to lead me right across
the drained lake to one of the three machines used for
pumping out the water, and one or other of which is occa-
sionally put in requisition when there has been an accumu-
lation of rain-water. We came just in time to see one of
these machines at work.

We went on to Haarlem, where we saw the fine park,
with the elegant royal palace, and likewise a portion of the
town. I noticed over the door of a house an oval disk,
about a foot and a half in length, covered with pink silk,
and ornamented with rich lace in ample folds. They told
me this was a sign that one of the inmates had recently become the possessor of a baby. A strip of paper projecting
above the disk indicates that the new arrival is a girl. The
custom dates from the old warlike times, when the rough
soldier respected the house where the suffering mother lay,
and the practice once prevailed throughout Holland. It
has now fallen into disuse, and is only kept up in Haarlem.

Besides Colonel Steuerwald, who paid me the kindest attention during my stay in Holland, I was fortunate enough
to meet another very amiable friend, the "Resident" van
Rees, whom the readers of my "Second Journey round the
World" will recollect I had encountered at Batavia. Herr
van Rees lived at the Hague; but as soon as he heard of
my arrival in Holland he came to Amsterdam to invite me
to make a short tour through his native country.

We began by an excursion to Utrecht, where a great
Students' Festival happened to be going on when we arrived. The students are in the habit of celebrating the
foundation of the University by an annual commemoration.
The festivities are kept up for a whole week. They com-

prise masked processions, concerts, balls, races, dinners, illuminations, and much more of the same **kind.** This year
the affair was to be particularly brilliant. The worshipful
students, it appears, were divided **into** two factions, the aristocratic and the democratic. Each party wished to out-
shine the other, and had stipulated for an entire week to
carry out their laudable purpose.

We arrived in Utrecht during the aristocrats' week. The
concourse of visitors was so great that we could not find
room in any hotel; fortunately for us, Herr and Frau Suer-
mondt, friends of Herr van Rees, received us with friendly
hospitality in their house.

In the afternoon there was a procession. The students
were all decked out in the most costly dresses; nothing was
to be seen but velvet, satin, lace, and ostrich feathers. Some
groups represented characters of the sixteenth century;
others figured as princes from Java, Hindostan, **etc., with**
their splendid retinues. There was even an Indian **deity,**
carried in a palanquin, and accompanied by **a Malay** band
of music. Whole scenes were represented in enormously
long wagons, and some of these were really very artistically arranged. Thus, for instance, a whole house was shown,
with the side walls taken out. A married pair sat at a ta-
ble; the wife had a child in her lap, and a second was play-
ing about at her feet; the **family** doctor and another friend
were paying **a** visit, chatting and drinking tea, while the
maid was scouring the step in front of the house.

On another wagon a wind-mill was perched; in front sat
a man building a boat, while a second mended his nets.

A third wagon showed the interior of a peasant's farm,
where butter was being churned, sail-cloth **woven, and ropes**
twisted. Next came a hunting procession, the huntsmen
carrying falcons on their wrists, and the whole thing really
capitally carried **out.** The procession was headed **by** mili-
tary music, and a second band brought up the rear. In

the evening the town was brilliantly illuminated with lamps of colored glass and gay paper lanterns arranged in festoons along the streets and on both sides of the canals. In some houses the whole façade was blazing with light, and the portals and balustrades of the bridges glittered with thousands of lamps. Some of the streets looked like fairy-land.

Toward midnight the procession came marching back with a number of torches spitting forth blue and dark purple flames. The feast was not over until two o'clock.

Gay and brilliant it was, I can not deny, but much too grand for students. It might be allowable if the celebration only took place once or twice in a century; even then a single day would be sufficient for it; but in its present form the effect can not be beneficial. The young men must occupy themselves for many weeks beforehand with their masks, costumes, balls, and other delectations, much more than with their studies. Moreover, the expenses are so great that only the rich can bear them with ease; the poorer students must therefore abstain or run into debt. For my part, I infinitely prefer the plain burlesque exhibited at the Artists' Festival at Munich, which, although inexpensive, was full of merriment and wit, lasted only a day, and afforded as much, if not more, pleasure to actors and spectators than could be extracted from this students' feast, with all its show and glitter.

The townspeople, too, are put to an amount of expense by the two evenings' illumination that must be any thing but welcome to the poorer classes among them; but if they neglected to illuminate, the students would be almost sure to break their windows or play them some other silly trick.

Another custom of which I could not approve was the practice pursued by the students of parading about the whole week in their fancy costumes, as princes, knights, etc.

The second entertainment at which I was present consisted of a horse-race and a few feats of horsemanship by

professional circus-riders. To say **the truth,** I expected
something better. Tilting at the ring, or a joust executed
by the students in their fancy costumes, would not have
cost more, as they had dresses and horses all ready provided, and would have been more worthy of the grand pro-
gramme. On this occasion I noticed how difficult it is to
rouse the Hollander from his phlegmatic repose. A Herr
Loisset brought forward a beautiful and marvelously trained horse, which performed such difficult feats as would
have **called forth** the loudest plaudits from any other audience. **To** my surprise, the people remained as cold as
ice, and Herr Loisset left **the** circus with his horse without
receiving the slightest token of approbation.

The town of Utrecht is surrounded by very pretty shrubberies and park-like plantations; **but here, as** every where
else in Holland, the want of hills and mountains **is** evident. There was **not** much to be **seen in** the place. **Of**
the churches, I only visited the Protestant cathedral, allured
by its majestic exterior. Unfortunately, I found **the** interior defaced in an incredible way. As the church is very
large, and the congregation found a difficulty in hearing
the sermons, a great and high partition of boards had been
erected—a church within the church. Of course, this hid-
eous plank-work, which occupies above half the entire
space, completely **destroys the** proper effect of the really
beautiful building.

My friendly host, Herr **Suermondt,** seemed reluctant to
part with me, **and I** readily accepted his hearty invitation
to prolong **my** stay a little while. The first days were devoted to the **town** itself and to the fortifications; and here
and there I snatched an hour for a visit **to** the fine picture-
gallery belonging to Herr Suermondt, and which he has
thrown open to strangers.

We also paid a visit to the favorite resort of the Utrecht-
ers—the little village of Zeigst, a few miles from **the town.**

The drive to this place is charming.   The road, paved with brick like most of the Dutch high roads, leads us past pretty country houses with handsome gardens; in many parts there are avenues of sturdy trees, of a thickness I have seldom seen surpassed.   Lime-trees, oaks, and beech-trees, and among the latter particularly the red beeches, attain a height in Holland perhaps unparalleled elsewhere.

In Zeigst there is an establishment of the Moravian brethren.

CHAPTER III.

On my return from Utrecht to Amsterdam, Herr van
Rees took me to Zaandam and Broeck, an excursion which
can be accomplished in a carriage in one day.

Zaandam is famous as the place where Peter the Great
worked for several months as a carpenter in order to learn
the art of ship-building. They still show the wooden hut
where he dwelt, and this is kept in the same condition in
which the great emperor left it. It consists of two plain
little rooms with a few wooden chairs and tables. To defend it from the effects of the weather, a roof of brick-work
has been built over it, and in winter this is covered in at
the sides with wooden planks. Zaandam, with its thirteen
thousand inhabitants, is a very cheerful little town. Nearly every house is surrounded by its garden.

No less celebrated than Zaandam, but for another cause,
is the little village of Broeck, which has acquired fame by
its exceeding cleanliness, and that, moreover, in a country
where the streets of the towns are often cleaner than the
interior of the houses in many other lands. I expected, of
course, to see something extraordinary, but must confess
that the reality surpassed my expectations.

The houses are all built of wood, and painted of some
dark color. The roofs are covered with glazed tiles, and
the windows adorned with handsome curtains, while every
door-lock is so brightly polished as to look as if it had been
just fixed. All the houses stand in little gardens, and each
has three doors. One of these is never used but on the

most important **events of** life: **when the** bridegroom and bride go forth **to** be married; **when the child is** carried to the font; **and when man is** borne forth **to take** possession of his last earthly dwelling. This strange fashion is found nowhere except in this village. Of **the two** remaining doors, one is used for daily purposes of entrance and exit; the other leads to the stable, which forms part of the building.

The somewhat narrow streets are bordered by wooden palings; behind the houses room is left to drive in the cattle, to stack the harvest of hay, etc. The streets were washed and swept so clean that, though they are skirted by trees, I did not see a single leaf on the ground. The people, I believe, keep no domestic animals except oxen and cows, for fear the streets should **be** dirtied. Verily, this is carrying cleanliness to extremes.

We went into several of the houses. The rooms showed the perfection of cleanliness and adornment. The **floors** were covered with plain carpets or mats, and every **piece** of furniture polished so highly that it looked like **new,** though, to judge from the shape of the different pieces, they evidently dated from the last century. The interior arrangements were handsome enough, with plenty of glazed cupboards, full of all kinds of rarities, particularly china, among which I noticed specimens of Chinese and Japanese manufacture. I saw no beds; their place was supplied by false cupboards in all the rooms, which are metamorphosed into couches at night; but great was the store of bed and table linen. The floors of these rooms must not **be desecrated** by shoes; like the Oriental, the Dutch peasant leaves his slippers at the door. It certainly does not **cost** him much trouble to divest himself of them, for they are of wood, and he has only to kick them off. Not but that he has better ones for Sundays and visiting days; it is only at his work that he is shod with wood.

The cow-stables were far handsomer than those I had seen at Herr Muysken's establishment in the Lake of Haarlem. They consist of long halls, with handsome ceilings, resting on pillars of wood. But a stable of this kind is, in fact, only half a stable, for the cattle only live in it during the winter. On the first of May the beasts are driven to pasture, and there they remain until the first of November, and during this time the farmer may be said to make a summer residence of his stable. The hall is divided into **compartments** or rooms by partitions four feet high, and in **these rooms the** family lives the whole of the day, only using the real dwelling-house at night. The walls and pillars of the hall are hung with glittering paraphernalia of china, plates, dishes, and metal cans, and even pictures are seen there. The implements for making butter and cheese are ranged in perfect order in the various compartments, and every thing glistens and gleams as brightly **as** if it had never been used. Not a stain, not an atom of dust is tolerated any where.

It happened to be on a Sunday that we visited Broeck, and the villagers were at church. We proceeded there to see them in their Sunday garb. There was nothing peculiar **in the** costume **of** the men, who were all very neat and **tidy;** but all the women wore that unhappy head-dress, common throughout Holland, which seems to have been invented to deprive the female sex of its chief natural ornament, for it entirely conceals the hair.

This head-dress, probably invented of old by some dame of high degree who had lost her hair, is worthy of a particular description. A hoop **of** gilt metal encircles the head. This hoop is about an inch and a quarter in width at the forehead, increasing to two inches at the back of the head. This fillet is surmounted by a white cap, fitting tight to the skull, and trimmed with broad folds of lace, while a long strip of the same fabric hangs down over the shoulders.

Chased gilt ornaments an inch and a half long, and an inch broad, are attached to each temple, producing very much the effect of the blinkers with which the bridles of carriage-horses are furnished. Three little locks of silk hang down over the eyes. This head-dress certainly has no pretensions to taste, but has the advantage of being subject to no change in fashion. It is expensive enough, costing generally from sixty to eighty Dutch guilders, and even some hundreds in the cases of rich people, who ornament their coifs with pearls and precious stones; but these are heir-looms, descending from generation to generation.

Many women absolutely place a structure of straw, with a broad brim bent upward in front and behind, on this wonderful cap when they go out, and this queer affair they call a hat. I was astonished to find that girls and women endowed by nature with beautiful hair subjected themselves to this foolish fashion—the motive could scarcely be vanity.

In the remaining costume of the women I found nothing very worthy of remark. On Sunday they all wear gowns of black merino. The fashionable world dresses as it does every where else; and some of the citizens' wives paid homage to the present fashion so far as to wear a stylish bonnet over their hideous Dutch caps.

On the following morning, my indefatigable Mentor, Herr van Rees, took me to the Hague to see his family.

The Hague, a city of eighty thousand inhabitants, does not look so ancient as Amsterdam, but is very much cleaner, principally from the fact that the Hague is not such a manufacturing and commercial city as Amsterdam. Like all Dutch cities, it is intersected by numerous canals. The Hague is the seat of government and the abode of the court, the foreign embassadors, and officials generally. The king has several palaces, not remarkable either for size or for their architecture. They look merely like handsome private houses. The old chief palace, built in the town itself, is a fortress surrounded by moats, **and built on a low** mound or redoubt.   The heavy gates, the **tower, and** especially the **dark** color with which it is stained all over, give **this place** an appearance of antiquity.

About the churches there is not much to be said.   **The** cathedral is a very handsome building, dreadfully disfigured by being surrounded by **a** number of mean-looking little houses.

The picture gallery, **here** called the "Museum," owes its celebrity chiefly to two pictures, which are reckoned among **the great masterpieces** of the Dutch school — a cattle-piece **in life size, by Paul Potter, and** Rembrandt's "Doctor," or "Anatomist."

The cattle-piece is so true to nature, **so warm in tone,** and powerful in execution, that **one almost wonders,** after a lengthened contemplation of the work, **to see the bull, the** sheep, the cow, and the shepherd **remain so** still **and motionless,** expecting them to begin to move.

The other picture is just as extraordinary in **its way, but** I thought the subject less attractive.   The surgeon **is** dissecting a corpse.   He has just laid open the palm of the hand **and** the arm sufficiently to expose the whole system **of veins** and nerves, and he is explaining these to his audience.   The calmness of the operator, to whom the business is familiar, and **the rapt attention of** his hearers, some **of** whom are hanging **upon his words, while** others gaze fixedly upon **the dissected subject, are** admirably rendered; in my poor opinion, this picture **is** the great painter's masterpiece.   Besides these two great paintings, there are many charming pieces by Steen, Ostade, Rubens, and others.

Herr de Boer's bazar is well worth a visit.   I have seen similar establishments in other great towns, but none to compare with **this.**   The objects **to be seen** are innumerable, **and are** arranged in the most attractive manner in large **halls.**   There is **a** great variety, in particular, of Chinese and Japanese objects. That Nature may not be forgotten amid the **charms of** Art, these halls are surrounded by beautiful green-houses, which, with their palms and cactuses, sugar-canes, and coffee-trees, remind the Hollander who has returned from India of the El Dorado he has left. Another arrangement, unfortunately not universal, is, that all who come to Herr de Boer's bazar, whether purchasers or visitors, **are** alike treated with great civility and **attention.**

The Dutch seat of government possesses a very fine park, whose fresh verdure, glorious trees, and blooming slopes **re-minded** me of the parks in England. Very charming, too, **is the** road from the Hague to Scheveningen, a fishing village on the coast, some half **a** dozen miles from the city, and a place much frequented by **the** townspeople in summer for bathing purposes. The action of the waves here is said to be particularly invigorating. Thick shady avenues for pedestrians, carriages, and horses extend to **the** entrance of the village. Scarce a sunbeam struggles through the thick foliage, so that there is coolness and refreshment on the hottest day of summer. Unfortunately, however, real summer days are very sparingly meted out to the Hollanders, the full power of the sun being felt only for a short period in this land. It was in June that I visited Holland, and yet it was only at noon that I found it agreeable to lay aside my warm cloak. **In the** evening and the morning the thermometer often **showed** only six to eight degrees Réaumur, and in the night the mercury must have sunk some degrees lower. They told **me,** however, that **this year was** an exceptionally cold one, and strong north winds were continually blowing.

From the Hague I made a few excursions—one to the city of Leyden, and another to the busy port of Rotterdam.

Leyden is a very dull place. In the busiest streets it is very easy to count the passengers, and it very seldom hap-

pens that one must step aside to avoid a passing carriage.
But the place possesses great Art treasures. The museums
of Leyden are celebrated for their great collections, particularly of specimens of animals, fishes, and reptiles, and likewise of skulls of men of almost every race. The Museum
of Antiquities possesses many rolls of Egyptian papyrus,
mummies, and Egyptian and Buddhist idols.

Messrs. Leeman and Schlegel, the curators of these museums, were obliging enough to conduct us through them
in person. Unhappily, our time was so limited that we
could only give a passing glance at all these wonders. The
museums are separated, because it was impossible, we were
told, to find a single building with the requisite number of
great rooms. The collections are at present deposited in
ordinary dwelling-houses.

The Japanese Museum, an exceedingly complete collection of the natural and artificial products of that country, is
the private property of Dr. Siebold.

If Leyden did not appear very attractive to me as a city,
I was much delighted with Rotterdam: if I had to fix my
residence in one of the cities of Holland, it should certainly
be here. In this rich commercial town there is business
and bustle all day long, especially on the canals, which are
broader and deeper than those of the other towns, and as
navigable for great three-masted ships as for little cockboats.

Few towns offer such an aspect as Rotterdam, where marine colossi with high masts, as well as smoking steamers,
are seen parading, as it were, through the middle of the city.
I stood for hours at the window, and was never weary of
gazing. Yonder a great East Indiaman is slowly getting
under way; here a ship has just arrived from a long voyage, and the sailors are shouting, waving their caps, and
calling to their wives, who, informed of the vessel's arrival,
stand waiting on the banks of the canal. Here weighty
chests of sugar and bags of coffee are being dragged out of

the hold of a ship and deposited in the huge warehouses;
there they are loading a brig with Dutch produce for conveyance abroad; steamers of all sizes are swirling by every moment, and hundreds of boats dart to and fro among
them. To be able to see all this from my own window
seems so strange, that I rub my eyes, fancy myself in a
dream, and refuse to believe in the reality.

Rotterdam has many great and handsome houses; some
are particularly remarkable for having flat terraces instead
of ordinary roofs. The park adjoins one of the best streets;
though less spacious than the Haagsche Bosch, it is charm-
ingly laid out.

In Rotterdam I took leave of my worthy and generous
friend, Herr van Rees. The good-nature of this gentleman
was so great, that he wished to take me through the whole
of Holland, as far as Gueldres and Friesland; but it would
have been more than encroaching on my part to take advantage of his liberal offer. I alleged that the time had
come when I must embark on my new journey, and that I
must proceed at once to London to make the necessary
preparations.

My stay in Holland had been a brief one—about a fortnight. During this time I had seen many interesting things,
but few scenes of natural beauty. In this respect Holland
is poor. A great portion of the land, having been won
from the sea, necessarily consists of a continuous plain, broken here and there only by low banks and "dunes," about
twenty or thirty feet high. In Gueldres and Friesland,
these "dunes," or sandy banks, are said to attain a height
of from fifty to a hundred feet. The views, therefore, show
the same features every where—green meadows, with cattle
grazing, a few fields, pretty shrubberies, great massive trees,
and neat farms and villages. The picture thus presented
is cheerful enough, but when one has it continually before
one's eyes it soon becomes monotonous, and creates a crav-

ing for the sight of mountains, or, at least, **of a range of hills.**

The most striking objects to the traveler in Holland are the numerous canals, great and small, which intersect both **town** and country **in** all directions. Every patch of field, every meadow, is, **as** it were, **a** little island, surrounded in all directions by canals two or three feet **broad.**

The part of Holland through which I passed **consists** principally of marsh land. As far as the eye can reach, it **rests** upon pastures full of fine-looking cattle, which constitute the chief wealth of the country. In Holland there are **about** 1,130,000 **head** of cows, oxen, and calves, to **a** population of 3,200,000 souls, a proportion **to** which **no** other country presents a parallel. No wonder that Holland provides half the world with butter and cheese.

The soil is decidedly fertile — witness the fat pastures and meadows, the plentiful crops of great heavy corn-ears, and the strong, lofty trees. A fruitful land is Holland, I **will not deny,** but certainly not a beautiful **one.**

CHAPTER IV.

London.—Paris.—Sitting of the Geographical Society.—News from Mada-gascar.—Popular Life in Paris.—Sights.—A Tale of Murder.—Versailles.—St. Cloud.—Celebration of Sunday.

ON the 2d of July I quitted Rotterdam, and embarked in a steamer belonging to Messrs. Smith and Ers for London (distance 150 sea-miles, time of passage 20 hours). This company was the first English one that refused to allow me to pay. I had already taken my passage; but, as soon as Mr. Smith heard my name, he insisted, in the kindest way, on returning me the passage-money.

In London I spent about four weeks with my worthy friend, Mr. Waterhouse, of the British Museum; and on the 1st of August I proceeded to Paris.

The chief aim of my journey was to visit the island of Madagascar, with whose government the French alone have relations. I was therefore obliged to go to Paris to obtain information respecting this, to me, unknown country. To say the truth, I was not sorry for this; for, strange as the fact may appear to many of my readers, in all my wander-ings through the world I had never visited Paris.

I reached that city on the morning of the 2d of August, and at once set about my work. My fortunate star led me to make my first visit to Monsieur Jaumard, the President of the Geographical Society, and on that very evening the society was to hold its last meeting for the present summer.

I had a very warm letter of recommendation to Monsieur Jaumard from Professor Carl Ritter, of Berlin. Monsieur Jaumard received me in the kindest manner, and invited me to be present at the sitting. I was introduced by the celebrated geographer, Monsieur Malte-Brun. **A place** was assigned to me at some distance from the table. **At** the commencement of the sitting the president made a speech in which he introduced me to the society, said a few words respecting **my** travels, and concluded by proposing that I should be received as an honorary member. The assembled members held up their hands in assent, and my **admission** was carried without **a** dissentient voice.

I was as much gratified as astonished at this distinction, which I had not anticipated in the least; my pleasure was **all** the **greater** from the fact that my old tutor, who had **taught** me history and geography, officiated as corresponding **member of** this same society. The president rose, and **led** me from my place to the table, at which I now took my place as a member, amid the cordial **congratulations of the** whole company.

I immediately consulted the gentlemen present with **respect** to my intention of undertaking a voyage **to Madagascar:** they were unanimous in thinking the plan quite impracticable under existing circumstances. During my stay in Holland I had already gleaned from newspaper reports that the French government intended sending a squadron **to** Madagascar, and that a serious war was considered imminent. I now learned some farther particulars. The French **have** for centuries possessed a little island, called St. Maria, **on** the coast of Madagascar. In the time of the late king Radama they succeeded in obtaining a footing in Madagascar itself by acquiring **a** district in the Bay of Vanatobé. In this district there is **a** rich depôt for coals; and the French employ 180 colored workmen, Indians, negroes, etc., from the Mauritius, under the superintendence of three white men. On the accession of Queen Ranavola, after the death of Radama, the new sovereign ordered these people to evacuate the district. They refused to obey the mandate, as they considered the place to be the property of the

D

French government. Hereupon the **queen** sent 2000 soldiers, **who fell upon** the community, killed two white men and a hundred negroes, and dragged away the rest and sold them **as** slaves. The French government naturally demanded satisfaction, though there **was little** chance of obtaining justice **without** resorting **to violent** measures; and thus every one was prepared, as I have said, **for** the breaking out of a serious war.

Wherever I made inquiries, these reports **were confirmed; and I consequently** found myself compelled, if not **to give up the plan of my** journey, at all events to modify it. As a matter of precaution, I took with me a letter of recommendation from the **French Admiralty to** the commanders **of their vessels on foreign stations. I was** asked to **wait for the return of the emperor, who had** gone to some bathing-place, **that I might be introduced** to him; but that would have kept me too **long; and I** quitted Paris with my business in a very unfinished state.

The few days which I spent in this **great** city **I utilized** as much as **possible** in getting at least a glance at its **many** objects of interest. Of course I should not dream of giving an accurate description of **what I saw.** The rage for traveling is so universal at the present day, and the facilities for getting over hundreds **of** miles **of** ground, **at** least in Europe, in a few days' time, are so great, that a large majority of my readers have probably been to Paris themselves; and **those who** have not **seen** the great city are sure to know, from the descriptions of other travelers, as much as I could **tell** them about it. I will, therefore, only describe in a very few words the impressions I carried away with me.

London and Paris differ as widely from one another as the English character from the French. In both cities there is plenty of life and bustle; but one can see at the first glance that **in Paris** it is not all, as in London, a *business life.* One does not see those rigid self-contained figures, wending their way with restless steps, careless of all that is passing around them, and seeming to consider every wasted minute as an irreparable loss. In Paris, lounging seems the order of the day, and even the bustling man of business finds time to greet his friends and exchange a few words with them, and to pause, moreover, for a few minutes in front of this or that shop, and admire the wares displayed with such really wonderful taste in the window.

The houses themselves don't look so grave as the London domiciles. They are of large size (for in some more than thirty families live), and are not nearly so much blackened by coal-smoke as the London houses are. The doors are all open, and afford a view into neat court-yards, which are sometimes adorned with flowers—decidedly a more agreeable aspect than the tightly-closed doors of London, which seem to give the houses an uninhabited look.

In the evening the difference is most perceptible, for then the characteristic restlessness and love of pleasure inherent in the French display themselves in full force. All the streets, the public squares, the places of amusement, are equally crowded; and the Englishman, accustomed to spend his evenings in the family circle, by the fireside, for seven or eight months in the year, and in the garden of his cottage during the remaining four or five, might fancy, on first seeing the pressure and crush in the streets of Paris, that some public festival was being celebrated.

The centres of all this life are the Boulevards; and very bright and fairy-like is the scene there, on a fine summer evening, with their magnificent cafés standing wide open, and splendid shops, bright as day with the glare of thousands of gas-lamps, and with their motley crowd of carriages in the roads and of pedestrians, either wandering to and fro on the broad pavements, or sitting at neat little tables in front of the coffee-houses.

The Champs Elysées are no less attractive, though they

scarcely realize their name of *fields;* for, except in the short space between the Place de la Concorde and the Rondpoint, trees and grass-plots have begun to **vanish** rather rapidly, to be replaced by handsome houses and hotels. The view in the Champs Elysées is closed by **one of the** finest monuments of modern architecture—the Arc de l'Etoile—a colossal triumphal arch, built by Napoleon the **Great, in the** style of the Roman gate of Septimius Severus. **The chief** victories of the great conqueror are sculptured with exquisite skill on this monument.

A broad road, or avenue, which in a short time will probably also be quite filled with houses, leads from this point **to** the celebrated Bois de Boulogne. The name of this wood was so frequently in every body's mouth, that I naturally expected to **see a forest of great** sturdy trees, something **in the** style of the **" Prater" at Vienna, or** the " Thiergarten" at Berlin; but **it was not so.** In spite of its age, the Bois de Boulogne has never become a forest. The trees have remained small and spare, and it is a difficult matter to find a shady spot. The new and tasteful arrangement of this locality, and the addition of a beautiful fountain, are due to the present emperor, Napoleon III. He seems to be so fortunate in all his undertakings, that I should not wonder if he succeeded in making the trees **grow.**

The Tuileries Gardens are not very spacious, but they contain glorious specimens of venerable old trees. Here, as in all public places in Paris, chairs in abundance are **to be** had. You must pay for them; but the sum asked is very moderate—one sou per chair, whether you are a tenant for five minutes or for half a day.

Between the Champs Elysées and the Tuileries Gardens lies the Place de la Concorde, one of the finest squares in Europe. In old times it was called the Place Louis XV.; **and** here it was that the guillotine worked with horrible industry during the years 1792, 1793, and 1794, numbering Louis XVI., Marie Antoinette, Philippe Egalité, Marie Helène of France, Robespierre, and hundreds besides, among its victims. Now this place is adorned by two beautiful fountains, and on the spot occupied by the guillotine rises the great obelisk of Luxor. This obelisk, seventy-two feet in height, and of five hundred thousand pounds weight, is hewn out of a single block of stone: 1550 years before the Christian era it was **set** up in front of a temple at Thebes, in Upper Egypt. Mehemet Ali presented it to the French government. Louis Philippe had a ship built at Toulon **expressly** for its conveyance to France, peculiarly fashioned, **so as** to ascend the Nile to Luxor, near Thebes. Eight hundred men were engaged for three months in removing the obelisk from the temple to the ship. In the month of December, 1833, it arrived in Paris, but its erection was not accomplished until October, 1836. The cost of transporting and setting it up amounted to two millions of francs.

Late building operations have completely united the palace of the Tuileries with the Louvre, so that the two now form a single structure—undoubtedly the grandest of its kind in Europe. A few years ago houses of irregular architecture separated these two palaces, and the quarter of Paris surrounding them is said to have been one of the most extensive and the dirtiest in the city. Louis Philippe intended to have these old buildings pulled down, and to build broad straight streets that should unite the Tuileries with the Louvre; **but** millions of money were required to realize the idea, and constitutional kings can not dispose of the **funds of the state** at their own sweet will. Napoleon arranged all that more conveniently; the Senate and **the** Corps Legislatif, far more accommodating than were their predecessors, the Chambers of Peers and of Deputies, are always happy to fulfill the wishes of their sovereign.

There is so much to be seen in both these palaces, in the

way of pictures, antiquities, models of fortresses, ships, and other curiosities, that one might wander about for weeks in the labyrinth of halls and galleries, quite unconscious of the lapse of time. One of the apartments is dedicated entirely to relics of Napoleon the First. Here are to be seen his tent-bed, his writing-table, his arm-chair, his robes, various uniforms and hats, many golden keys of conquered cities and fortresses, Turkish and Arabian saddles, and many other properties. The worshipers of this modern Cæsar attach a great value to the handkerchief with which the death-damps were wiped from his brow at St. Helena. Not one of the other members of the Bonaparte family is represented by any article in the collection, except perhaps the Duke of Reichstadt, one of whose coats is displayed there.

The Luxembourg Gardens, on the south bank of the Seine, are very prettily laid out. The palace, built in a severe style, possesses a rich gallery of pictures, mostly modern pieces. The halls and chambers are arranged with great splendor and true artistic taste.

Of the churches I visited but few. Notre Dame is distinguished by its pure Gothic architecture. The church of St. Geneviève is one of the oldest in Paris. It contains the tomb of the patroness of Paris, in a neat chapel, built in the Byzantine style, behind the chief altar. In the church of St. Sulpice, the façade, with its double rows of pillars and a gallery, is remarkable. In the background of this church, in a kind of niche, is a marble statue representing the Virgin Mary standing with the infant Jesus on a globe. A cupola-shaped roof, with a beautiful fresco of the Ascension, rises over the statue, which, exquisitely chiseled, and with the light falling upon it with magic effect, has a most solemn and impressive appearance. Again, I could not help remarking the amount of poetry and effect developed in the Roman Catholic religion—and what an advantage does this effect give it among the excitable masses of the people, over

the simple and rather monotonous forms of Protestant worship! It is unfortunate, however, that abuses, more or less
objectionable, have every where crept in, and are very dam-
aging, if not entirely destructive, to this poetic feeling.
Take, for instance, the wretched custom adopted in French
churches of paying for chairs. There are few or no benches,
but great stores of chairs are heaped up against the walls.
For each chair the charge is a sou; and at the end of the
year all these sous no doubt make up a round sum, which
is very welcome to the worthy dignitaries of the church;
but the devotions of the congregation are terribly disturbed. Every moment the verger comes pushing his way
through the people; first he brings a chair, then takes one
away; now he asks for money, and then he chats with
some regular customer. And is not the idea of being
obliged to pay, in a temple of God, for the right of sitting
down, enough in itself to drive away all serious and devout
thoughts?

The Pantheon is built in the Grecian style; the interior
forms a cross. This church contains monuments of many
celebrated Frenchmen. I felt the greatest interest in those
of J. J. Rousseau and Voltaire.

The Hôtel des Invalides is a magnificent institution for
the reception of 5000 old soldiers who have been frequently wounded in battle, or have lost an arm or a leg. The
building seems very conveniently arranged, and the old
pensioners are said to be well treated; but no one has
thought of providing a grass-plot for their delectation.
Even the courts are destitute of trees and benches. The
officers have had a small garden laid out at their own expense. The dome of the "Invalides" is of great size. The
interior is ornamented with a great number of captured
flags, and on the walls appear great tablets, graced with the
names of celebrated generals. Behind the high altar is the
chapel, where the remains of Napoleon, solemnly brought

from St. Helena in 1840, are to rest until the mausoleum is finished. It was nearly completed at the time of my visit. It consists of a beautiful rotunda, surrounded by twelve pillars, with twelve colossal statues of marble in the intervening spaces. The floor is likewise of marble, with a laurel wreath in mosaic surrounding the sarcophagus, which is cut out of a single block of porphyry. The entrance porch, from which two flights of steps lead downward into the rotunda, is supported by two gigantic statues. The gate **and** the statues, which are of bronze, are beautifully executed. **The part of the** church that rises over the mausoleum is **nearly covered with** gilding, and when the full light of day shines upon it the effect is magical.

With the celebrated cemetery of Père la Chaise I was greatly disappointed; but seeing the cemetery at New York had perhaps spoiled me for admiring any other. The graves are certainly adorned with tombs, flowers, and shrubs, but every thing **is so** crowded together that there is scarcely room to walk. The number of monuments distinguished by grace and richness of adornment is small, and their effect is lost by their position. The most interesting among these **is that** of Abélard and Heloise, who died in the twelfth century, and whose ashes were removed to this resting-place in the nineteenth.

The graves of the poor are in a division by themselves. **Here** I found on many—particularly on the graves of children—monuments that seemed to me much more attractive and more touching than the tombs of the rich. They consisted of little glass cases, containing tiny altars, on which the favorite playthings of the dead babies were displayed. In one I noticed a tiny basket, in which lay the thimble and sewing implements of some industrious little worker whose labor here on earth was finished—a simple memorial, but one that spoke eloquently to the heart!

The cemetery of Père la Chaise was not opened till the

year 1804; it contains 100 acres, and is entirely surrounded by a high wall. The view from the hill that rises in the midst is the best reward for a very toilsome walk.

I could only pay a flying visit to the Jardin des Plantes and the Museum. The wealth of the former in exotic plants and animals is well known; both institutions are reckoned among the most remarkable in Europe.

I was much pleased with my visit to the Manufacture des Gobelins, or, as I might term it, Picture Carpet. This tapestry is wrought with such perfection, that a close inspection is required to convince the beholder he is gazing, not at an oil-painting, but a woven fabric. The drawing is very correct, and the mingling and transition of the various colors delicate and finished, as if a practiced pencil had been at work. For hours I stood watching the workmen, without obtaining the slightest clew to the secret of the art they practiced. The workman has a kind of large frame before him, on which the threads, or tissue, or warp (I am unacquainted with the right term) are perpendicularly fastened; at his side he has a huge basket of Berlin wool, wound on shuttles, and of all imaginable hues and shades. The picture he has to copy is not a worked pattern divided into squares, but an oil-painting; and it is not placed in front of the artistic weaver, but behind him. He works at the wall of threads before him, beginning from below and making his way upward, without even sketching the picture he wants to copy; I noticed some workmen, however, who had indicated the part at which they were working— a foot, for instance, or a hand—by a few strokes on the edge of the frame. Those men who imitate Persian and Indian carpets, producing fabrics a quarter of an inch thick, and which resembles cut velvet, have the original, also an oil-painting, suspended above their heads. In some apartments the most gorgeous Gobelins were displayed. They are very dear; a piece of tapestry, fifteen to twenty feet in height by eight or ten in breadth, will cost from 100,000 to 150,000 francs. But then a workman has frequently to labor for ten or more years at such a piece. The wages of the workmen are not very high; I was told, however, that after a certain number of years of service they receive a pension, which is granted in a shorter period should they become blind over their work—a calamity which not unfrequently befalls them.

My last visit was to the Morgue, where the bodies of persons found dead are exposed for identification by relatives or friends. Many of my readers will perhaps wonder how I, a woman, could visit such a place; but they must remember that, during my journeyings, I have frequently been face to face with death, and that its aspect, consequently, was less terrible to me than to the majority of people; and I can therefore look at times even with a kind of mournful complacency upon its image, mindful of that last journey all of us must take.

The Morgue is a large vaulted apartment, divided into two halves by a partition of glass. In the division behind the glass wall are six or eight low tables, or slabs, on which the corpses are laid out. The clothes they had on when found are hung upon the walls. The other half of the room is for the visitors, among whom, if any of the bodies show marks of violence, secret agents of the police are accustomed to mingle, to glean from the expression of countenance, or from any chance remark, a clew by which to track the criminal. The corpses are thus exposed for three days, but the clothes are left hanging for a longer period. The most terrible sights are sometimes seen here. Thus I saw a male corpse that had lain for some months in the water, and on the next table a young girl whose head had been completely cut off; it had afterward been sewn on the neck. The poor creature had been murdered by her lover through jealousy. A remarkable incident in this murder was that the perpetrator, disturbed in the very fact, leaped from the window of a room on the sixth story without injuring himself. He scrambled up from the ground and ran away. Three days afterward, when I left Paris, he had not been apprehended.

I was told that a few weeks before, some fishermen had brought in a table-leaf with the body of a woman tied to it, but the head and feet were missing. The fishermen had discovered the body in the river by chance; it had been weighted with stones, and sunk. All possible measures were immediately taken by the authorities to find the head and feet; and, contrary to expectation, they were eventually found, though hidden in separate places. The body was then put together and exposed in the Morgue. One of the secret agents quickly noticed among the spectators an old woman who could scarcely suppress an exclamation on seeing the corpse. When she left the room the agent requested her to accompany him to the commissary, and on being asked if she knew the deceased, she replied that she recognized in the poor creature a likeness to a woman who had lived in her neighborhood a short time ago, but who had lately removed to quite another quarter of the town. Farther questioning brought out the fact that the murdered woman had come from the provinces a few months before with a sum of money, intending to carry on some small trade in Paris; she made acquaintance with a man who professed himself willing to serve her, and announced to her, after a short time, that he had found a better and cheaper dwelling for her. She accepted his offer, left her old domicile without giving the address of her new one, and since that time nothing more had been heard of her. Inquiries were made of the commissionaires, or porters of the neighborhood, one of whom remembered carrying her luggage, and pointed out the house where he had deposited it. A secret agent betook himself thither, but found the

door locked. At his summons the porter appeared. The
agent asked him if a Monsieur X—— did not live in that
house; **and** on receiving an answer in the negative, added,
"That is very singular, for the address is quite correct," at
the same time showing a paper. **The** porter declared there
must be some mistake, for the house belonged **to** Monsieur
L——, who passed the greater part of the year in the country, but had given particular orders that not a **single room**
should **be** let. The agent departed, but the **house was**
watched, and at about eleven o'clock at night two suspicious-
looking characters were seen to enter. After making sure
that there was no other means of exit, a sufficient number
of armed policemen rushed into the house, and secured the
porter and his two associates without much resistance. The
house was carefully searched, and in one of the rooms they
discovered not only the frame-work of the table on a leaf
of which the woman had been bound, but traces of blood,
and the bloodstained axe with which the unhappy creature,
lured into the house by the murderers, had been killed.
But enough of these horrors, of which, alas! **Paris** offers
but too many examples.

My excursions in the environs of the capital were limited to Versailles, Trianon, and St. Cloud, which I visited on
one **and** the same day.

The railway takes one, in an hour, to Versailles, past the
little town of Sèvres, celebrated for its great porcelain manufactory. Sèvres is picturesquely situated in a broad valley watered by the Seine. The railroad runs, throughout
nearly **the** whole distance, parallel with the valley at a considerable elevation, so that the traveler sees the charming,
highly-cultivated country gliding past like scenes in a magic
lantern.

As regards Versailles itself, I candidly confess myself unable to describe it. I can only assure my readers that such
splendor in buildings, gardens, halls, pictures, and general

arrangements could only arise in France, under a king like
Louis XIV., who rivaled the Romans themselves in luxury,
and held the modest opinion that *he* was the state, and the
people but an accessory to his greatness.

Hurrying through the lofty halls, and marking the innumerable pictures, representing battles, assaults, burning
towns and villages, with the inhabitants half naked and in
full flight, I could not help asking myself in what we are
superior to the wild Indian. Our civilization has refined
our customs, but our deeds have remained the same. The
savage kills his enemies with a club; we slay ours with
cannon balls. The savage hangs up scalps, skulls, and similar trophies in his wigwam; we paint them on canvas to
decorate our palaces withal; where, then, is the great difference?

At St. Cloud I could only visit the gardens, the palace
being occupied by the empress. The fountains here are
said to be very grand, but they do not play every Sunday.
It was on a Sunday that I went to St. Cloud, but, unfortunately, not on one of the high days; there were, however,
pedestrians in plenty, and, had I been an Englishwoman, I
should have been horrified; for there were children here,
and even young men and maidens, so lost to all sense of
propriety as to play at ball on a Sunday!

I have already observed that the good Parisians are
rather too fond of pleasure, and I am ready to allow that
too much of any thing is objectionable; but, on the other
hand, I submit, even at the risk of being anathematized as
unchristianlike by English ladies generally, that it is quite
natural for people who have to sit for the whole week
long at the work-table, in the shop, or in the counting-
house, to indulge in a little recreation on Sundays. I can
not imagine the bountiful Creator of all things looking with
displeasure upon really innocent relaxation. It is all very
well for rich people, who can amuse themselves every day

in the week, and let their children have a holiday on Saturday, to make it a rule to observe the Sabbath strictly; but to the poor man, who works hard all the six days to maintain himself and his family in honesty, the Almighty will surely grant permission to forget his cares in harmless pleasure on the seventh.

CHAPTER V.

ON the 12th of August I left Paris, as I have said, with my business unconcluded, and returned to London.

After mature deliberation, I had at length taken my resolution. The exceedingly kind reception I had met with in the Dutch Indies on my last journey aroused in me the wish to make a second voyage in the same direction, particularly as there were many islands yet to be explored. The state of affairs in Madagascar might also change during my absence, and on my return I might find it possible to visit this almost unknown region. I made inquiries about the price of a passage, but found it was £75—too much for my purse. As a special favor, I was to be allowed a reduction of five pounds; but I hoped to find more favorable conditions offered in Holland, and the sequel proved that I was not mistaken.

Before leaving London I paid a visit to Mr. Shaw, the Secretary of the Geographical Society. He had read in the papers of the honor accorded to me by the Geographical Society of Paris. He seemed somewhat embarrassed, and expressed his regret that a similar step could not be taken in London, inasmuch as it was expressly forbidden by the statutes to receive a woman as a member. I wonder what the emancipated ladies of the United States would say to such a prohibition! That I should not be received was natural enough, for I can not lay claim to a deep knowl-

edge of any branch of the science. But no one will doubt
the existence of many really scientific women at the present day, and to exclude such persons merely on account
of their sex I think incomprehensible. It might pass in
the East, where the female sex is not held in great estimation, but not in a country like England, which professes to
take pride in its civilization, and to keep pace with the spirit of the times.

So far as I am personally concerned, I have every reason to be grateful to the Geographical Society of London.
It made me a valuable present, without my having taken
any steps in the matter; for it never was my way to thrust
myself forward or to petition for any thing.

On the 22d of August I again set foot on Dutch soil, and
it was in Rotterdam. My valued friend, Colonel Steuerwald, had recommended me to Herr Baarz; and by this
friendly and exceedingly obliging gentleman I was received
in the heartiest manner, and spent some very agreeable
days in his house. Herr Baarz introduced me to Herr
Oversee, one of the principal ship-owners of Rotterdam.
One of his ships was just ready to sail for Batavia; she
was to be dispatched at the end of August. This was a
capital opportunity for me. But Herr Oversee tried to dissuade me from going in this ship, as all the berths were not
only taken, but overcrowded as far as the Cape of Good
Hope, where the vessel was to touch. Besides the cabin
passengers, there was to be a whole cargo of children, boys
and girls, of from ten to fourteen years of age, nearly a hundred in number, who had been bespoken by Dutchmen settled at the Cape, to be trained as men- and maid-servants.
As I heard that a separate part of the ship had been allotted
to the girls, and that they had been placed under the superintendence of a matron, and as I was anxious not to miss
this opportunity of starting, I urged Herr Oversee to give
me a berth in this portion of the ship. The kind man ac-

quiesced at once. He put **me on a** par with the first-class passengers as to diet and other details: **from the Cape to** the **end** of my journey I was to **have a separate cabin, and** the charge for the entire voyage was not more than twelve pounds ten shillings sterling.

This affair concluded, I went to Amsterdam to **take leave** of the amiable Steuerwald family, and came just in time to be present at some public festivities, celebrated, as it seemed to me, on very extraordinary grounds. The festival was in honor **of the** separation effected between Belgium and Holland twenty-five years before. This separation had **been any** thing but voluntary on the part of Holland, but it was nevertheless commemorated with great enthusiasm. The affair had already been going on for some days when I arrived, and was not to be finished under three or four more. Dutchmen seem to think it impossible **to** get through with a holiday under a week. On the other hand, **the** people are certainly very moderate in their requirements: **all** they want is license to parade about the streets from **morn**ing till late in the evening, to look at a few flags and wooden triumphal arches, and to see those who really do feast drive past on their way to banquets and to balls.

The chief solemnity was fixed for the 27th of August, the anniversary of the "separation." I arrived on the afternoon of the 26th, and found every window decorated with flags, little triumphal **arches** here and there, gay with green boughs and colored paper, and such a crowd in the streets that my carriage could scarcely force its way through.

Next day there was certainly something extra to be seen. In spite of the streams of rain which kept pouring from the heavens (perhaps in token of mourning for the "separation"), the military turned out on parade; the king appeared on a tribune erected in the cathedral square, opposite the palace, listened to the speeches of the burgomaster, and **of** the leaders of the troops who still survived from those days,

and made speeches in reply. Four hundred children sang
the national anthem and other hymns. A monument was
moreover uncovered—an obelisk, with the Goddess of Union standing thereupon, and its base resting on the heads
of many lions, from whose open jaws streams of water gush-
ed forth. In the evening we had a display of fire-works
and illuminations.

I should not like to incur the imputation of passing a
hasty judgment upon the people, nor do festivities of this
description afford much opportunity for forming an opinion, for the same curiosity and the same contentment are
found among the people all the world over when there is
any thing to be seen. I was, however, disagreeably impressed here, as I had been already at the Hague and at Utrecht,
by the frequent appearance of groups of slatternly women,
three or four of them arm-in-arm, pushing their way noisily through the crowd, and sometimes even heading troops
of half-drunken men, like so many Megæras, shouting and
dancing as noisily as the topers themselves. This the Hollanders call jollity. I call it shamelessness; and am always
grieved to see women fallen so low as to brazen out their
shame in the face of the world.

After a hearty farewell to my friends I returned to Rotterdam, and on the 31st of August I betook myself on board
the "Salt-Bommel," 700 tons burden, Captain Juta, master.

Our ship was the first that was to carry a cargo of children from their native land; and as the 31st of August
happened to be Sunday, and a very fine day, and as the
Hollanders are just as inquisitive as any other nation, it is
not to be wondered at that from the early morning the
quays and the shore were lined with thousands of spectators. The good people had the consolation of looking at
our ship all day long, for the steam-tug which was to take
us in tow as far as the Nieuwe Sluis did not make its appearance till four o'clock in the afternoon.

On board there was as much life and bustle as on shore. The children came trooping in, a few at a time, accompanied by their relatives, and laden with eatables and with little keepsakes. Here a mother might be seen pressing her child to her bosom for the last time; there a father gave his son a few last words of counsel and exhortation before the journey began; and many parents, after several partings from their children, came hastening back to take a last look at the beloved faces. And when the ship at last moved from the shore, many were there who could be *seen* crying "farewell" after distance had rendered the sound inaudible. Handkerchiefs and hats were waved to wish us God-speed, and mighty "hurrahs" were raised; the whole city seemed to take an interest in our outgoing, as though the children had belonged to the people at large. This universal sympathy and excitement was a good panacea against mournful reflections. Children and parents shouted their loudest with the rest; and if many a poor mother sat down and dropped a tear as she parted from her darling, her low sob was drowned in the louder accents of rejoicing and farewell.

Whenever we passed a village, the shouting and waving of handkerchiefs began again. Happy youth, that can thus look forward with light heart to the unknown future!

Our progress to-day did not extend beyond eight miles (I must always be understood to mean *geographical*, or sea-miles, sixty to a degree). The steam-tug took leave of us in the evening. On the following day we drifted lazily as far as the wharf of Helvoetsluys, and here we had to remain at anchor for some days, with what patience we might, waiting for a wind.

These few days were enough to convince me that I must prepare myself for a very uncomfortable voyage with very uncongenial companions.

The cargo of children was bound, as I have said, for the

Cape Colony. Some were to be landed at Cape Town, the
others at Port Elizabeth, a few hundred miles distant, on
the northeast coast. At the Cape it is almost impossible
to get respectable industrious servants or artisans: people
there are compelled to employ Hottentots and Caffres, who
will only hire themselves out for a few days, or at most for
a week or two; and they frequently run away, leaving their
work half done. The Dutch settlers, therefore, bespeak
children from their mother country, with the object of training them up as servants and artisans.

These children receive board, lodging, and clothing from
the day of their embarkation. On reaching their destination they serve without wages for the first two years and a
half, during which time they are considered as working off
the expenses of their journey. For every following year
they receive, besides board and clothing, sixty Dutch guilders (£5), one guilder per month being handed to them as
pocket-money. The other forty-eight guilders are deposited with the authorities, and on completing their twenty-
first year the balance is paid over to them. They have
then the right of leaving their masters, should they wish to
do so.

In several towns in Holland committees were formed for
the selection of these children. From the orphan asylums
none were taken. The children are asked, in the presence
of the authorities, if they are content to travel beyond sea.
Unfortunately, however, the committee seem to have taken
matters very easily, and to have troubled themselves very
little about the prescribed regulations. Thus the *children*
were not children at all; almost without exception they
numbered from sixteen to twenty years, instead of from ten
to fourteen; and they must certainly have been picked up
out of the streets, for in all my life I never saw such an
amount of riff-raff collected together. The grown-up girls
must have been lounging about for years in the sailor's tav-

erns; the younger ones followed the example of the elder, and the whole community swore like the sailors themselves, sang the most uproarious songs, and stole from one another. Their want of cleanliness was awful.

But I will not be too bitter against these poor wretches; and let him who would condemn them consider the curse that weighs from their birth-hour upon the children of poverty. It is not because they are wretchedly clothed and half fed that I pity them so heartily; their greatest misfortune consists in their having nobody to take charge of the education of their hearts and minds. The parents are **seldom capable** of fulfilling this trust, for did not the same **curse rest** u**pon their** infancy? They work hard through **the** day, and give their children the indispensable bread, **and** think they have done their duty. If several other children come, the loaf becomes insufficient, and they **are** obliged to put the elder children to work **at the earliest** possible moment. If this work to which they **are put were** but regular, it might be rather an advantage to the **child** than otherwise; but what can a little boy or a little girl of seven or eight years old do? Those who get into the factories, or are bound apprentices, are the best off; but there is not employment of this kind for all, and for many there **is no** refuge left but to do all kinds of little offices in the **streets,** hawk newspapers, sweep crossings, and run on errands. Left to themselves, without guidance, without definite notions of right and wrong, and too often, alas! with the evil example of their parents before their eyes, is it to be wondered **at if** they at last succumb to the temptations that hover round them in such varied forms?

Far more worthy of condemnation do those men appear to me to whom the education of the people is intrusted, and who so often leave their duty unperformed. They can not, like the children of the poor, plead ignorance in their own defense; **for** if they fail, they do so with a full consciousness of their offense.

I speak of the priests and schoolmasters, who, to my thinking, are the most important men among the people; for in their hands lies the real education of the rest. They are the chief personages in every village; they can, if they earnestly desire it, effect an incalculable amount of good, and the government ought to keep the most vigilant watch upon them. Is this done? Alas! I fear not.

The clergymen are generally so little attended to by their consistories, that the whole village will sometimes be crying out about the misconduct of its minister, while his superiors know nothing about it. And if the affair becomes too bad at length, what is the punishment? Simply his translation to some other parish.

The schoolmasters, moreover, are so badly paid, that scarcely any one will take up with this profession who can earn his living in another way.

With a few notable exceptions, clergymen and schoolmasters think they have done their duty when the former have preached a dry sermon on Sundays, and the latter have managed to teach their pupils to read and write. But how few, how very few, trouble themselves about the moral training of the children intrusted to their charge, by teaching them the difference between right and wrong, by endeavoring to rouse their hearts and minds to healthy action, and, above all, by setting them a good example!

We had a schoolmaster on board, Herr Jongeneel, and his wife: he was to superintend the boys and she the girls. These good people ate their rations with great perseverance, said many prayers and sang psalms, but they cared very little about the behavior of those who had been intrusted to them. The last note of the psalm had scarcely died upon the lips of the girls before they would be hurrying away to the deck, where they spent the evening and half the night bandying jests with the mates and sailors. Even in the daytime their behavior was so unbecoming that I and a married female passenger, with her step-daughter, were obliged to pass nearly all our time in the cabin.

I hear that Herr Jongeneel is to have a post as a missionary at the Cape. What is to be expected from such a man? He began the voyage with a falsehood. He had assured the committee he had no children, yet came on board with a child, and his wife was daily expecting another, which duly arrived on the 3d of September.

Under these circumstances, it was, of course, impossible for me to sleep in the girls' cabin. Captain Juta, a very good, obliging man, saw this, and as there was no other vacant place, he had a berth arranged for me on a settle in the chief cabin. It was not very comfortable, for the seat was not more than a foot broad, and it was a very difficult matter to maintain my place upon it, particularly when the ship rolled.

The rest of the company consisted—besides the young wife, her step-daughter, and myself—of eight or nine gentlemen, who were not the most eligible of fellow-passengers. They were generally very fond of seizing every opportunity of conversing with the girls, in a very sailor-like style. In the evening there was often such a disturbance that we quiet women could not find a peaceful spot on the deck where we might enjoy a little fresh air. The gentlemen and the girls raced wildly round the decks, pricked one another with needles, and shouted, laughed, and screamed like denizens of the lowest public houses. Mr. Schumann, a young chemist, was an honorable exception.

It was not till the 4th of September that a slight breeze arose, aided by which (and a little steam-tug) we made our way into the North Sea. The sails soon began to fill, and on the 5th we entered the English Channel, through which we sailed in two days and a half—the quickest run through this dangerous passage I have ever made in a sailing-vessel.

The 7th of September was a Sunday. The schoolmaster

and missionary expectant **read** the service with half-closed
eyes, and with such an appearance of unction and importance that **one would have thought he** had been born a
priest. His address or sermon was so dry and bald as to
be fit only for savages, who would not understand a word,
good or bad. At the dinner-table **he** seemed more at home
—ye powers, what an appetite he had! In the afternoon
we had **almost** a calm. The captain, who was ever ready
to give pleasure to **all, had** a fine organ on board. He had
it brought on deck, and played, that the young people
might dance. It was quite **a** little festival. Every one
was in good spirits, cheerful, and decorous, for the captain
remained present the whole time. The sailors also sang,
and danced among themselves or with the girls. The boys
clambered about the rigging, played with each other, or executed all kinds **of** gymnastic **feats.** We passengers stood
about in groups, watching the gambols of the merry young-
sters.

One of the girls took no part in the general hilarity.
The poor thing seemed the only one who felt how mournful it was to go forth into the wide world without staff or
stay. On the very first night which I passed in the girls'
cabin I had been struck by her mournful countenance;
she had cried herself to sleep, called for her mother in her
dreams, and in the morning when she awoke, and saw all
the strange faces round her, she seemed to lose all courage,
cowered in a corner, and wept long and bitterly. Great
indeed must have been the poverty of the parents **that in-**
duced them to part with a child **who** clung with such passionate tenderness to the remembrance of home, and bitter
the parting of the poor mother from the child that was going to the far country with such **a** slender prospect of returning. Surely there is a sharper sting in such a parting
than in following the remains of a beloved relative to the
church-yard. In the one case there is the consoling belief

that the soul is safe from harm, but alas for the perils that encompass soul and body on a life-long journey among strange faces!

Oh, that all into whose houses these orphan children come would endeavor to make up to them, by a little love, the mighty loss these poor creatures have sustained! I tried to console the girl as well as I could, and the good captain spoke kind words to her, and promised to take her back to Europe if she did not feel happy at the Cape. But as the girl's sorrow wore off from day to day, she began to take pleasure—as we find is too frequently the case—in the conduct of her companions, and in a few weeks home and parents were alike forgotten.

The only girl on board whose behavior was uniformly good was one from whom I should least have expected propriety of conduct. Mary, as they called her, was the daughter, by a first marriage, of a man who had married again shortly after the death of his first wife. There was a son by this marriage, two years younger than Mary. The second wife disliked her step-children, scolded them continually, and frequently ill treated them, particularly when she had taken too much brandy, which she appeared to do pretty frequently. When Mary had reached her eighteenth, and her brother his sixteenth year, she declared that they were old enough to earn their own living, and turned them out of the house. For three months the poor creatures slept in the streets or in any corner where they could get shelter; no one would receive them, no one would take pity on the poor, ragged, half-starved wretches. They had learned nothing, and could barely manage by begging, and by little earnings now and then, to get a few farthings to buy bread. Once they had a hope of seeing their condition improved. One evening, as they stood at the corner of a street, they saw an elderly man crossing the road, and leading a little girl by the hand. A merry boy of seven or

E

eight years of age was following them; he had loitered a
few paces behind, playing with his hoop. Just when he
was in the middle of the road a carriage came round the
corner. The startled boy tried to spring aside, but fell
over his hoop, and would probably have been crushed by
the wheels, or trampled under foot by the horses, if Mary's
brother, who happened to be close by, had not rushed toward him, and dragged him out of the way.

The old gentleman came hurrying up, took the boy in
his arms, examined him carefully, and could scarcely believe he had escaped entirely without injury. As a crowd
had begun to gather round, he beckoned Mary's brother to
follow him, and went toward his own house accompanied
by the children. He made the two beggars—for Mary had
kept close to her brother—come in with him, and asked
where they lived. They told him their history in a few
words. The old gentleman seemed touched, wrote down
the address of their father, and dismissed them with a small
gratuity and a direction to call again on the following
evening.

They were quite overjoyed; for the first time in three
months they could enjoy a warm meal and sleep under a
roof, and they hoped that next evening the good gentleman
would find them work, and perhaps even take them into
his house. With what impatience they waited for the appointed hour! At last the evening came, and with beating
hearts they knocked at the door. An old servant appeared, and desired them to wait; after a short absence he re-
appeared, put a few guilders into their hands, and said that
his master could do nothing more for them. Great was
the disappointment of the poor children; but they did not
dare to question the servant, and went away weeping silently.

The old gentleman had probably gone to make inquiries
at the parents' house, and finding the step-mother alone,

the wicked woman, to justify herself for having turned the children out of doors, had told some horrible tale about them.

The poor wretches were looking forward with great fear to the approaching winter, when fortunately they heard of the committee which sent out young people to the Cape. They went at once to the office, and were accepted.

A girl who remains good and virtuous under such circumstances deserves the greatest respect and admiration. Mary continued, like a heroine, unspoiled by the bad step-mother, by starvation in the streets, or by the bad example on board. God grant poor Mary happiness and blessings, for surely she deserves them!

On the 19th of September a very strange incident took place. We were going quietly before the wind, when suddenly it changed and took us "all aback." The sails could not be furled quickly enough to save one of the yards from being sprung and the sail torn to shreds. The whole affair was over in a few moments, and the passengers in the cabin knew nothing about it. The captain ascribed the occurrence to a great water-spout. We could not see it, but had probably come within the domain of the whirlwind it raised.

At the end of our passage, which was somewhat tedious and thoroughly uneventful, we had a death on board; the schoolmaster's eldest child died of the croup. I was very disagreeably impressed on this occasion by the behavior of the mother. With the child on her lap—it had only died a few minutes before—the bereaved mother eagerly asked for bread, butter, and cheese, and a glass of water. When she began to drink the water, and found it was not sweetened, she scolded the girl, and sent her off for the sugar. After she had satisfied her hunger and thirst, the poor little child was dressed, and the scene of grief began. She took it in her arms, wept and sobbed, and seemed as if she could not part from it. A few hours afterward all signs of mourn-

ing had vanished, and one would have thought the poor
child had never existed.

On the 16th of November, at noon, we at length cast
anchor in front of Cape Town. For a description of this
place, I refer my readers to my "Second Voyage round the
World."

It was Sunday, and I therefore refrained from going on
shore. Where English people form the majority of the
population, it is not customary to pay visits on this day;
the good folks are all day long either at church, or praying
at home, or supposed to be praying.

Cape Town is not so great but that the name of every
stranger is known within a few hours after arrival; and on
this first afternoon I received two friendly offers of hospitality for the time of my stay here—one from Madame
Bloom, the other from Mr. Juritz, an apothecary.

On the morning of the 17th of November, I was engaged
in packing up my few possessions before going ashore with
the captain when a gentleman came on board and inquired
for me. He introduced himself as Mr. Lambert, a Frenchman, and told me that he had been living in the island of
Mauritius some years, and had, in fact, landed here on his
return voyage to that island. He had heard in Paris of my
intention of proceeding to Madagascar, and that I had been
dissuaded from attempting the journey. Hearing yesterday of my arrival, he had hastened to invite me to go to
Madagascar with him, if I had not entirely abandoned my
project. He had been in the island about two years before,
and was personally acquainted with the queen. He had
written to her from Paris, requesting permission to pay a
second visit, for no one is allowed to land in Madagascar
without the queen's consent. He hoped to find this permission awaiting him at the Mauritius, and would write immediately on his arrival to obtain a similar permission for
me, which he had no doubt would be granted; only, if I

intended to **undertake the** journey, **I must make up my mind** at once, as **the** steamer would **start for the Mauritius on the** following day. In consequence of the rainy **season** having set in at Madagascar, the voyage from the **Mauritius** thither could not be commenced until **the** beginning of April; but, in the interval, Mr. Lambert assured **me** I should find the heartiest welcome in his house.

It would be difficult **to** picture my surprise and joy **at** this. I had given up all hope of carrying out my plan, and **now I should** be able to do it, and, moreover, in the **most agreeable and** the **safest** way. I hardly knew what **to say to Mr. Lambert.** I felt **ready** to shout for joy, and **tell** every one I met of my good **fortune.** Yes, I have had good luck in my journeyings—never-ending luck. At Rotterdam I found a ship which was **to touch at the** Cape—a thing that hardly occurs twice in the course **of a year, as** the Dutch have scarcely any communication **with the col-** ony; and here at the Cape I arrive just **in** time **to meet** Mr. Lambert, who would have been gone had **I landed** twenty-four hours later. These are the happy chances **one** reads of frequently enough in novels, but they very seldom **occur in** actual life.

I immediately sent my baggage to the steamer, and **hastened** ashore **to see my** friends. **An** adjutant of the governor, Sir **George Grey, came** with **an** invitation from his excellency **to visit him at his** country house. I could not **resist so** flattering **a** summons, and spent the whole evening **at his** excellency's. Sir George made me the tempting offer **of a** journey through the greater part of the Cape **territory** in his company; but nothing in the **world** would have induced me to give up Madagascar. **I there-** fore gratefully declined his liberal offer, the **value of which,** however, I fully appreciated, **and** that, under different cir- **cumstances,** I should have joyfully accepted. This **kind gentleman** seemed to take a real interest in my doings, and to be sorry that he could not in any way be of service to me. He made me promise to let him **know** by letter if I should require his recommendation or any other assistance on my journey.

On the morning of the 18th of November I was escorted back to the town to **Mr.** Lambert, and a few hours later we **were again at sea.**

CHAPTER VI.

I MADE the voyage from the Cape to the Mauritius in the handsome and entirely new steamer "Governor Higginson," Captain French, of 150-horse power. The vessel had been built in shares, Mr. Lambert being the chief shareholder. He refused to let me pay for my passage, and would not have allowed me to do so even had he not possessed a single share. He declared that I was now his guest, and must remain so till I finally left the Mauritius.

Our voyage of 2400 sea-miles to the Mauritius was very prosperous. The sea was certainly stormy when we set sail, and we had to struggle much against contrary winds; still, it was said that no other steamer had ever made so quick a passage.

Except some small water-spouts, we saw nothing remarkable till we reached the island of Bourbon.

On this steamer I learned the amount of the current expenses of navigation. Without reckoning coals, it exceeds £500 per month. The crew consisted of forty-seven persons. The consumption of coal was about twenty-five tons in twenty-four hours. These coals are in some places exceedingly dear; at the Cape, for instance, where they cost £2 10s. per ton.

On the morning of the 1st of December we discovered land, and in the afternoon cast anchor in the little-known harbor of St. Denis, the capital of the island of Bourbon.

This pretty little island, also called Ile de la Réunion,

lies between the Mauritius and Madagascar, in latitude 20°
21° south, and longitude 52° 53° east. It is forty English
miles in length by thirty in breadth, and has about 200,000
inhabitants. Discovered in 1545 by Mascarenhas, a Portuguese, it was occupied by the French in 1642; from 1810
to 1814 it was under English dominion, and since that time
it has been a French possession.

Ile de Bourbon has lofty chains of mountains and plains
of considerable extent, stretching parallel with the sea-coast.
The flats are planted with the sugar-cane, which flourishes
here famously, and gives the whole island an appearance of
luxuriant verdure.

The town of St. Denis is built far out into the sea, and
surrounded by evergreen trees and gardens. In the background rises a hill, crowned by a palatial edifice, which I at
first took for the governor's residence; but it has been built
for a nobler purpose — it is the hospital. The Catholic
church also stands upon the hill, and against its foot leans
a long building of only one story, and with handsome rows
of pillars, which make it look like a Roman aqueduct; but,
on a nearer inspection, one detects windows and doors, and
the place turns out to be the barracks. The whole picture
is closed in by a chain of mountains, which divides into two
parts, and affords a magnificent glimpse of a deep gorge
thickly shaded with plants and trees. All this I saw from
the steamer's deck, for we only staid here a few hours, and
these were passed in the usual formalities—the visit of the
physician, the officials from the post-office and custom-house,
etc. The business was no sooner over than the steam began to puff and gurgle, the wheels were put in motion, and
we were off to the island of Mauritius, a hundred miles away.

Next morning we had not only long lost sight of Bourbon, but the Mauritius lay before us; and in the afternoon
our steamer anchored in the safe harbor of Port Louis, the
capital of the island. But three hours passed before we

landed, and I took up my quarters in Mr. Lambert's country house.

The island of Mauritius, seen from the sea, presents a similar aspect to Bourbon, only that the mountains are higher, and are piled up in successive chains. The town has not so picturesque an appearance as St. Denis; it wants the fine stately buildings which give such an imposing effect to the latter place.

The Mauritius, formerly called " Ile de France," is situate in the southern hemisphere, between latitude 19° 20°, and longitude 54° 55°. It is thirty-seven miles long by twenty-eight broad, and has a population of 180,000.

Like Bourbon, the Mauritius belongs to Africa. It was taken possession of by the Dutch in 1570, but is said to have been discovered earlier by the Portuguese Mascarenhas. The Dutch gave it the name " Mauritius," but left the island in 1712. Three years afterward the French took possession, and called the island " Ile de France." In 1810 the English conquered it, and have kept it ever since. They have also restored its old name of Mauritius.

The island was uninhabited at its first discovery. The whites introduced slaves—negroes, Malabar Indians, and Malagaseys, from whose intermarriages all kinds of shades of color and nationality arose. Since the abolition of slavery in the year 1835, almost all the working-people have come from India. The Anglo-Indian government makes contracts for five years with people who wish to hire themselves out in the Mauritius; at the expiration of that time they have to apply to the government in the Mauritius, at whose cost they are sent back to their own country. Those who fail to report themselves lose their right to a free passage.

The hirer must pay to the government for each laborer two pounds the first year, and one pound every year following; this money covers the expense of the passage out

E 2

and home. To the laborer himself he has to give five or
six rupees a month, and board and lodging. This scale
only applies to common laborers; for cooks, artisans, and
skilled workmen, the wages are much higher, rising according to their capacity.

I found the inhabitants of the Mauritius in a state of
great excitement. Intelligence had lately arrived from Calcutta that the exportation of coolies, or laborers, was forbidden, as it had been alleged that the men were very badly treated in quarantine, which they are compelled to keep
on account of the cholera. They say, however, that the
government here is to redress the quarantine grievances
with all due care, and they therefore hope the prohibition
will soon be relaxed. If this is not done, the island will be
threatened with ruin in a few years.

At present it is in the most flourishing condition; the
income which this little island yields, not only to the planters, but to the government, is perhaps larger, in proportion
to its extent, than the amount yielded by any other territory whatever. In the year 1855, for instance, 2,500,000
cwt. of sugar were grown, the value being £1,777,428 sterling. The revenue of the government for the same year
amounted to £348,452. The expenses were much less than
the income; and as this is the case nearly every year, and
the surplus is not sent to England, but remains in the country, the treasury is always well filled. At the present time
it is reported to contain £300,000; and with every year the
wealth of this fortunate island increases. In the year 1857
the revenue increased by £100,000, this great sum being
raised solely by the new duty on spirituous liquors. That
the inhabitants partake of this prosperity is proved by the
difference between the exports and imports. In the year
1855, the former exceeded the latter by half a million sterling. Could the same be said of some of our great European states?

The government officials are exceedingly well paid, but not nearly so well as in British India, though the expenses of living are much greater here. The reason is, that the climate of India is considered very unhealthy for Europeans, while that of the Mauritius is salubrious enough. The governor has a house, and £6000 a year salary.

Mr. Lambert's country house, "Les Pailles," to which I proceeded, is seven miles from the town, in the district of Mocca. The whole island is divided into eleven districts.

At my kind host's I found every thing heart could desire—handsome rooms, good living, numerous servants, and the greatest independence; for Mr. Lambert drove to town every morning, and frequently did not return till the evening.

After a few days' rest I began my wanderings through the island.

First of all, I visited the town of Port Louis. There was little enough to be seen in it. Though of tolerable size (it has a population of 50,000), it possesses not a single fine public building, with the exception of the government house and the bazar. The private houses, too, are generally small, and never exceed one story in height. The bridge across the big river—frequently so destitute of water that it can be easily forded—is built tastefully enough, only they have been so sparing of its breadth that only one carriage can go across at a time; when two meet, one has to wait till the other has passed. Governments seem to act very much like private people: so long as they have little money, or, indeed, are in debt, they are generous, and even extravagant; but from the moment when they become prosperous they grow saving and avaricious. At least this seems to be the case with the government of the Mauritius, which is much more stingy, with its well-filled chest, than our European states that are burdened with debt. Does it not show a miserable want of spirit to have such a narrow bridge in the busiest part of the town?

Two other bridges of hewn stone fairly fell in during my stay; fortunately, no one was hurt. Each governor thinks only of filling the treasury; his greatest pride is in being able to say that under his rule the surplus of income over expenditure had increased by so many thousand pounds. Acting on this principle, the present governor objected strongly to the estimates given in for the building of the two bridges, ordered that they should be constructed at a cheaper rate, and—has the pleasure of building them twice over.

The town possesses a public walk, called the "Champ de Mars," which is, however, little frequented, and a theatre, in which a French company perform.

The rich people generally live in their country houses, and only come to town for the day.

The mode of life among Europeans and Creoles (under the latter term are understood people born on the island of white parents) is similar to that in the British or Dutch Indies. At sunrise we refreshed ourselves with a cup of coffee, brought into the bedroom; between nine and ten the bell summoned us to a breakfast of rice, curry, and a few hot dishes; and at one came a luncheon of fruit or bread and cheese. The chief meal was taken in the evening, generally after seven o'clock.

Living is very dear here. House-rent, the better kind of provisions, servants' wages, etc., are paid for at very high prices. The simplest establishment of a respectable family with three or four children costs from thirty-five to forty-five pounds per month. The staff of servants, though much smaller than in an Indian household, is as much in excess of a European one. Families who make little appearance must keep a footman, a cook, a man for carrying water and cleaning the crockery, another to wash the linen, and a couple of boys from twelve to fourteen years old. The lady of the house has, besides, a maid for herself and one or more for the children, according to their number. Those who have carriages keep a coachman for each pair of horses. The monthly wages of servants are from thirty to thirty-six shillings for a man-cook; twenty-four to thirty shillings for a footman or maid; and forty-five to ninety shillings for a coachman. Quite a common helper gets at least eighteen shillings, and the boys six shillings and their clothes: lodging is found for them, but not board. In British India fewer rupees are paid than dollars here. Domestics do not pay more for their board than four shillings a month at the most; they live on rice and red pepper, vegetables, and a few fishes, and these articles they can get for almost nothing. The servants perform their offices worse there than in any country I know, except perhaps at Amboyna in the Moluccas. Every where the visitor must bring his own servants; for if, for instance, he goes into the country and has no attendants with him, he stands a very good chance of finding his bed unmade and his water-jug empty at night. The poor housewives have great difficulty in keeping their houses in any thing like order. In India they are much better off: there the chief of the servants bears the lofty title of "major-domo," and has the supervision of all household details. All the articles in use in the domestic economy—the plate, linen, and china—are intrusted to his keeping. He is responsible for the safety of all; he superintends the servants—reckons with them, cashiers one and engages another. If cause of discontent should arise, application is at once made to the major-domo. But here the lady of the house must herself undertake this arduous office; and as the Creole ladies are not remarkable for carefulness and love of order, it may be imagined that the interior arrangements of all households are not in the best state. I would not counsel any visitor rashly to set foot in any but the reception-room.

Social intercourse does not flourish in the Mauritius.

There is not even a club here: the chief reason may be that the society consists of French and English in almost equal numbers—two nations whose characters and modes of thinking vary too much ever to amalgamate freely.

Besides this chief obstacle, there are other minor hinderances; for instance, the late dinner-hour, and the great distances between the various houses. As I have observed, the usual dinner-hour is between seven and eight o'clock, and thus the whole evening is lost. In other hot countries, when it is customary for people to live in country houses outside the town, the gentlemen generally come home from their business at five o'clock, and dine at six, so that at seven people are ready to receive visitors and friends.

But here all visits are paid before dinner, as it is too late to do so afterward, and whoever wants to assemble a few people for the evening must invite them solemnly to dinner. These dinners are conducted with great ceremony. Every one appears in full dress, the officials generally in uniform, as if they had received an invitation to court. At table, one is frequently seated between two perfect strangers, and after suffering the horrors of ennui for hours, a move is made at past nine o'clock into the reception-rooms, there to suffer ennui for some time longer. Music is very seldom introduced. Packs of cards are every where displayed on the tables, but I never saw them used. Every guest seems to be waiting with impatience for the time when he may take his leave without appearing rude: he is devoutly thankful when the evening has come to an end, and then accepts the next invitation with the greatest pleasure.

These dinners do not take place very often; for, ready as the good folks are to put up with the dreary ennui in consideration of the good company and the well-furnished table, the generous giver of the feast has to remember that each cover costs him at least from eighteen to twenty-four

shillings. Nor is the thirst of his honored **guests to be ap-**
peased on easier terms; for Frenchmen and Englishmen
are alike judges of good grape-juice, and the Mauritius
would be no English colony if the rarest wines of **Europe**
had not found their way there.

If the fortunate guest be not the fortunate possessor of a
carriage and horses, a dinner of this kind puts him to **some**
expense likewise; for he has generally four, or six, or more
English miles **to go,** and the hire of a coach costs fifteen
shillings **at least.**

There is more hospitality to be met with in the country
than in the town, but its practice is not universal. I received many **invitations,** among the rest one from the governor, Mr. Higginson, who has a **country house** at "Reduit,"
seven miles from the capital. **Most of** these invitations I
declined, particularly those in which I **suspected more** etiquette than real friendliness. I have **never been an** advo-
cate of ceremonious visits and stiff parties, **but a small** circle of kind, educated persons I am always glad to join. **In**
this respect I was gratified in some houses, particularly **in**
those of the English families Kerr and Robinson, who lived
in **the Mocca** district.

Mr. Kerr had lived long in Austria, and with the lan-
guage he had acquired all the friendly **ways** of my dear
countrymen; and his wife, **too, was** quite free from the pro-
verbial English **reticence.** I came to this friendly family
with **all my little** requests, and felt really at home with
them. **The Robinsons were also** very good, friendly people, and musical withal.

The district of Mocca has an advantage over **the other**
divisions of the island in its agreeable climate, especially **in**
that part distant five or six miles from the town, where **the**
land rises a thousand feet above the sea-level.

The region around **is very** romantic. The volcanic
mountains exhibit themselves in the strangest shapes.

The vegetation is most luxuriant. A peculiarity which I rarely noticed in the other districts was the presence of deep, broad clefts, forming gorges or defiles. I explored several of these; among others, one on a little plateau near Mr. Kerr's country house. It varied from eighty to two hundred feet in depth, and was about forty feet broad at the bottom; at the top the breadth was much more considerable. The sides were richly decked with stately trees, graceful shrubs, and climbing plants, while below, a foaming crystal streamlet, rushing onward, formed several pretty cascades.

One of the finest views, perhaps, in the whole island is to be obtained from Bagatelle, Mr. Robinson's country seat. On one side the eye rests upon picturesque mountains, on the other it roams over fields luxuriant in verdure, stretching over a sunny plain to the boundless ocean. It is said that on a clear day the island of Bourbon can be discerned from this point.

Of all the country seats I saw in the Mauritius, those of Mr. Robinson and Mr. Barclay seemed to me the handsomest. The dwelling-houses are surrounded by parks and gardens tastefully laid out, where tropical flowers, shrubs, and trees (particularly beautiful palm-trees) are seen in close community with the European plant-world. In Mr. Robinson's garden we had peaches as fine as any in Germany or France.

The houses of these two gentlemen stand in very advantageous contrast to the other houses in the island. The rooms are high and spacious, the arrangements very convenient; order and cleanliness reign every where.

These praises, unfortunately, can not be extended to the country houses of the Creoles. To speak frankly, I mistook most of the latter establishments for the dwellings of poor peasants. They are generally built of wood, are very small and low, and very much hidden by bushes; one would never believe that rich people are to be found living in these hovels.

The interior arrangements are quite in conformity with the exterior. The reception-room, and perhaps the dining-room, are passable; but the sleeping-rooms are so small that one or two beds and a few chairs fill them completely. And this in the Mauritius, a country where the heat is oppressive, and lofty and roomy apartments almost a necessity! To fill up the measure of inconvenience, many people have had the odd fancy of partly roofing their houses with white metal. The visitor who is unfortunate enough to be lodged in a room just under one of these roofs can form a lively idea of the sufferings endured by the unhappy captives of old in the lead-roofed prisons of Venice. Every time my unlucky destiny led me into such a house, I looked forward with terror to the night, which I was sure to pass in sleepless discomfort, burning with heat, and half stifled for want of air. In Ceylon the roofs are also sometimes covered with lead or zinc; but the houses are much more lofty, and the metal is not exposed to the burning rays of the sun, but covered with wood or straw.

I found many of the houses in such a dilapidated condition, and so tottering in appearance, that I marveled greatly at the courage of the people who dared to inhabit them; for my part, I am not ashamed to confess that I feared every gust of wind would blow the house to pieces, the more so as the winds in the Mauritius are very violent, and there are frequent hurricanes. The worthy Creoles quoted these same winds and hurricanes as an excuse for the mean architecture of their hovel-like homes, declaring that loftier buildings would be unable to resist the storm. If they were as badly built as these huts, certainly; but the country houses of Mr. Barclay and Mr. Robinson have always held their own against wind and storm, though they are lofty and spacious, and have been built many years.

I have often noticed that there is more true hospitality in the country than in towns; but the rule will not apply universally, as I found by personal experience. For though, in the houses of such worthy people as Mr. Kerr, Mr. Robinson, and Mr. Lambert, I felt thoroughly at home, it sometimes happened, on the other hand, that I allowed myself to be tempted by the seeming friendship of Creoles to accept invitations involving disagreeable consequences, which made me rejoice greatly when I regained my freedom.

Persons of high position and great influence must, of course, every where be received with consideration, but strangers and ordinary guests, from whom there is nothing to be expected, are sometimes very cavalierly treated in these parts. There is enough to eat and drink, but a "plentiful lack" of every thing besides. The unimportant guests are lodged in the "pavilion," a little hut frequently a hundred yards distant from the dwelling-house, necessitating a pleasant walk in the rain or in the broiling sunshine every time the family assembles for a meal; and as the main building itself is generally ruinous, the state of the pavilion may easily be imagined.

That delectable retreat generally consists of two or three little rooms, where neither door nor windows can be induced to shut, where the rain beats in through the broken panes, where the lock of the entrance-door is so rusty that the door must be barricaded from within, or every gust of wind would blow it open. Each of the little rooms is provided with a bed, a rickety table, and one or two chairs. Of a cupboard I never saw a trace. My clothes and linen could never be unpacked, and I was obliged to stoop and unlock my boxes whenever I wanted the most trifling article.

But these discomforts would have been of little moment if any friendliness or readiness to oblige on the part of host or hostess had made amends. Unfortunately, such readiness is rarely found. In most houses the guest **is** left to himself all day long. No one takes any trouble about him, or **cares** to do any **thing** to make the time pass pleasantly. Nearly every establishment boasts five or six horses; **but these** are intended exclusively for the master of the house, **or** perhaps for his sons. The guest is never offered the use of them, and the lady of the house herself is seldom able to say, "I will take a drive to-day."

Even the luxury of a cold bath, necessary as it is to health **in a hot climate like** that of the Mauritius, I found unattainable except when it rained. Then, indeed, I had it perforce—in my bedroom; for the roof was generally so ruin-**ous that the water** poured in on all sides.

CHAPTER VII.

THE greatest sugar-cane plantations are in the district of
Pamplemousse, in which also the Botanical Gardens are situated.   I visited the Monchoisy plantation, the property of
Mr. Lambert.   The manager, Mr. Gilat, was kind enough to
escort me through the fields and buildings, and to give me
such a lucid explanation of the method of growing and preparing the sugar-cane, that I can not do better than give
his own words, as nearly as I can remember them.

"The sugar-cane is not raised from seed, but pieces of
cane are planted.   The first cane requires eighteen months
to ripen; but as, during this time, the chief stem puts out
shoots, each of the following harvests can be gathered in at
intervals of twelve months, so that three crops are obtained
in four years and a half.   After the fourth harvest the field
must be thoroughly cleared of the cane.   If the land is virgin soil on which no former crop has been raised, fresh slips
of cane can at once be planted, and thus eight crops may
be obtained in nine years.   If this is not the case, ambre-
zades must be planted—a leafy plant, which grows to the
height of eight or nine feet, and whose leaves, continually
falling, decay on the ground and fertilize it.   After two
years the plants are rooted out, and the land becomes a
sugar plantation again."

For about the last ten years the custom has prevailed of
dressing the land with guano, and very good results have

been obtained. On good ground 8000 lbs. per acre have been raised, and on bad soil, that formerly yielded 2000 lbs. at the most, the produce has been doubled.

I was much astonished to see the beautiful widespread plains of Pamplemousse covered with great pieces of lava. It would appear as if nothing could grow under such circumstances; but I heard that this peculiarity of the soil is favorable to the sugar-cane, which will not bear a long drought. It is planted between these fragments of rock, and the rain-water, collecting in pools in the clefts and holes, keeps the ground moist for a long time.

When the canes are ripe and the harvest begins, no more is cut down each day than can be pressed and boiled at once, for the great heat soon spoils the sap in the canes. The cane is pressed between two rollers, turned by steam, with such force that it is crushed quite flat and dry; it is then used as fuel for boiling the kettles.

The juice runs successively into six kettles or pans, of which the first is most fiercely heated; the force of the fire is made to diminish under each of the others. In the last kettle the sugar is found almost half produced. It is then placed on great wooden tables where it is left to cool, and here the mass granulates into crystals of the size of a pin's head. As a final operation, it is poured into wooden vessels perforated with small holes, through which the molasses still contained in the sugar may filter. The whole process requires eight or ten days for its completion. Before the sugar is packed, it is spread out on great terraces to dry for some hours in the sun. It is shipped in bags containing 150 lbs. each.

Mr. Lambert's sugar plantation contains 2000 acres of land, but of course only a part of this is planted each year. He has 600 laborers, who are engaged for seven months in the year in the field, and during the other five in getting in the crop and boiling it. In a good year—that is, when the

rainy season sets in early and lasts long—Mr. Lambert gets
three million pounds of sugar from his plantation; but he
is well content with two millions and a half. A hundred
pounds of sugar are worth from nine to twelve shillings.

The largest planter in the Mauritius is a Mr. Rocheconte,
who is said to produce nearly seven million pounds of sugar
annually.

Sugar, and nothing but sugar, is to be seen in this island.
Every undertaking has reference to sugar, and all the conversation is about sugar. Mauritius might be called the
sugar island, and its coat of arms should be a bundle of
sugar-canes and three sugar-bags rampant.

During a residence of some weeks I had opportunities
of observing the condition and circumstances of the laborers. They are called "coolies," and come, as I have mentioned, from all parts of India. They hire themselves for
five years, and the planter who hires them has to give each
laborer 8s. or 10s. a month, 50 lbs. of rice, 4 lbs. of dried
fish, 4 lbs. of beans, 4 lbs. of fat or oil, a sufficiency of salt,
and a little hut to live in, besides the sum he has to pay to
the government for their passage.

The laborer's condition is not nearly so good as that of
a servant. He has to work heavily in the cane-field and
the boiling-house, and is much more exposed than the domestic servant to the arbitrary power of his master; for he
may not leave until his five years' contract has expired.
He may certainly go and complain if he is hardly used, for
there are judges to hear, and laws to redress his woes; but
as the judges are frequently planters themselves, the poor
laborer seldom finds the verdict given in his favor. The
laborer has also frequently to walk eight or ten miles before he gets to the court. In the week he has no time to
go, and on Sundays he finds it closed. If, after much
trouble, he at length succeeds in reaching the abode of justice, he finds, perhaps, that the court is engaged in a mul-

tiplicity of affairs, and is told to go and come again some other day. To make the thing more difficult for him, he is not admitted at all unless he brings witnesses. How is he to get these? None of his companions in misfortune will dare to render him such a service, for fear of punishment, or even corporal ill usage at the hands of his master.

I will relate an incident which happened during my residence in the Mauritius.

On one of the plantations ten laborers wished, upon the expiration of their contract, to quit their employer and take service with another. The planter heard of this, and three weeks before the articles of these ten men expired, he persuaded ten others to give in the papers of the malcontents as their own, and to have the contract renewed for a year. Then he called the discontented laborers separately before him, showed each one the contract, and told him he had another year to serve. Of course the people persisted that this was impossible, as they had not been at the court at all, and had never had the writing in their hands. The planter replied that the contract was perfectly valid, and declared that if they complained before the court they would not be heard, and that corporal chastisement would most likely be their reward. Moreover, if they went, he would not pay the wages he owed them for five months' work, unless under compulsion.

The poor fellows were at a loss what to do. Fortunately, an official of high position lived close by, and one who was known as an honest, philanthropic man. To him they went, told their story, and begged his protection, which he at once promised. The affair came before the court, but the trial went on very slowly, as none of the planter's people dared to give evidence. Even if they had the will, it would have been difficult for them to do so, as the planter forbade his people to go out, and had them carefully watched and prevented from communicating with any one all the time the action was proceeding.

In the course of some **ten weeks, five** sittings or hearings took place. The first three were held **before** a single judge, who was a planter into the bargain. **The** protector of the poor plaintiffs insisted that **three judges should be** appointed, **as the law demands, and** protested against **the one** judge, **who could not** but appear as influenced by his **position as a planter. As this** demand proceeded from a **man in a high position, and** was, moreover, strictly legal, **it was complied with, and the** first judge only attended the two subsequent **sittings to give** explanations respecting the former three.

At the fifth **sitting** the action was certainly decided in favor of **the coolies, but the verdict was given in a** manner I should never have thought possible in a land under English rule.

The judge, or planter, who had heard the plaintiffs in **the** first three sittings declared that **when** the ten people **first** came to him, he could not know whether they were **the real** proprietors **of the** papers, for that hundreds of laborers came to him **with** similar complaints every day.

He had written out the new contract on unstamped paper, **as he happened to have** none with a stamp by him, **and the people,** not one of whom could write, had attached **their crosses as signatures.** Afterward he had the contract rewritten on **stamped paper, as it** would otherwise have **been** invalid, **and in order not to** call up the people again, his clerk had affixed the crosses. As the people had, therefore, not signed with their own hands, the contract was void, and the coolies were free; and thus the action was decided.

The real circumstances of the case were entirely different. If the poor **coolies** had not found **an** influential protector, the planter-judge would have decided the affair in favor of the employer. **The** appearance of the official personage upon the stage compelled the judges to show at least an appearance of justice; and so they saved themselves by finding out a FORGERY, for which, in any other country, the judge and his clerk would not only have lost their places to a certainty, but have been provided with board and lodging, and a restricted number of companions, in a certain great public establishment.

The planter got off unpunished, though, even according to the Mauritian laws, framed with great regard for the planter's convenience, he should have been subjected to a fine and a year's imprisonment.

To crown his worthy action, he cheated the poor coolies, and mulcted them of a month's pay, under the pretext that they had done little work, broken some of their implements, and stolen others.

This paltry person is very much looked up to in the Mauritius, and is received with pleasure in society. He is rich certainly, and is a regular attendant at church, and here, as elsewhere, people have peculiar ideas as to wealth and religion—ideas which plain honest folks are too dull to appreciate.

I would not quit the district of Pamplemousse without visiting the Botanical Garden, which is under the superintendence of the accomplished botanist and director, Mr. Duncan.

Scarcely had I spent a quarter of an hour with this amiable man, a Scotchman by birth, before he invited me, in the most friendly manner, to spend a few days in his house, that I might be able to examine the treasures of the garden at my leisure. Though I had become somewhat careful in the matter of Mauritian invitations, I could not resist the real good-nature of Mr. Duncan. I staid with him, and had no cause to repent it. Mr. Duncan was a man of a few words, but he *did* what he could to make my residence in his house agreeable. When he saw that I was collecting

F

insects, he himself helped me in my search, and often
brought me some new specimens for my collection.

I walked several times with him through the Botanical
Garden, which is very rich in plants and trees from all
parts of the world.   Here I saw for the first time trees and
shrubs from Madagascar, indigenous to that island.   I particularly admired a water-plant, the *Hydrogiton fenestralis*,
whose leaves, three inches in length and one in breadth,
are quite pierced through, as if by artificial means pieces
had been broken out.   A tree, the *Adansonia digitata*, is remarkable, not for its beauty, but for its ugliness.   The stem
is of uniform clumsy thickness to a height of eight or ten
feet; then it becomes suddenly thin: the bark is of a light,
unsightly color, quite smooth and almost shining.

There were many spice-trees, and a few specimens of the
beautiful water-palm, which I have already seen and described in my "Second Voyage round the World."

I am no botanist, and therefore can give no detailed description of the garden; but competent persons have assured me that it is very judiciously and scientifically laid
out.   To look at the varied and numerous plants, and the
extensive plantations, sometimes requiring great labor to
cultivate, no one would believe that Mr. Duncan has very
restricted resources at his command.   The government only
allows him twenty-five laborers, Malabars and Bengalees,
who certainly do not get through as much work as eight or
ten strong Europeans would accomplish.

As I am on the subject of plants and trees, I will mention
the fruits produced in the Mauritius.   Among the most
common are many kinds of bananas and mangoes, citchy,
butter-fruit, splendid pine-apples, sweet melons and watermelons.   The watermelons here attain an enormous size,
some weighing more than thirty pounds, but they have little
flavor.   Peaches are abundant, but require much care to
bring them to perfection.   Pomegranates are also found of

great size, besides papayas and other similar fruits. I have described all these in my former works, to which I accordingly refer my readers.

As regards the animal world, the Mauritius is fortunate in possessing neither beasts of prey nor poisonous reptiles. The centipedes and scorpions found here are small; their sting is painful, but not dangerous. Ants are also not so numerous here as in India and South America. I could sometimes leave the insects I had collected for half a day together on the table, and the ants did not get at them, while in other hot countries these depredators would be devouring their prey within a few minutes. The musquitoes are troublesome enough, and sometimes drive strangers to desperation. Those who have been resident here for some years are said, like the natives, to enjoy a comparative immunity from their attacks.

The disagreeable kakerlak sometimes plays his pranks here, but is far less obnoxious than in other countries. They say that very exciting combats sometimes takes place between the kakerlak and the beautiful green fly called *Sphex viridi-cyanea*. I was not fortunate enough to witness such a fight, but only read the account of one in the "Voyages of Monsieur Bory de St. Vincent." The fly flutters round the kakerlak until the latter becomes motionless, as if magnetized; then she seizes him, drags him to a hole already selected for the purpose, lays eggs in his body, stops up the hole with a kind of cement, and leaves her victim to his enforced companions, by whom he is quickly devoured.

I had almost forgotten to mention an object of interest in the district of Pamplemousse—a tomb, in remembrance of the pretty story of "Paul and Virginia," the scene of which Bernardin de St. Pierre has laid in this island.

The month of April was already coming round, and, excepting in my excursions in the district of Pamplemousse

and a few drives in and about Mocca, I had seen nothing of
the Mauritius. I was loth to quit the island without at
least visiting the most interesting points, but how to manage this was the question. The friendly judge, Mr. Satis,
invited me to an excursion to the Tamarin waterfall. On
the way we passed the country house of Mr. Moon, who had
been invited by Mr. Satis to join our party.

We soon came to the waterfall, distant scarcely an English mile from Mr. Moon's country house; and just opposite to the cascade, under some shady trees, Mr. Satis had
taken care to have a good luncheon ready for us.

A more beautiful spot could scarcely have been chosen.
We encamped on an elevated plateau, 1160 feet above the
level of the sea; on one side was a gorge 800 feet deep, and
at least 500 broad at its top, but narrowing toward the sea.
Into this gorge the stream leaps headlong, forming seven
beautiful waterfalls, two of them more than 100 feet in
depth. It rushes, foaming in headlong haste, through a region clothed with the richest verdure, and closes in the
neighboring sea its short but troubled course. The appearance of the fall is said to be much more majestic after long
rains, when the smaller cascades become absorbed into one
great fall, and the whole mass of water rushes down into its
deep bed in only two leaps.

This delightful day will be always a bright spot in my
memory, not only for the beautiful spectacle I saw, but for
the pleasure I derived from my acquaintance with the amiable Moon family. I became as friendly with Mrs. Moon
as if I had known her a long time, and very glad was I
when she heartily invited me to stay some time in her house.
Unhappily, the time fixed for my departure for Madagascar
was at hand, and I could only spend three days with the
family—three happy days, which made amends for many
previous disappointments.

In Mrs. Moon I not only made the acquaintance of a very

amiable but of a very accomplished lady; her talent for painting is quite remarkable. At the request of the directors of the British Museum she has made colored drawings of all the 120 different kinds of mangoes, and also of the medicinal plants found in the Mauritius.

Mr. and Mrs. Moon, and their equally obliging relative, Mr. Caldwell, were at once eager to show me the "lions" of their island, and the next day they took me to "Mont Orgueil," from which the best view of the country and of the mountains can be had. On one side appears the "Morne Brabant," a mountain extending far out into the sea, and connected with the main land only by a narrow tongue of earth; not far from this rises the "Piton de la Rivière Noire," the highest mountain in the island, 2564 feet. In another direction the "Tamarin" and "Rempart" rear their heads; and in a fourth is to be seen a mountain with three tops, called "Les Trois Mammelles." Very near these summits there opens a deep caldron, two of whose sides have almost completely fallen in, while the remaining two rise high and steep. Besides these mountains there are the "Corps de Garde du Port Louis de Mocca;" "Le Pouce," with its narrow top rising suddenly up out of a little mountain plateau, like a thumb or finger; and the marvelous "Peter Booth." This mountain takes its name from the first man who ascended to its summit, which was long regarded as inaccessible. Peter Booth managed to do this by shooting an arrow, with a strong twine thereto attached, over the summit. Luckily, the arrow fell upon an accessible spot on the other side of the mountain. To this twine a strong rope was fastened, which was thus drawn over the mountain-top and secured on both sides; and Peter Booth hauled himself up by it, and attained at once the summit and the honor of immortalizing his name. The last of the mountains seen from this point is the "Nouvelle Découverte."

The mountains of this **island are** remarkable for their manifold and beautiful shapes. **Some are** in the form of broad perpendicular walls; others rise **like** pyramids; some are covered to their summits with rich **forests,** while others are only covered to half their height, **and their high rocky** points rise abruptly, smooth and bald, **from amid the green sea** of leaves. Beautiful valleys and deep gorges **lie between, and above** appears a cloudless sky. I could scarcely **tear myself away** from the charming picture, and the longer I gazed upon it, **the** greater **the** beauties I discovered.

Our next, **and,** unfortunately, our **last** excursion was to the "Trou du Cerf," or "Stag's Hole," a crater of perfectly **regular** form, filled with rich vegetation. This crater produces a very startling effect, for nothing betrays its existence till the visitor stands upon **its** very **brink.** Though the sides are steep enough, a **path leads** down to the centre, which is filled with **water during the rainy season.**

From the edge **of** the crater **the visitor has a striking** view over three fourths **of the island. Before him rise** majestic mountains with **their luxuriant** virgin forests, **from** which the steep, smooth mountain-tops come peering forth; wide-spreading plains, rich with sugar-cane plantations, **bright** with green foliage all the year round; and the azure **sea, whose** foaming waves fringe the coast with **a** margin of **white** foam—a wondrous landscape, wanting only a few rivers to make its beauty **perfect.**

The island **does** not suffer from want of water, but is **too** small to possess a real river; **this,** however, has not prevented the inhabitants from dignifying some of the larger streamlets with that title.

I left the Moon family with the greatest regret. It was through **their** friendship that I was **enabled to** visit any points of interest in the Mauritius: **in the** last few days of my stay I saw more than in the four long months I had previously spent in the island.

In most houses, especially in **those of the Creoles**, people made all kinds of protestations, and promised all manner of things; but the promises remained unperformed. **Not the smallest** service was rendered, **not one of those attentions offered which** are much more gratifying **to a stranger** than the board and lodging which **every one can procure** by paying for **them.** Still less did any **among them think** of making excursions to the more beautiful points. The people themselves **have** no idea that the beauties of Nature **are** pleasant **things to see,** and wonder that strangers should expose **themselves** to the slightest fatigue merely to see a **waterfall, a mountain, or a fine view.**

The men are solely and exclusively engaged **in** the business **of** acquiring wealth as quickly as possible: sugar **is a sort** of golden calf to them, and whatever has **no** reference to sugar is to them **worthless. The women are** not **much** better. They have **too little education, and too** much of the indolence so frequently found **in hot countries to take an** interest in any **serious subject.** With the exception **of the** care of their **own** valuable selves, the only thing **that can** rouse them **into life** is the agreeable occupation of inventing or disseminating slanderous gossip; and I have even found gentlemen who, in this charitable **and** exciting amusement, **would for** a few moments forget the **claims** of sugar. I did **not** escape the common fate. **The amiable** inhabitants, male and **female, of Port Louis, have absolutely** done me **the honor to represent me as** a *poisoner;* they **absolutely asserted that I had been hired by** the English **government to** poison Mr. Lambert!

That gentleman had brought from Paris **some very valuable** presents **for** the Queen of Madagascar, **and had been** so wanting in proper consideration **for the** feelings of people generally as to neglect to **tell every one** what the object **of these** presents really was. **Of** course, said Mauritian good-**nature,** it **must** be some secret political movement of the

French cabinet, which the English government had found out, and had commissioned me accordingly to put this dangerous man out of the way.

Stupid as this fiction was, it obtained credence among the Creoles, and even among the French, **and** prevented me from undertaking an interesting little journey. Before setting out on his journey to Madagascar, Mr. Lambert went **to** Zanzibar and Mozambique, commissioned by the French government to hire negroes and bring them to the Ile de Bourbon. This is a new kind of mitigated slave-trade, dis**covered** by France and countenanced by England. The **negro is only** in servitude for five years, and receives two dollars per month from his master, besides board and lodging. After five years he has leave to continue toiling, or he may die of hunger if he **does not** choose to work. He may buy himself this privilege **earlier** for fifty dollars (between seven and eight pounds), and may even return to his own country if he has money enough to take him home.

Mr. Lambert, knowing my fondness for traveling, **and my** eagerness to avail myself of every opportunity **of seeing** new lands, offered to take me with him. The French agent heard of this, and immediately went to Mr. Lambert to request him not to take me, alleging that I was employed as **a spy** by the English government. Whence this hatred of **Creoles** and French toward me, poor insignificant being that **I was?** The only reason I can suggest is that I associated almost exclusively with English families. But it was surely not my fault that English families sought me out, and always treated me with great kindness when I accepted their invitations? Why did not the French do likewise? All the favors and all the kindness I received **came** from English people: among **the French** residents, only Mr. Lambert and Mr. Genève showed **me hearty** friendship. The rest, like the Creoles, contented themselves with empty promises. I must confess that I contracted such a dislike to the French population of this part of the world, that I could not make up my mind to visit the neighboring island of Bourbon, gladly as I would, under other circumstances, have done so.

I am glad indeed that, when the desire to travel awoke so strongly in me fourteen years ago, I did not begin with the Mauritius. My zeal would soon have grown cold. Well—perhaps my readers would have been saved many a wearisome hour.

But then, on the other hand, I should not have visited Russia, and learned the notable fact that, in this much-abused despotic empire, there are many institutions more liberal in character than those of a colony of England, the country especially proud of its progress.

And yet it is so—notably as regards the passport system. If a traveler wishes to leave St. Petersburg, or any of the great towns in Russia, to start on a journey, he has to give notice of his intention a week before he departs. The traveler's name is published three times in the newspaper, so that, if he has debts, his creditors may take the requisite steps. Here, on this vast and extensive island, a week is considered far too short a notice. Three weeks are required, or, as in Russia, a surety must be provided.

I was so little prepared to find such an old-world regulation in force in an English colony, that I did not take any trouble about my passport. A few days before my departure, however, I asked the French consul for his *visa*, more, as I thought, as an attention than from necessity.

By chance, I heard at dinner the same day that this was not enough, and that the permission of the police to depart was also necessary. I was dining at Mr. O——'s, a partner of Mr. Lambert; and as several gentlemen were present, I asked if any of them would have the kindness to go through what appeared to me a mere formality on my behalf, and be bail for me. To my great astonishment, the gallant, refined Frenchmen **exhausted** themselves in empty excuses; **not one would** do me **the** service I required. **Next morning I went to** Mr. Kerr, **an** Englishman, and **in a few hours I had my** passport.

To my sorrow, I must confess that **at last I was** treated with **lack of courtesy by an** Englishman, **and** that Englishman was the **governor.**

When **I first arrived in the** Mauritius, this gentleman had **received me** very **courteously;** he even asked me to his country **house, and had, unasked,** offered me a letter to **the Queen of** Madagascar. On my going to him, a short **time before my** departure, for the promised letter, he likewise **put** me off with an excuse. **I was going to** visit the **Queen** of Madagascar **in company with Mr.** Lambert, and he pronounced **my companion to be politically a** dangerous man. Verily great **honor was mine in the** Mauritius; the French **took me for an English spy, and the** English governor for **a spy of the French government!**

After all **these** pleasant experiences, **no one will wonder** when **I say** that I looked forward with longing expectation **to** the moment when I might leave this little island, with its still more little-minded inhabitants. I will try to keep **no** other remembrance of it than the memory of its natural **beauty, and of the** friendship **and** kindness I received from **the good people** whose names I have mentioned, and from **some others. I have not had an** opportunity **of** naming **them** all; for others, Messrs. Fernyhough, Beke, Gonnet, etc., rendered me many a **good service.** To one and all I return **my** heartiest thanks.

CHAPTER VIII.

A Geographical and Historical Account of the Island of Madagascar.

WITH the exception of certain strips on the coast, the island of Madagascar is almost an unknown land; only here and there has a traveler been able to penetrate into the interior, and none have had an opportunity of studying the country at their leisure. So far as I am concerned, I have unfortunately not sufficient knowledge to describe the country in a scientific way. The most I can do is to give a simple but truthful account of what I have seen; beyond this my powers do not extend. It would, perhaps, be not uninteresting to my readers, therefore, if, before I relate my own experiences in Madagascar, I give an historical and geographical summary, compiled from the various works that have appeared concerning this island.

Madagascar is said to have been known to the ancients. In the thirteenth century Marco Polo makes mention of the island. The Portuguese visited it in 1506, and the first European nation that attempted to form settlements thereon were the French, in the year 1642.

Madagascar lies to the northeast of Africa, from which it is separated by the Mozambique Channel, seventy-five miles in breadth. It stretches from latitude 12° to 25° south, and from 40° to 48° east longitude. After Borneo, it is the largest island in the world. Its area is about 10,000 geographical square miles. Estimates of its population differ greatly, some writers giving from a million and a half to two millions, others raising the numbers to six millions.

The island contains woods of immense extent, far-stretching plains and **valleys, many rivers and** lakes, and great chains **of mountains, whose summits rise** to a height **of** from **ten to twelve thousand feet, and** even higher. The vegetation **is exceedingly** luxuriant, **the climate very** hot. **The coasts, where** there are many **swamps, are very** unhealthy for Europeans, but the interior of **the island is** more salubrious. The chief productions are some peculiar **balsams and gums, sugar, tobacco,** silk, maize, indigo, **and** spices. **The** forests **yield** the handsomest kinds of wood for buildings and furniture, and trees bearing almost every **fruit of the torrid zone.** Among the various descriptions **of palms, the** beautiful water-palm is frequently found. In **the** animal kingdom Madagascar **also** possesses some peculiar species; for instance, the **maquis, or half ape,** and the black parrot, besides much **horned cattle, many** goats, sheep, and beautiful birds. **The woods and savannas** swarm with wild cattle and pigs, **wild dogs and cats; but** there **are no** dangerous animals beyond these. **The snakes are innocuous; and** there are very **few reptiles, none of them being** poisonous except the **centipede,** and the little black spider which lives underground, and whose sting is said to be deadly; but this spider is seldom met with. In metallic substances, too, this island is said to be very wealthy, especially **in iron** and coal; but its mineral treasures have as **yet been very little** explored.

The population consists of four distinct **races.** On the south side dwell the Kaffirs, on the west the negroes, while **the** Arab race predominates on the east, and the Malay family in the interior. These chief **races** are subdivided into various tribes, **among** whom **the** Hovas, who belong to the Malay race, are the most numerous and most civilized in the whole **island.** The Hovas occupy the greater part of the interior; and **as far back as the** period of the first discovery **of** Madagascar, they **formed a** powerful empire, **of** which the capital was Tananariva, situated in an elevated plain in the district of Emir, and consisting of a union of many villages. Least known, or, to speak accurately, quite unknown, is the southwest coast, where the inhabitants are considered the most inhospitable of all, and the most inveterate foes of Europeans.

Like most nations in their infancy, all these various races and tribes are very indolent, superstitious, inquisitive, and unprincipled. As I have stated, the French have been endeavoring, since the year 1642, to establish themselves in Madagascar. They conquered certain strips of land, and erected *comptoirs* and little forts here and there, but could never maintain their position. All their efforts failed, partly in consequence of the unhealthy climate, partly through the harshness and cruelty with which they treated the natives, and partly because they were never assisted with money and troops from home, when these were required.

Neither the French government nor the "Société de l'Orient" could ever come to a decision respecting this island. At one time they wanted to conquer it entirely, at another to abandon it altogether. Troops and ships were several times dispatched, and then left to their fate, and nothing was accomplished. The last of these undertakings occurred in the year 1733, under the command of the Polish Count Benjowsky, who received beforehand the title of Governor of Madagascar. Count Benjowsky seems to have been a very capable and resolute man, and as he had a larger force under his command than had been engaged in any previous expedition, he would perhaps have succeeded in annexing Madagascar definitely to France, or at least in founding a permanent and important colony on the island, had he not been treated as badly as, or even worse than, his predecessors; for not only did the promised succors fail to arrive, but the Governor of Bourbon, who was to have assisted him, proved a most dangerous enemy. Instead of sending him money and troops, he tried in every

way, from jealousy, to weaken the power of his new rival;
and so it happened that, in spite of his first successes, Count
Benjowsky was soon scarcely able to hold a few unimportant forts and factories. After his death even these were
lost, and in the year 1786 the French left Madagascar altogether. Of all their conquests they only retained the little
island of St. Maria.

After the beginning of the nineteenth century the English attempted to found settlements in Madagascar, but
they too were unsuccessful. They took possession of the
harbors of Tamatavé and Foul Point, but only kept them
a short time. Meanwhile the empire of the Hovas in the
interior had increased considerably. Dianampoiene, the
chief of Tananariva, carried on successful wars against the
petty chiefs, and annexed their states to his own. He is
reported to have been a very active and intelligent man,
and to have given good laws to his people; under his rule
the use of spirituous liquors and of tobacco was forbidden.
Dianampoiene died in the year 1810, and left his kingdom,
which had already become powerful, to his son Radama.

This potentate was only eighteen years old when he
came to the throne. Like his father, he was intelligent, upright, and very ambitious. He loved the Europeans, and
sought to increase his knowledge by consorting with them.

The English very cleverly made use of this disposition
of the king's, and managed to get into high favor with him.
Radama was soon so prepossessed by them that he allowed
them distinctions of every kind, and sometimes even wore
an English uniform. He likewise made a treaty with England, by which he bound himself to give up the export
slave-trade. As an indemnity he received money and presents to the amount of about £2000; and the English government farther undertook to send ten young men from
Madagascar to England, and ten others to the Mauritius, to
be instructed in various handicrafts and trades.

Radama kept the **treaty** strictly; but not so did **the En**-glish General Hall, who succeeded Mr. Farquhar as **Govern**-**or of the** Mauritius. General Hall seems to have held **the doctrine that** savages are not men. He was not ashamed to declare openly that **a** contract made with **a** chief of **sav**-ages was entirely invalid, and accordingly he constantly broke the treaty. A natural consequence of this manner of dealing was, that Radama again licensed the slave-trade, **and** began to favor the French **at** the expense of the English, giving **his** new friends a small strip of land in the Bay of Vanatobé.

The **English strove** for a long time to regain their influ-**ential** position, but in vain. They had made themselves so hateful not only **to** Radama, but **to** the people, that every thing false and mendacious used to be called "English." Nevertheless, they succeeded at last in getting **the** treaty renewed, and even obtained fresh privileges. **They got** permission to bring in missionaries, to build schools, **and to** teach the Bible. In consideration of a duty of five per cent. they were allowed **to** enter all the harbors, to carry on trade, to cultivate the ground, and to found industrial establish-ments.

Radama died in his thirty-sixth year, on the 27th of July, **1828.**

Following out the ambitious projects **of his** father, he had succeeded in **extending his rule** over the greater part of the island, and had made **himself** King of Madagascar. Besides the country of **the Hovas, the** land of the Teklaves, on the northwest coast, with its capital, Bambetock; Mozangage, on the west coast, and the countries of the Antawares **and of** the Betimsaras, on the north, obeyed **his** sceptre; **the** southwest coast and the district of **the** Anossij, in the south-**east, had** alone maintained their independence.

Radama possessed great oratorical talents, and was very fond of exhibiting them. He was altogether very vain and exceedingly open to adulation: his people were obliged to worship him as if he had been a god, and the influence the missionaries obtained under his government they doubtless owed chiefly to the praise and flattery with which they continually plied him. They compared him **to the** First Napoleon, of whose great deeds the **French** had told him, and whom he appeared to have taken as his model. **The** parallel was not altogether inapplicable, however, and the title, Radama **the** Great, may be allotted to him when we consider how much he achieved during his short reign. The **conquest** of a great portion of the island, the abolition of **capital** punishment for many offenses, the prohibition of the export of slaves, the establishment **of a** tolerably well-disciplined army, the **introduction of** many European handicrafts—all this **was his doing.** He was **the first** to open a door to civilization in Madagascar; **in his** reign the first public schools were built, and **the Roman letter taken as** the character wherein the national language was to be **written.** Bent in every way upon improving the condition **of his** empire, he made an exception only in one particular—he set his **face** resolutely against every proposal to construct roads, declaring, like most rulers of half-savage tribes, that the bad roads were his best defense against the Europeans. During the last years of his life he unfortunately gave himself **up** to lamentable dissipation, which probably caused **his** early death; many, however, declare that he was poisoned.

At Radama's death, not only the English, but all European influence ceased. His first wife, Ranavola, succeeded him on the throne, **and** added to her name the regal title "Manjaka." This cruel, bloodthirsty woman began her rule by the execution of seven of the nearest **relatives** of the late king; indeed, according to the account given by a missionary, Mr. William Ellis, not only were all killed who belonged to Radama's family, but those nobles also who stood near the throne, some of whom Ranavola feared might advance a claim to it.

The treaty which Radama had made with the English she abrogated at once. Her hatred for the British was very great, and extended to every thing that came from England, even to the cattle introduced from that country. All people of English descent were to be killed, or at least banished from her dominions; nor did the French find favor in her eyes. She set her face generally against civilization, and tried hard to stifle its every germ. She drove away the missionaries, prohibited Christianity, and made all communication with Europeans difficult. Her subjects, especially those who do not belong to the race of the Hovas, from which she came, she treated with great severity and cruelty: for the smallest offenses the most rigorous punishments were inflicted, and sentences of death were, and still are, executed daily.

One only among those related by ties of blood to the late King Radama had succeeded in saving his life by timely flight. This was Prince Ramanetak. This prince had just claims to the throne; and as Queen Ranavola soon made herself hated by the people for her cruel and bloodthirsty rule, he might well have succeeded, with French help, in effecting a revolution and taking possession of the throne. This would have been very advantageous to the French, for Prince Ramanetak was very favorably inclined toward that nation. But the government in France remained true to the policy pursued toward Madagascar for the last two centuries, and the magnificent aid they offered to the prince consisted of—sixty muskets and twenty kegs of powder.

As I have already stated, when describing my visit to Paris, the French were ultimately expelled by Queen Ranavola even from the strip of land given them by Radama in the Bay of Vanatobé. Whether France will demand satisfaction, and show the insolent rulers of Madagascar the might of a European people, or whether she will let the opportunity pass by as she has done on former occasions, I can not take upon myself to conjecture. Time will show.

CHAPTER IX.

Departure from the Mauritius.—The old Man-of-War.—Arrival in Madagascar.—Mademoiselle Julie.—Account of Tamatavé.—The Natives.—Comical Head-dresses.—First Visit in Antandroroko.—Malagasey Hospitality.—The Europeans at Tamatavé.—The Parisio-Malagasey.—Domestic Institutions.

ON the 25th of April, 1857, I quitted the Mauritius. Thanks to the good offices of Mr. Gonnet, the owners of the "Triton" gave me a free passage to the harbor of Tamatavé, on the coast of Madagascar, distant 480 sea-miles. Our vessel was an old worn-out brig of war, which in her youthful days formed part of the British fleet at the great victory of Trafalgar in 1805. Deeply had she fallen from her former high estate; for now, in her old age, she was used for carrying oxen during the fine season of the year from Madagascar to the Mauritius. Accommodation for passengers there was none, all the space being divided into berths for the oxen; and as to the security of our vessel, the captain gave me the consolatory assurance that she was utterly unfit to do battle with any thing approaching to a storm.

My desire to leave the Mauritius behind me was nevertheless so great that nothing could dissuade me from going. I commended myself to Heaven, embarked with a light heart, and had no reason to repent my boldness. If the ship was bad, her captain, Mr. Benier, was a remarkably good one. Though not of high birth, for he was half Creole in color, he behaved with a courtesy and consideration which would have done honor to the most cultivated man. He at once gave up his cabin to me—the only place in the ship not monopolized by preparations for the four-footed passengers—and did all in his power to make the voyage

as agreeable to me as possible.   For the first three days our
passage was rather a quick one.   The wind was in our favor, blowing from the east, as it always does in these seas
from April to the end of October.   A quick-sailing ship
would have made the voyage in three days; but not so our
old war-craft, wending painfully on her way.   We were
still far distant from our goal, and, to our dismay, a strong
contrary wind arose in the night between the third and
fourth day of our voyage.   Notwithstanding the consoling
verdict of the captain with regard to the safety of the ship,
I sat expectant every minute of some catastrophe.   But the
night and the following day passed away without accident,
though the wind, still contrary, compelled us to cast anchor
toward evening off the island of "Prunes."   On the fifth
day we came to Tamatavé, but could not run in there; at
length, on the sixth day, we came to anchor in the harbor.

Violent falls of rain, frequently of long duration, had con-
tributed their share in rendering the voyage irksome; I had
no books with me, and the good captain's library consisted
of a cookery-book and an English and French dictionary.
But such minor inconveniences are easily forgotten, particularly when a long-sought goal is in view, as was now the
case with me.   The land I had ardently wished, during
many years, to visit, now lay before my eyes.

I wished to quit the ship at once; but it appears that, in
spite of her contempt for civilization and her dislike of European institutions, Queen Ranavola has adopted the two
among them most obnoxious to travelers—police and custom-house.   Just as though I had been in France or any
other European country, I was compelled to wait till the in-
specting officers had come on board, and looked very carefully at the ship and at me.   As I had the queen's royal
permission to set foot in her kingdom, no farther difficulty
was made, and I was free to land.   Here certain custom-
house *employés* of Madagascar at once took possession of me,

and led me to the custom-house, where all my baggage was opened and searched. How they searched! not the smallest object escaped their eyes, not the tiniest paper packet was overlooked. The officials exhibited the keenness of bloodhounds, and could hold their own beside the sharpest *douaniers* in France or Germany. Fortunately, nothing was stolen from me; and I looked complacently on a scene that so whimsically reminded me of my own country.

At Tamatavé I was to meet Mr. Lambert, who intended not to return to the Mauritius after his visit to the eastern coast of Africa, which he had undertaken on behalf of the French government, but to proceed to Madagascar at once. Mr. Lambert had not yet arrived, but he had already told me in the Mauritius that, in the event of having to wait, I should put up at Mademoiselle Julie's, and he would take care to inform her of his arrival.

My lady-readers will probably expect to be introduced, in the person of Mademoiselle Julie, to an unmarried European female, cast by some strange freak of fortune on this distant island. Unfortunately, I must disenchant them: Mademoiselle Julie is a true Malagasey woman, and, moreover, a widow, and the mother of several children. In Madagascar, the strange custom prevails of calling every member of the sex feminine "Mademoiselle," even though she may have a dozen little olive-branches to show, or may have been married half a dozen times.

Mademoiselle Julie is, nevertheless, no ordinary personage, and decidedly one of the most interesting characters, not only in Tamatavé, but in the whole island. She was left a widow about eight months ago, but continued to carry on her husband's business, and with a better result, it is rumored, than the deceased himself could attain. She is the possessor of sugar plantations and a rum distillery, and engages in commercial speculations of various kinds. Her penetration and industry would render her a remarkable woman any where; and they are the more surprising in a country like Madagascar, where the women are generally completely ignorant, and have a very low place in the social scale.

Mademoiselle Julie received part of her education in Bourbon. She speaks and writes French perfectly. Unfortunately, she has retained some of the usages, or rather *ab*-usages, of her native land. Her greatest delight is to lie for hours extended on the ground, resting her head on the lap of a friend or a female slave, who is engaged in clearing mademoiselle's head of certain little occupants which shall be nameless. This agreeable occupation, by the way, forms a favorite diversion of the women of Madagascar, who pay visits to each other in order to indulge in it *con amore*. Mademoiselle Julie was also violently addicted to using her fingers at dinner instead of fork and spoon; but she only indulged her inclinations so far when she thought herself unobserved.

Mademoiselle Julie did not receive me in the most cordial way exactly. She surveyed me from top to toe, rose in a leisurely way, and led me to a neighboring little house, worse appointed than even the pavilions of the Mauritius. The one room contained no furniture except an empty bedstead. Mademoiselle Julie gruffly inquired where I had left my bedding. I replied that I had brought none with me, as Mr. Lambert had assured me I should find every thing necessary in her house. "I can give you none," was her curt rejoinder; and although, as I afterward found, she had a store of bedding sufficient for the need, not of one, but of half a dozen travelers, she would have let me, old as I was, sleep on the bare bedstead. Fortunately, another woman, a Madame Jacquin, was present, who at once offered to supply me with bedding, and gave mademoiselle her opinion of her conduct in some rather strong expressions. Very grateful was I to good Madame Jacquin for her friendly offer, but for which I should have had to make shift as best I could till the arrival of Mr. Lambert with my cloak, and a pillow which I usually carry with me.

All other comforts were, of course, out of the question, and I had to provide every thing I wanted for myself. My stay at Tamatavé lasted for some weeks, for Mr. Lambert arrived much later than he had intended.

The harbor of Tamatavé is the best in the whole island; and in the fine season, from April to the end of October, many ships arrive here from the Mauritius and Bourbon, to take in cargoes of oxen, of which between ten and eleven thousand head are exported annually. About two thirds of the number go to the Mauritius, and only one third to Bourbon, although there is no great difference between these two islands, either in extent or in population. But there are many Englishmen in the Mauritius, who are more ardent admirers of roast-beef than the French.

It is a singular circumstance that Queen Ranavola does not allow the exportation of cows; she thinks, in her cunning wisdom, that if she allowed cows to be taken away, the recipients would soon breed cattle for themselves, and the demand for them from Madagascar would cease. Of course, she has no idea that the two islands derive far greater profits from their sugar plantations than the land would yield as mere pasture-ground for cattle. A fine ox, worth about £2 5s. in Madagascar, would cost four or five times that sum if reared in Bourbon or the Mauritius.

Besides the oxen, rice, rabanetas, and poultry are exported. Rabanetas are a kind of mats, on which the sugar is spread out to dry when it comes out of the last pan. They are also used as tapestry to cover the walls and floors of rooms, and the poorest classes even wear them as clothes.

During the fine-weather season there is much bustle in Mademoiselle Julie's house. There are sometimes four or five ships in the harbor at once. The captains are all friends of my hostess, who gives them a general invitation to dinner, and may be said to **keep free** table. **At the time** of my visit, which, however, was quite at the commencement of the fine season, the concourse was certainly not so great. **I never saw more** than two ships **in** the harbor at once.

Tamatavé may one day become a very important place, when this fruitful island is thrown open to Europeans, and free trade allowed to **all** nations.

Now, the place looks like a poor but very large village. Its population, including that of the district immediately around, is reckoned at four or five thousand souls: among **these** are 800 soldiers, and about a dozen Europeans and Creoles from Bourbon. Except the few houses belonging to these latter, and to a few well-to-do Hovas and Malagaseys, one sees nothing but little huts, some scattered about without order or arrangement, others forming narrow streets. These huts rest on poles from six to ten **feet** in height, are built of wood or of bamboo, thatched **with** long grass or palm-leaves, and contain a single room, **of** which the fireplace occupies a large part, so that the family can scarcely find sleeping room. Windows there are none, but two doors, at opposite sides of the wall; the door on **the** windward or weather side is always kept closed.

The houses of the wealthier inhabitants are built of the same materials as the habitations of the poor, but they are larger and loftier. They contain only one room, which is, however, divided by low partitions into three or four portions; these houses **of** the wealthy have also windows, but they are not glazed.

The bazar is situate in the midst of the village, on an ugly, uneven plot of ground, and is remarkable alike for its poverty and its dirt. A supply of beef, some sugar-cane, rice, rabanetas, and a few fruits, are generally all that is to be found there; and the whole stock of one of the dealers, who squat about on the ground, is often not worth more than a quarter of a piastre. The **oxen** are slaughtered **in** the bazar itself, and the skins are not taken off, but **sold** in strips with the meat, being considered a great delicacy. Meat is not bought according to weight, but according to the size of each piece, measured by the eye. Whoever wants to buy or **sell** any thing in this country must provide himself with a small pair of money-scales, for there are no coins in Madagascar except the Spanish dollar; and it is only within the last two years, since Mr. Lambert came here for **the first** time and brought some five-franc pieces with him, that the last-mentioned coins have become current. In the absence of small change, the dollars and five-franc pieces are cut into greater and smaller portions, often into more than five hundred chips.

To my great surprise, I heard that, in **spite of their** ignorance and savagery, the natives knew **so well how to** counterfeit these dollars, that it requires some practice and a close inspection to detect the spurious coins.

The natives of Tamatavé are principally Malagaseys. They appeared to me more repulsive than the negroes and Malays, whose ugliest features are found united in their physiognomy. They have wide mouths, with thick lips, broad flat noses, protruding chins, and prominent cheek-**bones.** Their complexion varies through **all** shades of a muddy brown. As a sole redeeming point, some of them have regular **teeth of a pearly** whiteness; and sometimes a handsome pair **of** eyes may be seen. Their hair, on the other hand, is marked by peculiar hideousness; it is coal-black, but as woolly as the negro's, and much coarser and longer, sometimes attaining a length of two feet. When this hair is worn in all its native luxuriance, it has a horribly disfiguring effect. The face seems quite lost in a virgin forest of thick frizzled hair, standing out in all directions. Fortunately, few wear it in this way. The men often have their hair cut off quite short at the back of the head, and leave only a length of six or eight inches in front, which looks comical enough, as the hair stands upright, and forms a woolly topknot; but it is not so bad as the virgin forest. The women, and some of the men too, who are exceedingly proud of their hirsute ornaments, and can not make up their minds to shorten them, plait them into a number of little tails. Some let these tails hang all about their heads, while others unite them into bands or bunches, so as to cover the whole head. This kind of head-dress takes a good deal of time in preparing, particularly in the cases of the richer Malagaseys, who have their hair plaited into an infinite number of these little tails. On the head of one of these native beauties I counted above sixty plaits. The good lady's slaves must have had a good day's work in bringing them to the right pitch of perfection. On the other hand, it may be urged that such a head-dress does not require renewing continually, but will remain in all its pristine loveliness for several days.

To leave the hair free in all its natural beauty is considered a token of mourning. The Malagaseys are generally above the middle height, and I saw many tall, powerful figures, especially among the men.

Their costume is that generally adopted by half-civilized nations who do not go quite naked; the only difference is in the name. The two chief articles of clothing used by the Malagaseys are called *sadik* and *simbu*. The first of these is as primitive as can well be imagined, consisting only of a strip of cloth worn round the loins. Many of the natives consider this garment as sufficient, and do not extend their wardrobe beyond it. The simbu is a piece of white stuff, about four yards long and three broad. The natives wrap themselves in their simbus like the Romans of old in their togas; and they really often wear them gracefully enough. Sometimes, to leave their movements unimpeded, they roll up the simbu and wrap it round the upper part of their bodies.

The dress of males and females is the same, except that the women have a little more drapery, and often wear, besides the sadik and simbu, a third garment—a short, very tight jacket, which they call *karrezu.*

The simbu gives its wearers continual employment. It is always coming loose, and has to be adjusted every minute. It might almost be said that men and women here had only one hand to work with, the other being monopolized by the management of this refractory garment.

The food of the Malagaseys is as primitive as their clothing. Rice and anana are the staple of every meal. Anana is a kind of vegetable very much resembling spinach, and which would be very agreeable to the taste if they would not prepare it with rancid fat. The people who live on the banks of rivers or on the sea-coast sometimes eat fish, but very seldom, for they are far too indolent to carry on a systematic fishery: meat, too, and poultry, though they are to be had in great quantity, and at the cheapest prices, are only eaten on special occasions. The natives usually eat two meals, one in the morning, the other in the evening.

The usual drink is *ranugung,* or rice-water, which is prepared in the following way. Rice is boiled in a vessel, and purposely burned, so that a crust forms at the bottom of the vessel. Water is then poured on, and allowed to boil. This water assumes the color of very pale coffee, and, like every thing else that is burnt, tastes abominably to a European palate. But the natives consider it delicious, and when they have drunk the rice-water, they eat the burnt crust with the greatest relish.

The Malagaseys keep many slaves, who are not considered very valuable here. A slave usually costs from thirty-six to forty-five shillings, and no difference is made with regard to age, though children of eight or ten years find readier purchasers than adult slaves. They start on the principle, ordinarily correct enough, that children may be brought up as their owner likes, but that a grown-up person who has contracted bad habits can not often be made to mend his ways. Adult males are also rarely offered for sale, except men who, once free, have been condemned as a punishment for some crime to be sold by public auction, and those among the slaves who have behaved ill to their masters. Female slaves are generally higher in price than males; and a great value is set upon those who can weave silk. A slave who is expert at this work often fetches as much as £30.

The position of the slaves is here, as among all half-civilized nations, much better than that of their fellow-bondmen among Europeans and Creoles. They have but little work to do, are fed about as well as their masters, and are seldom punished, though the laws do not at all protect them. On the contrary, a master may beat his slave to death; but the stick he uses in administering the chastisement must not be tipped with iron; for if it be thus shod, the master is liable to fine or some other punishment.

In Tamatavé the thievish propensity is very much developed, and that not only among the slaves, but it is widely diffused among almost the whole inland population, not excepting officers and exalted personages; I had to learn this to my cost. In the little hut assigned to me by Mademoiselle Julie as a dwelling, there was no lock to the door; but as my quarters were in close proximity to her dwelling-house and other buildings, and Mademoiselle Julie had not informed me of the predilection entertained by her fellow-countrymen for the goods and chattels of others, I did not think of being suspicious about it. One day, on being summoned to table, I happened to leave my watch, a valuable keepsake from a lady friend at New York, on the table, and when I returned in the evening it had vanished.

I returned immediately to Mademoiselle Julie to inform her of this circumstance, and to ask what steps I should take to regain possession of my watch, declaring myself ready to give a reward of some dollars to whoever would restore it to me. Mademoiselle Julie replied with the most perfect coolness that there was nothing to be done; the watch had probably been stolen by one of the domestic slaves, for that here every body stole; and that another time when I left my hut I should do well to lock the door and close the window apertures. She did not even take the trouble to question any of her slaves; and the only result that accrued from my loss was, that three days afterward I managed, with much difficulty, to get a lock put to my door.

The country immediately surrounding Tamatavé consists of nothing but sand, vegetation not beginning to show itself for one or two miles inland. I could not undertake long walks, as it rained every day, and it behooves Europeans in this country neither to expose themselves to wet nor to go out immediately after rain, for the slightest dampness is likely to bring on fever.

By chance I learned from Mademoiselle Julie that she was the possessor of two estates, lying seven miles from the town, very near the woods, and that her sons resided there. I hoped to be able to take good walks there, and to gather treasures for my collection of insects, and accordingly begged Mademoiselle Julie to have me taken there. In this country journeys are made in a light kind of sedan-chair, called *tacon*, suspended between two poles, and carried by four bearers. Even if one has to go only a few hundred steps, the sedan-chair is brought into requisition. No one goes on foot except the slaves and quite poor people. On long journeys eight or twelve bearers are taken instead of four, so that they can continually relieve each other.

I quitted Tamatavé betimes in the morning. The road

to Antandroroko, as one of the estates of my hostess was
called, was very good, particularly when we got out of the
domain of sand into that of vegetation. Where there were
no hills the bearers ran along with me as if I had been no
weight at all for them, and we accomplished the seven miles
in an hour and a quarter.

At Antandroroko lived Mademoiselle Julie's younger
son, a young man of twenty-two, who had been partly educated at Bourbon. I should not have suspected this, for he
differed in nothing from his fellow-countrymen save in his
European garb and his knowledge of French, and had again
become a thorough Malagasey.

A clean little room was allotted to me in his house, with
mats on the floor, but no furniture. I seated myself on my
carpet bag and waited patiently for breakfast. Mademoiselle Julie had allowed me to depart fasting, and thus my
anxiety on the subject of the commissariat was natural
enough. But hour after hour went by, and no one called
me to table. I ascribed this delay in the appearance of
breakfast to my arrival, and flattered myself that some special dish was being prepared on my account—perhaps even
a fowl was being sacrificed, and thus the meal was naturally retarded; so I waited and waited, until at last a slave
entered, and said a few Malagasey words which I could not
understand. But I very well understood the signs he made,
inviting me to follow him, and obeyed joyfully.

I was conducted into another room, unfurnished like my
own, and with a mat spread out on the floor in the midst.
On the mat lay a large leaf, surrounded by several smaller
ones; the first representing the dish and the latter the
plates for the entertainment. They had been obliging
enough to put a real plate, with a veritable knife, fork, and
spoon for me, and likewise a chair. As for my hosts, they
crouched upon the ground. A slave appeared with a kettle of rice, and emptied the contents into the improvised

dish. Then he brought boiled beans, and a great pot containing a dried fish boiled up in water, and smelling **so** badly that I could scarcely remain at table. The much-desired fowl never appeared. I thought with a gentle regret of the Dyaks of Borneo, who are considered so savage and cruel, and who, while they themselves ate rice, could always find a chicken for me; and here, in the house of a semi-European host, and in a country where poultry is so cheap and plentiful, I had to content myself with rice and beans.

The manner in which the natives ate was any thing but appetizing. Instead of a spoon, they make use of a piece of leaf, which they fold very dexterously, and wherewith they manage not only to eat rice and beans, but even to carry fluids safely to their mouths. This leaf-spoon being very large, they distend their mouths to the utmost extent, and then shovel the provisions in. This might pass without comment, for it will not do to be too particular on **one's** travels; but the worst of it is that they all take their **sup**plies with their own spoons from the common store in **the** dish.

Near the fish-kettle a slave is generally posted, whose duty consists in ladling the broth out of the kettle, and pouring it over the rice as the company take it up in their spoons. The fish is taken in the hand in pieces, and eaten like bread. I do not wonder that a Malagasey who has **never left** his own country, or seen any thing better than its usages, should be content to live in this way; but how the young man who had been educated among Europeans could so entirely readopt the customs of his countrymen, I can not understand. Not only in the manner of eating and drinking was this peculiarity shown, but in every thing **else** likewise. He could sit for hours in his arm-chair **with**out reading or otherwise occupying himself. In fact, he did nothing all day long but rest, smoke tobacco, and talk to the highly intellectual slaves who continually surrounded him.

With true sorrow I had already noticed at Tamatavé that the few Christians who lived there—namely, a few Europeans and some Creoles from Bourbon—instead of setting a good example to the natives, and seeking to improve them by their own respectable lives and the purity of their behavior, seemed to have sunk to the level of the people among whom they dwelt, and adopted all their immoral habits. Thus, for instance, they contract no regular marriages, but, like the natives, change their wives at their pleasure, and sometimes even keep two at the same time, **besides** being attended on exclusively by female slaves.

Some of these people send their children to Bourbon, or even to France; but for what purpose? When the young man 'has really learned something—when he has contracted better habits and customs—he returns, and every thing is spoiled only too quickly by his father's bad example. But what passes my wit to understand is the fact that a European who has earned money enough to **live comfortably in** his native land, can of his own free will remain in this country; and yet such a wonder did I most certainly behold **in** the person of a certain Mr. N——.

This man has made a considerable fortune by commerce, and **went to** his native France a few years ago with the intention of remaining there. But the intercourse with cultivated men and women seemed to him no equivalent for **the** idle, entirely animal life in Madagascar. So he soon returned to Tamatavé, to his slave-women, and there he will probably end his days. The European is truly a wonderful creature. In Europe he can scarcely find a girl to his taste, and his chosen one is expected to possess all the perfections under the sun; and here **he is** charmed by black, or muddy-brown coarse beauties, **whom** I really would almost as soon class among the genus Simia as among the human race! I pity men who can sink so low as to lose all taste for the noble and beautiful, and all recognition of the dignity of humanity; and evil indeed are the effects of their example upon the natives, and lamentably is the progress of civilization checked thereby.

But to return to my amiable host. The splendid breakfast was over, and my hopes had been shattered; still, I firmly bade defiance to despair, and built my trust upon the principal meal, which is always taken in the evening. With the greatest impatience I awaited the hour—alas! of new disappointment; the same dishes appeared that had decked the morning meal; not one less, and not one more. It was too much for human endurance. Fortunately, however, the elder brother of my host had come over from the second estate. He was a young man who had not only been in Bourbon, but had lived for nine years in Paris. Although, like his brother, he ate his supper in true Malagasey fashion, by means of the leaf-spoon, I felt more confidence toward him, and invited myself without ceremony to breakfast with him next morning, certain that I could not be worse entertained than I was here.

In the evening a very good bed was made up for me on the floor of my room; but, unfortunately, the musquito-net was forgotten. The consequence was that I could not close my eyes all night. Before retiring to rest I had begged my host to send me up a cup of coffee, with milk, to my room in the morning. But what was the result of my request? They brought me a washing-basin of milk and some sugar, but neither coffee-cup nor spoon. The sight of the basin was of course quite sufficient to take away my appetite, though the milk looked refreshing enough. I modestly hinted at coffee, and heard that they were going to look for some, and that it would then be roasted and ground. I therefore declined to wait, took leave of my obliging host, and again set out on my journey breakfastless.

A boat took me up the pretty river Foondro, which falls into the sea half a mile from this place, to the dwelling of the Parisian Malagasey. He lived in a handsome house; came out some distance to me, and—oh happy hour!—led me at once to the dining-room, where, to my great jubilation, I found the table covered in European fashion, and a good, plentiful repast spread out upon it.

This young man in many respects presented a favorable contrast to those of his countrymen who had been, like himself, in Bourbon or in Europe. He is, I think, the only one who does not endeavor to forget every thing he has learned in Europe as quickly as possible. I asked him if he did not miss Paris, and if he did not feel a desire to live there. He replied that he should certainly like to dwell in a civilized land, but that, on the other hand, Madagascar was his native country—that his whole family lived here, and he could not make up his mind to leave them altogether.

His manner showed that these were not mere words— that he *felt* what he said. It greatly astonished me, for in general there is nothing more ridiculous than to hear a Malagasey speak of his family and of domestic ties. I have never met with a more immoral people than the inhabitants of Madagascar; and where there is such demoralization, family ties must be of the loosest. I dare not trust my pen to chronicle the many immoral customs which prevail, not only among the people generally, but in the highest families in the island, and appear quite natural to the people here. I can only say that female virtue is looked upon as quite valueless, and that the laws regarding marriage and progeny are of a stranger kind than any where else in the world. Thus, for instance, a man may divorce his wife and take another as often as he chooses. The woman may live with another man, though she may not marry again; but all the children born to her after she has been separated from her husband are looked upon as belonging to him; the second husband has not the slightest claim to them, and the mother is compelled to deliver them up to her first hus-

band immediately upon his claiming them. When a man
dies, too, any children his widow may afterward have are
looked upon as his; and it is in consequence of this law
that Prince Rakoto, son of Queen Ranavola, though he was
born long after King Radama's death, is looked upon as the
són of that monarch.

It likewise frequently happens that men who have no
children by their own wives marry girls who expect to become mothers, so that they may be able to call the child
that is about to be born their own. This craving for progeny is caused by an existing law, which declares the property of any man who dies childless forfeit to the state.

To speak of domestic ties in such a state of society would
sound like mockery; and if I had not noticed in my host,
on several occasions, a rare amount of real feeling, I should
have attached little credence to his words.

I had a good deal of conversation with him, and asked
him farther if he did not feel any craving for intellectual
companionship—for the agreeable domestic relations found
in Europe; if it did not seem hard to him to live continually among coarse, uncultivated men? He acknowledged
that the total want of cultivation among his countrymen
rendered their society any thing but agreeable to him, but
that he sought relaxation in books and study. He mentioned to me several very good works which he had brought
with him from France.

I felt truly sorry for this young man. I will not assert
that he showed any extraordinary amount of quickness or
depth of intellect, but he has an adequate amount of talent,
and so much real sensibility and feeling that he could not
fail to gain friends in any country in the world. I pity
him; for, amid this complete dearth of congenial society, it
will be wonderful indeed if he does not become a true Malagasey at last.

I remained with Mr. Ferdinand Diche—for so my host

was called—for a whole day. The weather continued so bad that I could neither walk out nor occupy myself in hunting for insects. On the following day I returned to Tamatavé.

CHAPTER X.

At length, on the 13th of May, Mr. Lambert arrived. On the 15th I witnessed the preliminary celebration of the great bath-feast of the queen. This is the only national feast in Madagascar, and it is kept with great solemnity in all the dominions subject to the sceptre of Ranavola.

I did not see the great feast itself, and can therefore only repeat to my readers the description I received from several eye-witnesses. It is celebrated on the first day of every year, and may thus be called the New-year's feast of Madagascar. But the Malagaseys do not follow our method of reckoning time, though they divide the year into twelve months as we do. Each of their months is *lunar*, and when the moon has renewed itself twelve times their year is past.

On the eve of the feast, all the high officers, nobles, and chiefs appear at court, invited by the queen. They assemble in a great hall, and presently a dish of rice is carried round, each guest taking a pinch in his fingers and eating it. That is the whole extent of the ceremony on this first evening.

Next morning the same company assemble in the same hall. As soon as they have all met, the queen steps behind a curtain which hangs in a corner of the room, undresses, and has water thrown over her. As soon as she has been dressed again, she steps forward, holding in her hand an ox-horn filled with the water that has been poured over her. Part of this water she sprinkles over the assembled company. Then she betakes herself to a gallery overlooking the court-yard of the palace, and pours the rest over the military drawn up there on parade.

On this auspicious day nothing is seen throughout the whole country but feasting, dancing, singing, and rejoicing, continued till late at night. The celebration is kept up for eight days, dating from the day of the bath. It is the custom for people to kill as many oxen on the first day as they contemplate consuming during the other seven: whoever possesses any oxen at all, kills at least one at this feast. The poor people get pieces of meat in exchange for rice, sweet potatoes, tobacco, etc. The meat is still tolerably fresh on the eighth day. It is cut into long thin strips, which are salted and laid one upon the other. The preliminary celebration of the feast occurs a week earlier, and consists of military processions. The votaries of pleasure then begin their feast, and thus have a fortnight's jollity— a week before the feast, and a week after.

The soldiers whom I saw in the processions at Tamatavé pleased me well enough. They went through their drill and manœuvres with tolerable accuracy, and, contrary to my expectation, I found the music not only endurable, but positively harmonious. It appears that, some years ago, the queen sent for a European band-master and a complete set of instruments, and her worthy subjects were inducted into a knowledge of music, probably by means of the stick. She succeeded in her attempt, and many of the pupils are already become masters, and spread the science among their fellow-countrymen.

The soldiers were dressed in a simple, neat, and perfectly uniform manner. They wore a tight-fitting jerkin, reaching to the chest and covering part of the loins. The chest was bare, and covered by the gleaming white belts supporting the cartridge-box, which had a good effect in contrast to the black skins of the soldiers. Their heads were uncovered. Their arms consisted of a musket and the national lance, called *sagaya*.

The officers looked comical enough. They went about in threadbare civilian suits, that forcibly reminded me of the fashions which prevailed when I was a child.

To these quizzical costumes, the ugly black faces and woolly hair gave such an effect that the whole was overwhelmingly funny, and I lamented that I had no skill in drawing, for I might have produced some wonderful caricatures from the models before me.

Except on parade and at exercise, the officers, like the soldiers, wear a costume that suits them. The soldiers live in a kind of barracks, in the court-yard of which the exercise is performed and the courts-martial are held. Europeans are strictly prohibited from entering these barracks.

The Queen of Madagascar can easily put herself at the head of a powerful army. Nothing but her potent word is needed to bring it together; for the soldiers receive no pay, and are obliged, moreover, to clothe and feed themselves. They procure provisions by going out to work, with the permission of their superiors; or they go home to cultivate their fields. But the soldier who wants his officer's permission for frequent absence must propitiate the latter by giving him a part of his earnings—at least a dollar annually. The officers are generally very little richer than the soldiers. They certainly receive, like the civil officials, a remuneration for their services from the customs revenue; but the pay is so small that they can not live upon it, and are compelled to have recourse to other means, not always of the most honest description. According to the law, a very small portion of the customs revenue ought to come to the private soldier; but I am told the officers find the amount so trifling that they do not take the trouble to give any account of it, and prefer keeping it entirely for themselves, so

that the poor soldier who can not find work, and is too far
from his home to be able to visit it from time to time, is literally in danger of being starved to death.   He is obliged
to endeavor to support life with herbs and roots, and all
kinds of makeshifts (sometimes very nauseous ones), and
may think himself lucky if he gets a little rice now and
then.   This rice the poor fellow throws into a large vessel
filled with water, drinks the thin rice-water in the daytime,
and only at evening allows himself a handful of the grain.
But in war-time, as soon as he is on an enemy's territory,
he makes amends to himself for the hardships he has endured; then he plunders and steals right and left; villages
are burned to the ground, and the inhabitants killed or
dragged away to be sold as slaves.

After parade was over, the officers drew up, accompanied
by the band, before our (or, more properly speaking, Mademoiselle Julie's) house, to salute Mr. Lambert, and invite
him to a feast in the queen's name.   This is the only expense the queen is in the habit of incurring for people
whom she wishes to treat with distinction.

Mr. Lambert treated the officers to some good wine,
whereupon they marched off to the strains of the national
hymn, which really sounded melodious enough.

On the 17th of May, the solemn banquet was held in the
house of the first judge of the kingdom.   The hour was
fixed for three o'clock, but they did not come to fetch us
until five.   We betook ourselves to the house, which stood
in the midst of a large square or court-yard, with palings
around it.   The soldiers stood in a double line from the
entrance of the court to the house, and the national hymn
was played as we passed.   We were conducted at once to
the dining-hall.   Two sentries, with crossed muskets, stood
before the door, but this did not prevent any one who listed .
from going quietly in and out.

The company, consisting of about thirty people, had already assembled to receive the guest of the day, Mr. Lambert, with due honor.

The first governor, who is at the same time commandant at Tamatavé, wore black European clothes, and across his chest a broad red satin ribbon, like that of an order; but, wonderful to relate, there are no orders yet in Madagascar. The second governor had donned an old European suit of faded sky-blue silk velvet, richly embroidered with gold; and the other gentlemen were likewise dressed in European fashion.

The table was covered with dishes of meat of all kinds, tame and wild fowl, fish, and other marine productions. I do not think I exaggerate when I say there were above forty dishes, great and small. The principal show-dish was the head of a calf of rather large size, so stripped of flesh that it looked like a skull, and produced any thing but an agreeable effect. There were likewise many different kinds of beverages, French wines and port, English beer, etc. After the meat, little badly-made tarts of various kinds were served, and the banquet ended with fruit and Champagne. Of the last-mentioned wine there was plenty, and it was drunk out of tumblers.

As far as I could see, all the guests seemed blessed with extraordinary powers as trenchermen, nor did they forget to do honor to the wines, and great was the number of toasts proposed.

Whenever the health of the commandant, of the second governor, or of an absent prince was proposed, one of the officers went to the door and shouted out to the soldiers in the yard the name of the person thus honored; thereupon the music struck up, and all the gentlemen drank the toast, standing.

The dinner lasted full four hours. It was nine o'clock at night when we quitted the table and betook ourselves to an adjoining room, where English beer was again offered to us. After this, to my great astonishment, two of the highest officers danced a kind of *contre-danse;* others followed their example and indulged in a polka. At first I considered this fancy for dancing to be a consequence of the Champagne they had imbibed; but Mr. Lambert enlightened my ignorance, and told me that these dances were part of the etiquette of the occasion. I thought it a strange custom, but was infinitely amused at the grotesque figures of the performers, and felt quite sorry that they did not continue the exercise longer. As a conclusion to the solemnity, the health of the queen was drunk in a liqueur flavored with aniseed, and to the accompaniment of the national hymn. After the royal toast nothing more may be proposed; to do so would be considered an offense against her royal majesty, who, like her deceased husband, exacts something very like worship from her people.

Accordingly we broke up. When, on my way out, I went for my parasol, which, on entering the room, I had deposited in a corner, I found it was gone—it had shared the unhappy fate of my watch.

Though theft is punished with great severity, frequently even with death, and though it is lawful to kill a thief caught in the fact without any explanation to the authorities, there is more thieving in Tamatavé than any where else. As I have already said, it is not at all unusual for officers and men of rank to take part in nocturnal burglaries. A few years ago a robbery of some magnitude was perpetrated in Tamatavó, and the majority of the stolen articles were discovered in an officer's possession. The man who had been robbed did not receive back the chief part of his property; but he got some, with an injunction to say nothing about the robbery, unless he wished to expose himself to very disagreeable consequences; and so the affair ended.

It is seldom that any one gives information to the authorities of a theft. In small affairs it is not worth while, as the detection of the thief and restoration of the property scarcely ever follow; and in robberies of any magnitude, persons of high position are almost sure to be implicated, and it would be dangerous to proceed against these. That the soldiers are among the most confirmed thieves is not to be marveled at, considering their miserable position. The officer or employé certainly has only a very small salary, but, at any rate, he gets something. Besides, he is a merchant or a landed proprietor, has slaves who work for him, and even makes a profit out of the soldiers who serve under him; but the poor private generally receives nothing at all, and it is almost too much to expect that he should submit quietly to die of hunger.

On the 19th of May we at length set out on our journey to Tananariva, the capital of the island. Our party consisted of Mr. Marius, Mr. Lambert, and myself. Mr. Marius, a Frenchman by birth, had been living for twenty years in Madagascar. He accompanied Mr. Lambert on his journey from a feeling of friendship, and undertook the office of interpreter and the general direction of the journey, and his kind assistance was of the greatest value to us.

The whole previous day and half of the present one we had been fully employed wrapping up the chests and boxes containing presents for the queen and Prince Rakoto, and our own baggage, in great dry leaves, to protect them against the rain.

Mr. Lambert had bought the presents for the queen and her court with his own money, and not, as they asserted in the Mauritius, with funds from the French government. The presents consisted of full and very expensive toilets for the queen and some of the princesses, her relations, rich uniforms embroidered with gold for Prince Rakoto, and valuable art-objects of all kinds, including several musical clocks, barrel organs, and similar toys. On these presents

Mr. Lambert had **spent** more than 200,000 francs. For the conveyance.of these treasures to **the capital** more than four hundred persons were **required, who** received the same pay as the soldiers; that is to say, **none at all,** for service of this kind **is** compulsory. Along **the** whole route the convoy had been announced, and the poor bearers had to be **at** certain stations on the road at an appointed time.

The people, about two hundred in number, who were **to carry us and** our personal luggage, were paid by Mr. **Lambert.** The fee for **a bearer** from Tamatavé to Tananariva, **a** distance of two hundred and twenty miles, is only a dollar; **and even provisions** are not found by the hirer. Mr. Lambert promised them good food **besides the dollar,** whereupon they expressed their **gratitude by loud shouts** and rejoicings.

The first day **we** only traveled seven **miles,** and passed the night at Antandroroko, the **estate** of Mademoiselle Julie's younger son. Here things **looked** very differently from the appearance they had presented on the **day when** I came alone. I am far from being vain enough **to** suppose that I should have been received like Mr. Lambert, **the** powerful friend of the queen; but the difference need **not** have been quite so glaring. To-day every thing was **done in** European style, and the table was hardly large enough to hold the dishes piled together **upon it.**

But so it is all the world over—rich people find friendly **faces** every where, **and** are received with every mark of good-will and **respect; but** when the poorer guest arrives, the mask is taken off; and whoever travels as I do, gets to know human nature **as it** is, and the verdict can **very** seldom be given in its favor. How different from **my** description of this country would an **account be from the** pen of Mr. Lambert! What encomiums might he not pass on the hospitality of the people who often received me with frigid, uncourteous welcome! I fancy it was only to the consideration with which Mr. Lambert treated me that I owed the boon of a musquito-net, which was actually provided for my bed on this occasion.

May 20th. To-day we traveled the whole day long on lakes and rivers. The largest of the former was the No-sive Lake, which is about eleven miles long by five broad. The Nossmasay and Rassaby are almost of equal extent. As we approached a small island in the last of these lakes, our boat's company suddenly began to yell and execrate with all their might. I thought some accident had happened, but Mr. Marius gave me the following explanation of the affair:

Many years ago a marvel of female beauty is said to have dwelt near this lake, but her life was the reverse of virtuous. This Messalina of Madagascar attained great fame, and considered herself greatly flattered thereby. She died young, and, in order to keep her memory green in future days, she besought her numerous admirers, on her deathbed, that she might be buried on this little island, and furthermore expressed a wish that all who passed by should roar and swear as loudly as they could, in remembrance of her.

Her admirers complied with her wish, and gradually the custom became universal.

The other lakes which we had to traverse were very small, and so were the rivers. A great loss of time was occasioned by the fact that very few of these silent highways communicated with one another. Between almost every lake and stream and its neighbor lay a little tract of dry land, from a hundred to a thousand paces in length, so that our boats were continually being unloaded and carried over. This was a hard day's work for our people; but, at any rate, they had the satisfaction of being well fed on their journey. Mr. Lambert had quite a paternal care for their comfort, and there was always fresh meat and rice in abundance.

Our way lay near **the sea-coast, and** we constantly heard the sound of the breakers. The land was flat and monotonous, but **the** rich vegetation gave it a cheerful appearance; in our progress we noticed some very flourishing plantations, and water-palms in abundance.

Our quarters for the night were fixed in the village **of** Vovong, in a house belonging to the government. On the way from Tamatavé to the capital there are houses of this description in many villages, and these houses are open **to** all travelers. The interior is spread with clean mats, which the inhabitants are bound to furnish; they are also responsible **for** the repairing the houses, and keeping them in proper condition.

May 21. To-day our journey was again on the waters: first, a short distance on the River Monsa; then our bearers had to carry the boat for at least half a mile, after which we embarked again on a little stream, very narrow, and so overshadowed by small trees, bushes, and aquatic plants that we could often scarcely force the boat through. This journey reminded me of similar trips in Singapore and **Bor-**neo, with this difference, that in the latter places our way lay through virgin forests of gigantic trees. After a few miles we came to a broader stream, of peculiarly transparent **and** limpid **water,** in which every object was reflected with **a** clearness and brilliancy I had never before seen.

In these lower lands, and, with few exceptions, along the whole coast of Madagascar, the climate is very unhealthy, and dangerous fevers are prevalent. The chief reason for this probably is, that the land lies deep, and the rivers **are** choked up with sand at their mouths. In the rainy season the water pours unchecked over the plains, forming swamps and morasses, the exhalations from which, in the hot months from November till the end of April, produce a malignant miasma. Even the natives who live in the healthy districts, in the interior of the island, are just as liable to its effects as the Europeans themselves, when they come to the unhealthy lowlands in the hot season. Of the Europeans, I saw a few in Tamatavé who were attacked every **summer** by the fever, though they **had** lived there for three or four years.

Our journey to-day did not exceed eight or nine **miles;**. betimes in the afternoon we halted **at** the village of Andororanto to wait for our baggage, which had been taken overland by another route.

May 22. This morning **we** traveled three hours by water on the River Fark, which falls into the sea not far from **the village where we** had passed the night. This river is **very broad,** but has few deep parts. Its banks afford a **greater** variety of scenery than the rivers we had hitherto **seen.** The uniform flats begin now to alternate with little clusters of hills, and in the far background **a low ridge** becomes visible.

Coming to a great bend in the river, we disembarked. The boats remained behind, and our journey by land began in earnest. This day we accomplished eight miles more inland toward the east. The road was tolerably good, except in the neighborhood of a few wretched villages which we passed.

As far as I have yet seen of this country, it is exceedingly fertile, except a few sandy tracts. Capital pasture-grass grows every where luxuriantly. The plains at the higher level are said to be excellently calculated for sugar plantations, and the low-lying lands for rice-fields, and yet all was lying fallow. The population is so scanty that we hardly passed a tiny village in every three or four miles. **This is** certainly inevitable in a country whose government seems determined to lay waste and depopulate the land. In Madagascar scarcely any one is a landed proprietor except the queen and the high nobility. The peasant may cultivate the land and sow seed where **he** finds a tract unoccupied,

without asking permission of any body; but this gives him
no proprietary right, and after he has cultivated the land
the owner may take it away from him. This circumstance,
added to the natural indolence inherent in all savage tribes,
readily accounts for the fact that the peasant only culti-
vates just as much land as he finds necessary to grow
enough for himself.

The taxes are not oppressive. The peasant has to deliver about a hundred weight of rice to the government annually; but compulsory service and other exactions are very
burdensome, for they prevent the peasant from attending
properly to his work.

Rice is the plant principally cultivated in Madagascar.
The crop is sown twice a year, and the government pre-
scribes a month each time to be devoted to the work. With
an active people this would be enough time to get the harvest gathered, and the new crop put into the ground; but,
unfortunately, the natives of Madagascar are very far from
being an active race, and so it often happens that the month
has passed away before the work is finished. After the
month is over, the government requires the men for all
kinds of services, of more or less importance, just as the
queen or the officers appointed by her majesty may please
to order. Those are worst off who live on roads leading
from the harbors to the capital, for they have to do so
much compulsory service as bearers that they have scarcely any time left for agriculture. At one time many left
their huts and fields, and fled into the interior of the country to escape this hardship, so that the villages began to be
deserted. To check this, the queen condemned every fugitive to death; but, on the other hand, she relieved the inhabitants of villages on the roads from military service, the
most hateful of all obligations to the people. A few little
villages were also stocked with royal slaves, who had no
other duty assigned to them but to act as carriers. If the
people had only to transport the royal luggage and goods,

their service would not be a heavy one; but every nobleman, every officer, can procure an order for similar service,
and even compel the people to work without showing any
authority at all. They can not complain, for a peasant
would never gain a cause against a nobleman or an officer,
and so they pass the greater part of the year working on
the roads. In the districts where there are no goods and
chattels to be carried, other work is found for them; and
if there happens to be nothing to do, they are summoned in
a body, not only the men, but the women, children, and all,
to attend a *kabar* at some place or other. Kabar is the name
given to public judicial sessions, councils, audiences, and as-
semblies of the people, where new laws and royal orders are
promulgated, and much similar business enacted.

The kabars are sometimes held in distant places, so that
the poor people have to travel some days to get to them.
Nor are the laws at once read out to them; this part of the
business is often postponed from day to day, so that they
are sometimes kept away from their homes for weeks. On
such occasions many die of hunger and misery, from having
taken an insufficient supply of rice; money they have none,
and must therefore seek to sustain life as best they may
with roots and herbs. Their destruction seems to be the
object of the queen; for she hates all the people who are
not of her own race, and her greatest desire would seem to
be to annihilate them all at one blow.

So far as the cultivation of the land is concerned, there
are people enough in Bourbon and the Mauritius who would
be glad enough to lay out large plantations. A few even
have tried it, clearing great tracts of land and planting sugar-canes. But they met with the greatest difficulties; for,
as the land every where belonged to the queen, or to one or
other of the nobles, the new-comers were obliged to propitiate the owners by presents of money to obtain permission
to carry on their operations. Besides this, the government

H

demanded ten per **cent. on their profits,** and, in spite of all
the heavy sacrifices, **they were not much better** off than the
natives; **for the peculiar** judicial institutions of Madagascar
allowed the owner to break off the contract at any moment,
and drive away **the** planter.

Some preferred **to** make a treaty with the queen herself,
her majesty therein engaging to provide the ground, the laborers, wood, **iron, in a** word, every thing necessary **to a**
plantation; the planter, on his part, undertaking to **set the**
work in motion, and to find provisions for the hands; while
the produce **was to be** divided equally between the con-
tracting parties. **The** queen entered into several contracts
of this kind, but never kept **to them.** In King Radama's
time, the land, **they told me,** had been more populous; under the **rule of the present queen, not** only have **innumer-**
able towns sunk down to a **few** scattered huts, but others
have altogether vanished. **Spots** were often pointed out to
us where fine villages had once stood.

We passed the night at Manambotre. **At a little dis-**
tance from this village we passed a place where great **blocks**
of rock lay scattered here and there. Their appearance **in**
this place astonished me not a little, as the soil consisted
every where of vegetable earth on which not the smallest
stone was to be found. Mr. Lambert had two oxen killed
this evening for the benefit **of our** bearers. They were
dragged out in front of our hut by ropes passed round their
horns; then several men armed with knives crept up from
behind, and cut the sinews of the **poor** creatures' hind legs,
so that they sank down powerless, and could be dispatched
without danger. **As I** have already remarked, they are
not flayed, but **the** skin is roasted with the meat; nay, the
natives even prefer it to the flesh, because the greater portion of fat adheres to it.

The oxen are fine large animals, and very tame; they
are of the buffalo kind.

May 23. To-day **the** bad roads began. I did not **feel**

afraid of them, for, in many of my journeyings—for instance, in Iceland, when I ascended the Hecla; also in Kurdistan, in Sumatra, and other countries—I have seen far worse; but my companions seemed horrified at the sight. They were certainly far from good, I must allow. The land is here more than wave-like in form: it consists of a succession of lofty hills sufficiently steep, and so closely packed together that barely a few hundred yards of level land are left between. Instead of winding along by the foot of these hills, the roads go straight up and down each of them. The soil, too, a rich loam, becomes as smooth and slippery as ice, from the rain, and there are, moreover, innumerable holes made by the cattle, thousands of oxen being driven this way from the interior.

Our bearers won my unfeigned admiration; indeed, surprising strength and skill are required to carry heavy loads along such roads. The bearers, whose duty it was to transport my little meagre figure, were the most lucky. I felt almost inclined to be angry with them, for they trotted with me, up hill and down dale, as if I had been no weight at all, and that was not quite the case. And when the ground happened to be somewhat level, they almost ran, although I tried in vain to induce them, by all kinds of deprecating signs, to moderate their ardor; for the long, quick strides they made were as disagreeable as the trot of a heavy horse. The hills were covered with rich grass; some also were clothed with plants. Among the latter there was much bamboo, with delicate clusters of leaves of a light green color, and of a luxuriant freshness I had never seen elsewhere. Like shade alternating with light in a picture, the bright bamboo stood near the Kafia palm, with its feathery dark leaves fifteen feet long. This palm is a very valuable tree to the natives, who plait their rabanetas with the fibres of its leaves—those coarse mats which I have mentioned in my account of Tamatavé.

Of the water-palm I saw some splendid specimens. This

tree flourishes here, in **the interior of** the country, much better than on the sea-coast.   I remember to have read in some
works of travels that this palm only occurs in situations
where **water is** scarce, and that it is called water-palm, and
also traveler's palm, because a small quantity of water col-
lects between each leaf and the stem, to the great delectation of the thirst-tormented wayfarer.   The natives here
assert, on the contrary, that this palm only flourishes in a
damp soil, and that water is always to be found in its neigh-
borhood.   Unluckily, I had no opportunity of investigating
the subject, so as to judge of the truth of these reports ; but
I hope the time will come when botanists will roam at pleasure through this great island, and settle, not only this, but
many other doubtful **questions** in geography and natural
history.

The sago-palm is another variety that flourishes greatly
in Madagascar.   Strangely enough, the **natives** dislike its
pith, although they are in general any thing but squeamish
in their diet, for they devour not only herbs and roots, **but**
insects and worms likewise.

The time passed very quickly to-day, for from every hill
and mountain a fresh view opened before us more beauti-
ful than the last.   But the population became thinner and
thinner ; in the whole day's journey we only passed by a
few very insignificant villages.

This night we stopped at a village called Ambatoarana.
The arrival of Mr. Lambert had been every where announced, and as it was known that he stood high in favor
with the queen, the inhabitants of the village received him
with the greatest demonstrations of respect, and **vied** with
each other to propitiate the influential man.   Here, too, the
judge came at once to call upon us, and in the name of the
community presented to Mr. Lambert a couple of oxen, besides a great quantity of rice and poultry.   Mr. Lambert
accepted these presents, but gave others of far greater value
in return.

CHAPTER XI.

Celebration of the National Feast. — Song and Dance. — Beforona. — The elevated Plateau of Ankay.—The Territory of Emir.—Solemn Reception. —Ambatomango.—The Sikidy.—The Triumphal Procession.—Arrival in Tananariva.

MAY 24th. It had not rained for four-and-twenty hours, and, consequently, we found the roads in somewhat better condition than yesterday. The hills we encountered were also less high and steep.

We generally divided our day's journey into two parts. At daybreak we started, and marched for three or four hours; then we stopped to breakfast on rice and poultry, frequently diversified by wild birds of some kind, often black parrots, and other beautiful specimens which Mr. Lambert shot on our way. After a rest of about two hours we set out to accomplish the second portion of our day's march, which generally about equaled the first in length.

To-day, however, we contented ourselves with getting through the first stage, for it was the day for celebrating the great national feast. The queen had no doubt taken her auspicious new-year's bath this morning. Mr. Lambert would not rob his bearers of the pleasure of participating in the enjoyments of the day; so, at ten o'clock in the morning, we halted in the village of Ampatsiba.

The first business was to slaughter the oxen. The rule of the feast, which enjoins that as many shall be slain as are sufficient for the day and the seven following, was not strictly carried out, for the weight of meat would have been too great for the men to carry; but five of the finest animals

were offered up as a sacrifice to the day; for Mr. Lambert
entertained not only our people, but the whole village.   In
the evening four or five hundred people assembled—men,
women, and children—in front of our huts; and, to complete the enjoyment of the feast, Mr. Lambert had their
favorite drink, *besa-besa*, served out to them.   This beverage, which seemed to me the reverse of agreeable, is made
from the juice of the sugar-cane mixed with water, and the
bitter bark of afatraina.   The water is first poured on the
cane-juice, and when the mixture ferments, the bark is added, and a second fermentation takes place.

The festal character of the day, assisted perhaps by the
besa-besa, put the little community in such good spirits that
they volunteered an exhibition of their songs and dances,
which were all equally stupid and uninteresting.

Some of the girls beat a little stick with all their might
against a thick piece of bamboo; others sang, or rather
howled, at the top of their voices: the noise was horrible.
Then, two of the ebony beauties danced; that is, they
moved slowly to and fro on a small space of ground, half
lifted their arms, and turned their hands, first outward, and
then toward their sides.   Now, one of the men approached
to exhibit his capabilities as a dancer.   He was, most likely, the "lion" of the village.   He tripped to and fro much
in the style of his charming predecessors, only in rather
more energetic fashion.   Whenever he approached any of
the women or girls, he was not deterred by our presence
from making very expressive gestures, which were received
by the assembled company with shouts of laughter and ob-
streperous applause; but the same thing is done at the public balls in Paris.

On this occasion I saw that the natives do not smoke tobacco, but take it in the form of snuff.   The pinch is not
inhaled through the nose, but inserted in the mouth.   Both
men and women enjoy their tobacco in this way.

In asserting that the "queen's bath" was the only feast celebrated in Madagascar, I was right to this extent, that the aforesaid solemnity is the only occasion of universal rejoicing. The natives, however, practice the custom of circumcising their children, and these occasions are celebrated with much rejoicing. The ceremony takes place in the larger villages designated for the purpose by government, and to these places the parents have to bring their children at a certain period of the year. The happy fathers invite their relations and friends to the solemnity, and recreate themselves with song and dance, eating and drinking as long as their stores of beef, rice, and besa-besa hold out.

May 25th. After yesterday's jollification, our bearers had hard work to-day. The hills were very steep, and far loftier than the former ones, averaging from five to seven hundred feet in height. Fortunately it had not rained, and on the dry earth climbing was not so very difficult a matter.

All the hills and mountains are here covered with virgin forests; but I looked in vain for the thick, lofty trees I had been accustomed to see in the wilds of Sumatra and Borneo, and even of America. The greatest trunks were scarcely four feet in diameter, and not more than a hundred in height. There was likewise no great profusion of flowering trees, orchidaceæ, and climbing plants; and the only remarkable feature in these forests seemed to be the large and varied genera of ferns, in which Madagascar rivals the Mauritius. I was informed that in the neighborhood of the roads all the great trees had already been cut down, but that in the depths of the forests splendid specimens might be met with, and that flowers, climbing plants, and orchidaceæ likewise abound in those solitudes.

From the summits of a few of the higher hills we had to climb we enjoyed glorious views of quite a peculiar kind. Never yet have I seen so great an expanse of land as this, consisting entirely of hills, lofty mountains, and narrow val-

leys and gorges, with not a single plain between.   Twice
we could descry **the sea in the** far distance.

This region must be admirably adapted **for** the cultivation of coffee; for it is well **known that** the coffee-tree
grows best on the sides of steep hills.   The land here is
said, moreover, to be well adapted for pasture, especially
for sheep.   In future times flourishing plantations will **per-**
haps arise here, adding life and variety to the glorious landscape.   To-day, alas! all around is an unpeopled desert;
hardly a miserable hut to be seen here and there half hidden in the verdant screen.

We slept in a village called Beforona.

May 26. Our journey to-day has been a repetition of yes-
terday's march, with the single additional incident that we
met a drove of oxen in **a steep, hollow way.   It** was fear-
ful to see how **the** creatures clambered **about.**   Almost at
every step they slipped, and I expected every moment they
would come tumbling down upon us.   With difficulty we
found a place where we could stand, **pressing against the**
bank till they had gone by.

Rather late in the afternoon we arrived at our station for
the night—a very little village with a very long name—
Alamajootra.

May 27. The hills to-day were less lofty and steep, the
gorges and valleys somewhat broader, and the roads better.
A few miles from our station for the night, on the only high
hill we had to **cross on** this day's march, the wooded region
suddenly came to an end, and **a** charming landscape lay **be-**
fore us.   In the foreground, extending in wavy lines, extending north and south, rose a chain of hills, which **we**
could overlook from our high post of observation; and behind these lay the beautiful elevated plateau Ankay, at
least fifteen miles broad (and of much greater length still)
from north to south.   Toward the east, in the background,
two low ranges of mountains rose up against the horizon.

Our station for the night was a village called Maramaya.

May 28. We came to the elevated plateau Ankay, on which we found tolerable roads, so that our journey now proceeded rapidly. On the other hand, we lost a great deal of time in crossing the River Mangor. There was nothing to be had in the way of boats but a few hollowed trunks of trees, each of which would scarcely hold three or four people; thus several hours were consumed in ferrying over our numerous train and multifarious baggage. The rivers which I have as yet seen in Madagascar, including the Mangor, are very broad at certain spots, but they have no depth; the largest of them would not be navigable for a craft of fifty tons. They are very well filled, but, unfortunately, there are many more caymans in these rivers than fishes.

We crossed the low mountain ridge of Efody, and then the way wound onward through pleasant little valleys to the village of Ambodinangano, where we passed the night.

Near many villages I had noticed great upright stones, always placed at some miles' distance from the village. Some of these, I was told, were funeral monuments; the rest were to mark the spots where the weekly markets are held. It would really seem as if the inhabitants of Madagascar were determined to do every thing differently from other nations, and so, instead of having their markets in the villages, they hold them in lonely desert places, miles away from every human dwelling.

May 29. To-day my traveling companions were fully justified in complaining of the roads, which were so bad that, in spite of my enlarged experience in this particular, I was compelled to acknowledge that I had seldom seen any thing to equal them. But the chief problem was how to cross the second little mountain chain of Efody, the sides of which are exceedingly steep. Even my bearers seemed to-day to feel that my frame was decidedly composed of mundane materials, and not of air. Right wearily did they

drag me up over the steep heights, resting for a few moments, from time to time, to take breath and gather new
strength.

After scaling this ridge we came into the territory of
Emir, the native region of the Hovas, in the midst of which
the capital of the island is situated.

The territory of Emir consists of a lofty, splendid, elevated plateau, nearly four thousand feet above the level of
the sea.   Many isolated hills rise up from this plain; we
pass no more forests, and, as the capital is approached, some
amount of cultivation, in the shape of rice-fields, begins to
appear.   Where there were no rice-fields, the ground was
covered with the short bitter grass of which I had noticed
so much in Sumatra.   Unfortunately, it is entirely useless,
as the cattle will not eat it.

The district of Emir did not appear to be very populous;
even in the neighborhood of the rice-fields I looked in
vain for villages—perhaps they were hidden behind the
hills.

In the few villages we passed I noticed that the houses
were not built like those at Tamatavé, and in the wooded
regions through which we had passed, of bamboo or timber,
but of earth and clay.   They are also loftier and more
roomy, and have exceedingly high roofs, thatched very
neatly with a sedgy grass that grows here in abundance beside all the rivers.   But the internal arrangement is just
the same.   The house generally contains only one room;
in very few is a small portion walled off by a partition of
matting.   Furniture is entirely wanting.   The majority of
the inhabitants of Madagascar possess nothing of the kind
beyond a few straw mats with which they cover the bare
floor, and a few pots of iron or clay wherein to cook rice.
Nowhere did I see beds, or even wooden chests in which
clothing or other articles could be kept.   Certainly they do
not feel the want of either of these conveniences, for they

sleep on the floor, and their wardrobe generally consists of a single simbu, which they draw over their head at night. The most luxurious among them go so far as to cover themselves with one of the straw mats of their own plaiting. Nowhere else have I found such an entire want of all the comforts of life, except among the Indians of Oregon Territory, in North America.

Some of the little villages, and a few separate houses also, are surrounded with ramparts of earth, a custom originating in the times when the country was divided among a multitude of small tribes who were continually at war with one another.   It has already been mentioned that the two great chiefs, Dianampoiene and Radama, put an end to these feuds by reducing most of the tribes beneath their dominion.   A few miles from the village of Ambatomango, our resting-place for this evening, a great procession of men came to meet us, accompanied by military music.   This was a kind of deputation sent by Prince Rakoto, the son of Queen Ranavola, and heir-apparent to the throne, to receive Mr. Lambert, and assure him of the prince's respect and affection. The deputation consisted of twelve adherents of the prince, a number of officers and soldiers, and a complete troop of female singers.

The "adherents" of Rakoto, forty in number, are young noblemen who love and honor this prince so much that they have bound themselves by an oath to defend him in every danger to the last man.   They all live near him, and in his expeditions he is always surrounded by at least half a dozen of these faithful followers, although he has no need of such a guard, as he is said to be much beloved by all the people, commons and nobles alike.

Mr. Lambert was received by this deputation with the honors usually accorded to a prince of the blood royal, a distinction which has never yet been shown to any of the high nobles, much less to a white man.

As often as our procession passed by a village, the whole
community turned out to see the strangers.   Many attached themselves to **the** train, so that it grew as it went, like an
avalanche.   The good people might well be astonished to
see white men received with such honor, for the like had
never been witnessed before.

In the village **of** Ambatomango, Mr. Lambert was surprised by a mark of affection on the part of Prince Rakoto.
We found the prince's only son, a little boy five years old,
waiting for us.   Prevented by the illness of the queen from
coming himself to meet Mr. Lambert at Ambatomango, he
had sent his child, which Mr. Lambert had adopted during
his first stay at Tananariva.

The custom of adopting children prevails widely in Madagascar; in most cases this is done by the adopter for the
sake of possessing a child, but in **others it arises** from the
fact that the father of the child wishes to give the man who
adopts it a striking proof of his friendship.   The adoption
is announced to the government, which, in a written document, accords to the second father full authority over **the**
child.   The infant receives the name of the adopted parent,
is admitted into his family, and possesses every right enjoyed by his own children.

Prince Rakoto had conceived such an affection for Mr.
Lambert upon their first becoming acquainted, that he wished to give him a striking proof of his respect and friendship, and thus offered him his best treasure—his only child.
Mr. Lambert adopted the infant, but did not avail himself
of all the rights his position gave him; the child received
his name, but was left in the care of its own father.

This **child is** not by birth **a** prince, his mother being a
slave.   Her name is Mary; but she is not, as her name
would imply, a Christian.   I am told she is very intelligent
and good-natured, but, nevertheless, of a firm character.
The prince loves her exceedingly, and, in order to have her

continually about his person, he has nominally married her to one of his faithful followers.

Till late at night, a good **deal of jollity was kept up in** our camp. A great feast was prepared, of which we partook in native fashion, seated on the ground; **on the** other hand, toasts were drunk in true European fashion, and the healths of all imaginable people proposed. Merry **music** and loud shouts of rejoicing accompanied every fresh toast.

The choir of female singers sent by Prince Rakoto to do honor to our arrival consisted of twenty girls, who crouched down in a corner of the room, and tortured our ears with their harsh, grating voices. They screamed and howled just like the women and girls in the village where we celebrated the feast of the queen's bath. They had a man with them as a leader or teacher, but he wore a woman's garb, and that of a European too; as the features of the two races vary very little, their beauty or ugliness being much the same, I should not have suspected this comical figure to be a man if the fact had not been mentioned **by** Mr. Lambert.

May 30th. This morning a deputation of villagers came to invite Mr. Lambert to a bull-fight which they proposed **to** give in his honor. After getting through the important business of breakfast, we proceeded to the scene of action, but found the preparations for the promised spectacle in a very backward state. It was evident that some time would **be required** for their completion. We thanked the people for their offer, but thought it best to take the will for the deed. We particularly wished to get to the capital, still **a** good half-day's journey distant, as quickly **as** possible—the more so, as the Sikidy, or oracle, had designated the **pres-**ent day as a fortunate one for our entry into Tananariva, and the queen wished that Mr. Lambert should not let the auspicious moment go by.

Throughout Madagascar, but particularly at court, it is

customary to consult the Sikidy oracle on every occasion, great and small. It is done in the following manner: A certain number of beans and small stones are mixed together, and from the figures they form, the people learned in the art of divination predict the favorable or unfavorable result of an undertaking. Of such oracle-interpreters or augurs there are more than twelve appointed at court, and in the most trifling matter the queen is accustomed to consult them. So devoted a believer in the Sikidy is she, that she in many things entirely sacrifices her own will, and is thus the greatest slave in the country she governs so despotically. If, for instance, she wishes to make an excursion any where, the oracle must decide on what day and at what hour this can be done. She will put on no garment and partake of no dish till the Sikidy has spoken, and the oracle must even decide from what spring the water she drinks is to be taken.

A few years ago a universal custom prevailed of asking the Sikidy, when a child was born, if the hour of its birth was fortunate. If an answer in the negative was returned, the poor baby was laid in the middle of one of the roads along which the great herds of oxen were driven. If the animals passed carefully by the child without injuring it, the bad magic influence of the oracle was considered to be broken, and the child was carried back in triumph to its father's house. Few were, however, fortunate enough to go through this dangerous ordeal unscathed; the majority of the infants were killed. The parents who were unwilling to submit their children to such a test turned them adrift, especially if they were girls, and took no more trouble about them. The queen has forbidden both the ordeal and the exposure; and this is, perhaps, the only humane law she has passed during her whole life.

All travelers who wish to come to the capital must apply to the queen for permission, and halt at least a day's journey from the city to receive the verdict of **the Sikidy,** which determines on what day and **at what hour they may** make their entry. Day and hour must be kept with **the** greatest strictness; and if the traveler should fall ill in **the** interim, and find it impossible to present himself **at** the gates of the city at the appointed time, he must **send a new** embassy **to** the queen, and await a second decision **of the** Sikidy, whereby he **loses some** days, and may be detained for weeks.

In this respect we were very fortunate. The Sikidy was obliging enough not to keep us waiting **a** single day, and designated that day as a fortunate one on which, according **to** the arrangements already made for **our journey,** we could reach the capital.

I vehemently suspect that the curiosity **of the queen had** some influence on the speech of the oracle. **The good lady** was naturally impatient to be put in possession **of all the** treasures which she knew Mr. Lambert had brought **for her.**

Our journey to-day seemed like **a** triumphal progress. In the van marched the military band; then came many officers, some of them of very high rank; next we came, surrounded by the adherents of the prince; the female singing choir, with a number of soldiers and people, bringing up the rear. As was the case yesterday, old and young came thronging round in every **village** through which we passed. All were desirous **of seeing** the long-expected **strangers; many,** too, joined **the procession, and** accompanied **us for miles.**

Our way wound onward through the beautiful elevated plain of Emir. How splendid an appearance would this glorious tract of land make if it were properly cultivated and populated! There are certainly many more fields and **villages** to be seen here than in the other districts through which our way had as yet led us, but very few could compare with this in fruitfulness of soil and fortunate position.

A peculiar charm is imparted to this plain by the numerous hills intersecting it in all directions, the majority rising quite isolated and unconnected with any of the rest. There is no lack of water; for, although no great rivers are seen, there are numerous small streams and ponds.

About forty years ago, the whole plateau of Emir was covered, they say, with forests; but now, for an area of about thirty square miles, it is so treeless that only the rich people use wood, procured from a distance by their slaves, as fuel. The poorer people make shift with a kind of short prairie grass, with which hills and plains are thickly covered, and which gives a fierce but not a very lasting flame. Fortunately, the people only require fire for preparing their food, and can dispense with fuel for their rooms, though in winter the thermometer falls to three or four degrees, and sometimes even to 1° Réaumur; but the houses are built with clay walls of tolerable thickness, and the roofs are thickly covered with long grass, and so the houses are sufficiently warm, in spite of the cold out of doors.

The roads were now exceedingly good, and our bearers ran jauntily on, as if they had nothing to carry. From afar we could see Tananariva, the capital of the country, situated almost in the midst of the plain, on one of the highest hills, and early in the afternoon we came to the suburbs, by which the city itself is surrounded on all sides.

These suburbs were at first villages; increasing gradually in size, they have at last been united into a whole. The majority of the houses are built of earth or clay; but those which belong to the city must be constructed of planks, or at least of bamboo. I found all the houses here greater and more roomy than the dwellings of the villagers; also much cleaner and better kept. The roofs are very high and steep, and have long poles reared at each end by way of ornament. Here I again noticed that many separate houses, and in other instances three or four attached, were sur-

rounded by low ramparts of earth, for no other apparent purpose than to separate the court-yards from the neighboring
tenements.   The streets and squares are all very irregularly
built: the houses are not placed in rows, but stand about in
groups, some at the foot of the hill, and others on its shelv-
ing sides.   The royal palace stands on the summit.   The
portion of the suburbs through which we passed was, to my
great astonishment, kept very clean, and this cleanliness was
not confined to the streets and public places, but extended
to the court-yards.   The only places that showed signs of
neglect were the narrow lanes between the walls of earth.

I was astonished at the number of lightning conductors
that every where appeared still more than by the general
aspect of cleanliness; each large house seemed provided
with one.   They were introduced by Mr. Laborde, a Frenchman, who had lived for many years at Tananariva, and
whose adventurous history Mr. Marius told me during our
journey.   I shall soon have to introduce my readers to
this extraordinary man.

I was told that there is, perhaps, no place in the whole
world where thunder-storms rage so fearfully, and where
the lightning strikes so frequently as is the case here.   At
Tananariva about three hundred people are stated to be
killed by lightning annually, and last year the number is
said to have risen to four hundred.   In one house a single
flash killed ten persons.   These fearful storms take place
chiefly from the beginning of March to the middle of April.

In the mean time we had arrived at the city gate, before
which we found a guard of soldiers drawn up with crossed
muskets, who refused, in the most polite manner possible,
to let us pass.   It appears to be the custom at this court to
surround every thing with a kind of halo of despotism.
Although every stranger who wishes to come to the capital
is obliged to obtain permission from the queen, and she is
therefore informed of the intended journey long before its

commencement—the traveler is moreover obliged to send
on a messenger when he has arrived within a day or two's
march of the capital, and to receive the report of the Sikidy
as to the day on which he may make his entry—he is again
obliged to halt at the city gate to announce his arrival to
the queen, and petition for admittance. If her majesty
happens to be in a bad humor, she often lets the poor stranger stand waiting some hours for her answer, exposed to
the broiling summer heat or to the pouring rain.

We were so far favored as to obtain leave to enter the
town after waiting only half an hour.

The interior of the town looks much like one of the suburbs, with this difference, that, in compliance with the law
I have mentioned, all the houses are built of planks or of
bamboo.

We proceeded to the house of Mr. Laborde, a very warm
friend of Mr. Lambert's, and who is also a great protector
of every European that arrives at Tananariva.

CHAPTER XII.

OUR host, Mr. Laborde, favored us with the following account of his life.

He was born in France, and is the son of a well-to-do saddler. In his youth he served for several years as a cavalry soldier in the French army, but, being always prompted by a desire to see something of the world, he gave up the service after his father's death, found a substitute, and embarked for the East Indies. In Bombay he established several workshops, repaired steam-engines, manufactured weapons, set up a saddlery, and did very good business; but his restless spirit would not let him remain long in one place, so he gave up his workshops to a friend, and in the year 1831 shipped himself off to the Indian Archipelago. The ship, driven out of its course by a storm, was wrecked on the coast of Madagascar. Mr. Laborde not only lost all he possessed, but his liberty into the bargain; for, as is well known, all shipwrecked men are made slaves of in this hospitable island. Mr. Laborde was taken, with a few of his companions in misfortune, to Tananariva to be sold.

Fortunately, tidings of his skill in manufacturing weapons and other articles reached the queen's ears. She sent for him to court, and promised him his freedom if he would serve her faithfully for five years. Mr. Laborde did this. He established a workshop, and furnished the queen with all kinds of weapons, even to little cannons, and also with

powder and other **articles.   In spite of** her general hatred
toward Europeans, **he gained** the **queen's** confidence, and
she soon got to **value him so** highly **that she** took his advice in several important affairs, and he succeeded, not unfrequently, **in** dissuading her from pronouncing sentences
of death.

But it is not only in the queen's estimation that Mr. Laborde stands high.   The people and the nobility also **set**
great store by him; for his many good qualities have made
him popular every where, and all **who** need counsel or help
come to him, and never come in vain.   He is physician,
confidential **friend,** and helper to **them all.**

The five years Mr. Laborde was to pass in the queen's
service extended to ten.   His patroness gave him house
and home, lands and slaves; and as he is married to a native woman, and has a son by this marriage, he will probably remain here to the end of his life, though he has long
been free and independent, and may leave the island whenever he chooses to do so.

Besides his manufactories for arms and powder, this **in-**
dustrious man has also established works for glass-blowing,
indigo-dyeing, soap and tallow boiling, and a distillery for
rum.   He wished also to stock the island with European
fruits and vegetables, and most of those he planted flour-
ished wonderfully, but his example remained unfollowed.
The natives preferred to live on in their pristine indolence,
and to continue eating nothing but rice, with the addition
of a piece of beef now and then.

If Mr. Laborde, however, did not succeed in producing
all the results he expected from his undertakings, they have
at least done good service in showing the capability of this
beautiful land for cultivation.

It was toward four o'clock in **the afternoon when we ar-**
rived in Mr. Laborde's house.

Our friendly host immediately introduced two Europeans

to us, the only ones then staying at Tananariva.   The two gentlemen **were** clergymen ; one of them **had been living** for two years, the other for seven months, **in Mr. Laborde's** house.   It was not the time to appear as missionaries, and they concealed the fact of their belonging to a mission very carefully, the prince and the Europeans being the only persons admitted into the secret.   One passes as a physician, the other as tutor to Mr. Laborde's son, who had come back two years since from Paris, where he had been sent by his father to be educated.

We were soon assembled at **a good** dinner round our **host's table.**   Every thing was arranged in European style, with the exception that the dishes **and** plates were all of **massive** silver, and silver goblets supplied the place of drinking-glasses.   I observed **jokingly to Mr. Laborde** that I **had** never met with such luxury at any **table, and** that Tananariva was the last place in the world where **I should** have expected to find it.   He replied that similar **luxury** prevailed in all the houses of the rich, but that there **were** certainly not many houses of this description.   He said **he** had himself introduced the fashion, but not from ostentation, but, on the contrary, on economical grounds.   He found that china-ware had continually to be replaced, as the **slaves** were perfect adepts in the art of breaking any given number of articles in the shortest possible time, so that the use of china became very expensive.

Before we had nearly concluded our pleasant meal, while Champagne was being handed round, and the toasts were beginning, a slave came running up in hot haste to announce the approach of Prince Rakoto.   We rose hastily from table, but had little time to go and meet the prince, for, **in his** impatience to see Mr. Lambert, he had followed close at the slave's heels.   The two men **held** each other in a long **embrace,** but for some time neither of them could find a word to express his joy.   It was easy to see that a deep and true

friendship existed between **them, and** we who stood round
could not view the **scene without** feelings of pleasurable
emotion.

Prince Rakoto, or, to **call him by his full** name, Rako-
dond-Radama, is a **young man twenty-seven** years of age.
Contrary to my **expectation, his** appearance **was** far from
disagreeable.   He is short and slim in stature, and his face
does not betray a likeness, in form or color, to any of **the**
four **races who** inhabit Madagascar.   His features **have**
quite the type of the Moldavian Greeks.   His black hair is
curly, but not woolly; he has dark eyes, full of life and
fire; a well-shaped mouth, and handsome teeth.   His feat-
ures wear an expression of such childlike goodness that
one feels drawn toward him from the first moment of seeing **him.   He often goes about in** European costume.

The prince is honored **and beloved alike** by high and
low; and I was assured by Mr. Laborde that he fully deserved all this affection and honor.   The son is, in fact, as
kind-hearted as the mother is cruel; he is just as **averse to**
the shedding of blood as his mother is addicted to it, **and**
his chief efforts are directed toward mitigating the severe
punishments the queen is continually inflicting, and obtaining a reversal of the sentences of death which she is always
too ready to pronounce upon her subjects.

He is always ready to listen to the unfortunate, and to
help them; and has strictly forbidden his slaves to turn
any applicant away on the score that he is sleeping or engaged at his meals.   Well aware of this, people often come
in the middle of the night and wake the prince from his
sleep, with petitions for their relations who are to be executed early next morning.   If he can not obtain a pardon
from his mother, he manages to pass **as** if by accident along
the road by which the **poor** culprits are led, bound with
cords, to meet their fate.   Then he cuts their bonds asunder, and either tells them to flee, or to go quietly home, ac-

cording as their offenses have been grave or venial. When the queen is informed of what her son has done, she never makes any remark, but only tries to keep the next sentences she pronounces as secret as possible, and to hasten their execution. Condemnation and punishment thus often succeed each other so rapidly, that if the prince is absent from the town when sentence is passed, the application to him for assistance is almost sure to come too late.

It is strange, considering how radically different their dispositions are, that mother and son should love each other so tenderly. The prince is devoted to the queen with the utmost affection; he tries to excuse her deeds of severity by every conceivable argument, and it is a bitter reflection to him that she can be neither loved nor respected by the nation.

The prince's character is the more remarkable, inasmuch as he has had his mother's bad example before his eyes from his earliest youth, and can not escape from her influence; moreover, not the slightest care has been taken of his education. In most similar cases, the son would certainly have imbibed the prejudices and acquired the vices of the mother.

No one has attempted to teach him any thing, with the exception of a few words of the English language; what he knows, and what he is, he owes entirely to himself. What might this prince not have been had a judicious education opened his mind and developed his talents? I had frequent opportunities of seeing and observing him, for a day seldom passed without his paying Mr. Lambert a visit. I found no fault in him except a certain want of independence and a distrust of his own abilities; and the only thing I fear, should the government one day fall into his hands, is, that he will not come forward with sufficient energy, and may fail in thoroughly carrying out his good intentions.

A few of the actions of this man will sufficiently prove the nobility of his mind.

It frequently happens that the queen orders hundreds of her subjects to perform the heaviest labor for months together for some favored personage—such work, for instance, as hewing timber for building, and then dragging it thirty miles along the road; hewing stone, and kindred occupations; for all which the poor people get not the slightest reward of any kind. When the prince hears of a case of this kind, he manages to pass by the neighborhood where the people are at work, meets them as if by chance, and asks for whom they are laboring thus. On receiving their reply, he farther inquires if they are properly fed, for wages are of course out of the question. Then it generally turns out that they not only have no food provided for them, but frequently have consumed all the provisions they have brought with them, and are trying to satisfy their hunger with herbs and roots. The prince then has one or two oxen killed, according to the number of the laborers, and this meat, with a good supply of rice, is by his command distributed among them. If the owner should come forward in surprise at this order, and attempt to remonstrate, the prince sends him away with this assurance: "Whoever works for you has a just claim to be supported by you; and if you will not make the arrangement yourself, your steward must."

A few years ago, a ship was wrecked on the coast of Madagascar, and the majority of the crew perished. Five sailors who had escaped from the wreck were sent, according to the usual custom, to the capital, to be sold there as slaves. The prince met them during an excursion he was making, about a day's journey from Tananariva, and noticing that one of the sailors had no shoes, and was limping painfully after the rest, he drew off his own and gave them to him. He also took care that the poor men were well fed. Mr. Laborde bought these five sailors, clothed them, gave them money and letters of recommendation, and helped them to get back to their own country. The prince is seldom in a position to carry out his benevolent designs, for he has no money, or, at any rate, very little; his whole wealth consisting in slaves, rice-fields, and oxen given to him by his mother.

Another time the prince saw a European being led as a prisoner to the capital by several natives. The poor wretch was being urged on like a brute beast by his guards with blows and pushes; he was so exhausted and weak from the long journey and the bad roads that he could drag himself no farther. The prince reproved the guards for their cruelty, himself alighted from his tacon, or sedan-chair, and told the captive to take his place.

The prince, moreover, found an opportunity of showing his generosity toward one of our bearers. True to the habits of his country, this poor wretch had stolen an ox in the vicinity of the capital, driven it to one of the markets, and tried to dispose of it; but he was caught in the fact, and brought to the capital. In cases of this kind, justice in Madagascar is very quick in taking its course; on the same day sentence of death was passed upon him, and toward evening he was to be executed in the manner of the country, with the lance or gagaya. Mr. Laborde heard of this, and sent in all directions in search of the prince to obtain his mediation. Luckily, the prince was found in time, scarcely half an hour before the execution was to have taken place. He proceeded at once to the prison, opened the door for the captive, and recommended him to flee to his own home as fast as he could.

Many similar traits were told me of the prince, and seldom, it is said, do many days elapse without his saving lives or performing some generous action. He often gives away his last dollar, distributes all his stores of rice and other provisions, and is doubly glad when he can help some unfortunate being without letting the recipient of his bounty know who is his benefactor.

I

The following words, which I heard from his own mouth, speak more eloquently **than** my weak pen could do the praises of this really noble man.   He declared it to be a matter of indifference **to him whether** the French **or** the English, or any other nation, took possession of the island, if only the people were properly governed.   For himself, he wished neither for the throne nor for the regal title, and would at any time be ready to give a written abdication of his claims, and retire and live as a private man, if he could by such a course insure the prosperity of the people.

I must confess that this declaration moved me deeply, **and inspired** me with a high respect for this prince—such respect as I feel for very few human beings.   To my mind, a man of such sentiments is greater than the most prominent among the ambitious and egotistical monarchs of Europe.

May 31. This morning the queen sent one of the grandees of the empire to inquire after our health, **and** to invite us to take the *sambas-sambas* next day in the house of the Lady Rasoaray.

On this occasion she sent Mr. Lambert a present as **a** mark of her favor.   The gift consisted of a magnificent fatted ox, of proportions I had rarely seen equaled even in Europe, besides some very fine poultry and a basket of eggs.   The presents of the queen never consist of any other articles, and are generally confined to poultry and eggs; oxen are only added when she wishes to confer on **the recipient** a mark **of** peculiar distinction.

The sambas-sambas is a dish made of fine strips of beef broiled in fat, and of rice.   It is customary, **in** the first month of the new year, to regale friends and relations who come to visit you with this dish.   Every one takes a pinch of it, rises from his seat, turns to the right and to the left, and says, "May the queen live a thousand years."   After this he may eat as much as he likes of the preparation, or may leave it untouched, as he pleases. This ceremony is somewhat equivalent to wishing a happy new-year among us.

As we happened to arrive in the first month of the new year, and the queen wished to show Mr. Lambert all kinds of attention, she invited him to this feast, and my humble self and the other Europeans were included in the honor as friends of Mr. Lambert.

All the banquets to which friends are invited are not held in the royal palace, but at the house of the Lady Raso-aray, who is of very high birth, and whose spacious, richly-furnished dwelling is well adapted for such purposes. To eat in the palace of the queen, or, still more, in her company, would be considered too great an honor for a stranger; so far the condescension of this haughty, self-opinioned potentate extendeth not.

I made use of this day to visit the town, of which, however, I can say nothing more than that is is very bustling, and extends over a large space of ground, especially if the suburbs be taken as part of it. It is said, with its immediate environs, to contain 50,000 houses, or " roofs," as they are called here, and 100,000 inhabitants. This estimate is probably much exaggerated; but certainly the proportion of dwellings is unusually great, from the simple reason that the houses themselves are particularly small, consisting of no more than one room, or at most but two. If the family is large, two or three additional little houses are built up around the original dwelling; all who have any pretensions to wealth have their kitchen under a separate roof; and, of course, the slaves are also quartered in various small houses. Still, I do not think Tananariva can contain many more than 15,000, or, at the most, 20,000 houses.

Mr. Laborde, for instance, is the owner of nine small dwellings, tenanted by seven free men and thirty slaves; here, then, the proportion of inhabitants to houses would be as four to one. But Mr. Laborde is a European, and does not live with his people in such a crowded manner as the natives affect—with them six, or certainly at least five, inhabitants may be reckoned to every roof.

June 1. At two o'clock in the afternoon we betook ourselves to the house of the Lady Rasoaray, and were conducted to a large hall, the walls papered in European fashion, and the floor covered with handsome mats. In the middle of the room stood a table, elegantly spread, in a style of which no prince in Europe need have been ashamed. The other arrangements in the room were simple, but tasteful. Many an English lady would have been exceedingly scandalized by the fact that in the room in which we were to dine stood two beds — two very handsome beds, with heavy curtains of rich silk. As I am, however, not an Englishwoman, but only a simple German, I took no notice of the circumstance, and the presence of the two beds did not prevent me from eating my share of beef and rice in all peace and quietness of spirit. These two dishes are the only ones admitted at the sambas-sambas, and water is the only beverage allowed on these occasions.

I particularly admired two silver vases, with carving on them in relief, which stood on the table; and my wonder rose considerably when I was informed that they had been executed by native artificers. They would certainly have met with high approval even in Europe. Like the Chinese, the natives are gifted in a high degree with the faculty of imitation, but they lack originality.

Among the high personages invited with ourselves to the feast were many who spoke either French or English, English being the more common. The knowledge of this language dates from the time of King Radama, in whose reign English missionaries came to Madagascar, and a certain number of young men were sent to the Mauritius or to England for their education.

The ceremony of the sambas-sambas was very soon ended, and we returned home early; in the evening we were surprised by a visit from Prince Rakoto. He brought with him the mother of his little five-year-old son, to introduce her to me. As I have already mentioned, the prince can not, according to the laws that prevail here, marry this woman, because she is a slave, and her son has, therefore, not the smallest claim to his father's rank; nevertheless, they are both honored with the princely title. It may certainly be said that in this country the laws are of little importance in so far as they affect the ruler; they depend solely and entirely upon the will of the reigning sovereign; and as soon as Prince Rakoto comes to the throne, he can alter them at his pleasure, and make his former slave his queen and her son heir-apparent.

I have spoken of the character of this woman. As regards her beauty, if it is to be discovered, it must certainly not be judged of by European eyes, or the beholder should have lived long enough among the natives to have become accustomed to their ugly features, and to consider the least hideous among them as handsome.

June 2. To-day we were present at a great review on the Field of Mars, a beautiful meadow spreading out at the foot of the hill in front of the town. It is asserted that from ten to twelve thousand soldiers are always assembled at Tananariva; but, like the estimate of the houses, this number must probably be reduced about one half. The military who appeared on this occasion did not certainly exceed 4500 or 5000 men. The soldiers formed a great double square, with the officers and band in the centre.

A review of this kind is held every fortnight—namely, on the third day of every second week; its object is to ascertain that the soldiers who should be on duty are present; that they are in health, and their weapons and clothes in proper condition. Their names are called over, and if in a company only a few are missing, the captain merely receives a reprimand; but if the list of absentees is a long one, the commanding officer is punished on the spot with a dozen blows or more. The latter incident is reported to be of frequent occurrence; for among such a large number of soldiers, there are many whose homes are several days' journey from the capital, so that they can hardly find time, between one review and another, to go thither, cultivate their fields, provide themselves with food, and return punc-tually.

No military manœuvres were undertaken, and I was told that war is carried on entirely without system, as among the wildest tribes. Especially when a company thinks it-self lost, all subordination ceases, and the men take to flight on every side.

Horrible is the fate of the sick and wounded soldiers, not only during a flight, when, of course, no one cares about them, but even during ordinary marches. Their comrades are bound to take care of them, and to carry and feed them; but how can people be expected to do this who are them-selves in want of every thing, and often so much weakened by hunger and toil of every kind that they can scarcely drag themselves along and carry their weapons? It fre-quently happens that efforts are made by the soldiers to rid themselves of these poor wretches. They are not killed outright, which would be rather a benefit to them, under the circumstances; but their comrades drag them along the ground, without giving them any food, or even a refreshing draught from the nearest spring. When they have ceased to give any sign of life, they are left by the wayside, no one caring to ascertain whether they are dead or not.

On these marches a fearful number of lives are sacrificed. In the last war, for instance, which the queen waged against the Seklaves two years ago, ten thousand men were sent into the field. More than half died on the march for want of food; many deserted; and when the army reached the scene of action, its force is said to have scarcely exceeded three thousand men.

The prisoners are much better off, for care is taken of them, as a profit is derived from their sale; and **even as** slaves they are not in nearly so unhappy a condition as the soldiers and peasants. Their owners feed, clothe, and **lodge** them; nor are they overworked; for, by transgressing in this respect, the owner runs the risk of losing his bondman, for his slave runs **away;** and fugitive slaves are seldom captured, there being no police or similar institution in the country. The master certainly has the power of beating his slave to death; the government will not interfere with him; but his own interest will deter him from any extreme measures. Many slaves pay their owners a small yearly tax in money, and live like free men; others even keep slaves themselves, who work for their master-bondmen.

After the review, the officers and music **marched past our** house to welcome Mr. Lambert.

The officers were mostly clothed, like their brethren at Tamatavé, in European garb, and looked ridiculous and comical enough. One wore a dress-coat, the tails of which reached almost to his heels; another had a coat of flowered chintz; a third, a faded red jacket, which had once done duty as part of a marine's uniform. Their hats were just as diverse in character. There were straw hats and felt hats, of all sizes and shapes, caps and head-coverings of fearful **and** wonderful forms. The generals wore the regulation cocked hat of Europe, and were mounted.

The military grades are modeled quite on the European plan; there are thirteen gradations from the private soldier up to the field-marshal.

I succeeded also in finding European titles in **Madagas-**car; there were crowds of barons, counts, and princes, as at the most aristocratic **European** courts.

The whole population of Madagascar is divided into eleven castes. The eleventh caste consists of the regal personage; the tenth of the descendants of the royal family. In this caste alone brothers and sisters may intermarry, probably in order to prevent there being too many scions of the blood royal. The six following castes, from the ninth to the fourth inclusive, comprise the nobles of higher and lower rank; the people belong to the third caste, the "white" slaves to the second—a class including all who were once free, and have been sold as prisoners of war or as a punishment for crimes; and the first, or lowest caste, consists of the "black" slaves, namely, those who have been born in that condition of life.

A noble may take a wife not only out of his own caste, but out of the two immediately below him, but never from a higher one. On no account may he marry a slave-woman; and the law does not even allow any other kind of connection between a noble and a slave. In this respect, by the way, Madagascar might serve as a model to those countries governed by white men where slavery exists; for the morality of the entire community would be greatly benefited if this custom were observed. This law was in former times very stringently enforced, and on the discovery of a connection of the kind alluded to the noble was sold as a slave, and the slave-woman beheaded. If the woman in the case was a noble and the man a slave, both were beheaded. In these latter days, however, this strictness has been much relaxed. Indeed, in the universally low state of morality prevailing here at the present time, the greater number of the nobles and officials would have to lose their heads or their freedom; and what would then become of the court? Some amount of good is, however, still effected by the law; for when such an affair between a nobleman and his slave is suspected, he is compelled to set her free to escape punishment.

As polygamy has been introduced here, every man may

have as many wives as he pleases; but among the nobles only a certain number of these women have a claim to the actual title of wife, and the first wife always keeps precedence over those taken subsequently. She alone lives in her husband's house, and great respect is shown to her; her children, too, have privileges beyond those of the other wives. The other children, like the subsequent wives, live in little separate houses. The king may take twelve lawful wives, but they must be all members of the highest families. The ruling queen and her sisters and daughters have the right of sending away their husbands and taking new ones as often as they choose so to do.

Our breakfast was just over, and I had retired to my room, when Mr. Lambert came to announce that the queen had summoned us to an introduction or audience. This honor is generally accorded to strangers eight or ten days after their arrival; but her majesty seemed desirous of showing distinction to Mr. Lambert above all Europeans who had ever visited her court, and so, not later than the fourth day, we had the happiness of appearing before that exalted personage.

All these tokens of honor and consideration astonished Mr. Lambert not a little. He had already told me in the Mauritius that he had very many good friends at the queen's court, and dangerous enemies also, who might have taken advantage of his absence to slander him in the vilest manner, not only in her eyes, but in Prince Rakoto's too. But a circumstance that Mr. Lambert now confided to me for the first time was, that attempts had been made in another quarter to prejudice the queen against him, and that he expected not exactly to be coldly received, but to be looked upon with some degree of suspicion.

And now, for the first time, I got an insight into Mr. Lambert's real plans and intentions, which were certainly not calculated to prepossess the queen in his favor.

I 2

When Mr. Lambert came to Tananariva for the first time in the year 1855, and saw with what cruelty the queen ruled, a wish arose in his mind to free the unhappy people from this tyrant. He succeeded in gaining the friendship of Prince Rakoto, who was also deeply moved by the people's misery, and who at that period told Mr. Lambert that he cared not who ruled over the nation so long as the government was good and just. They soon came to an understanding, and Mr. Lambert made a treaty with Prince Rakoto, and conceived the design of seeking help from either the French or English government.

In the year 1856 he went to Paris, and in a private interview with the emperor he made him acquainted with the boundless misery of the people of Madagascar, and tried to induce the French autocrat to come to the assistance of that unhappy country. But it is difficult to enlist the sympathy of a European government where philanthropy and not state interest is in question. This audience had no result, and an interview of Mr. Lambert with the English minister, Lord Clarendon, also led to nothing; nay, instead of any advantage accruing from this step, it was productive of difficulty and discomfiture, for every thing Mr. Lambert had done in reference to Madagascar came to the ears of a great missionary society in England. The society feared that, in the event of the French occupation of the island, the Roman Catholic religion might be the only form of worship introduced and licensed, which, in their opinion, would be, of course, a much greater misfortune for the inhabitants than the mere fact of their being ruled by an utterly cruel woman, like Queen Ranavola, who plays with human lives and sacrifices them at her pleasure! The society accordingly formed the notable resolution of opposing Mr. Lambert in every possible way, and immediately dispatched a chosen member, a missionary, to Tananariva to acquaint the queen with Mr. Lambert's design against her.

To judge from what occurred, as it was reported to me, it would appear that even an English missionary is capable of abandoning truth and sincerity in order to effect a purpose, and, upon occasion, to employ arts of a Jesuitical kind.

In the Mauritius, where the missionary made some stay before proceeding to Madagascar, he ventured to assert that Queen Ranavola had summoned him to Madagascar!

On his arrival at Tananariva he took care to impress upon the queen that he had been dispatched to her by the English government for the purpose of assuring her that England desired nothing more than to continue the same friendly relations with her country which had existed in the time of George the Fourth. He farther informed the queen of every thing that Mr. Lambert had undertaken against her in France and England; represented that gentleman as a very dangerous person, and a spy in the employ of the French government; and predicted that Mr. Lambert would speedily make his appearance, accompanied by a body of French troops, to depose her in favor of her son.

If even these misrepresentations had been made to effect some noble purpose, they could only have been justified by the very Jesuitical axiom that "the end sanctifies the means." But the object sought here was to impede, or perhaps altogether to frustrate, a truly Christian and philanthropic work, an undertaking calculated to promote the well-being of the entire nation. A missionary society ought surely to understand the principles of brotherly love better than this, and keep in view the maxims of religion, and especially to remember that they are not to be made subservient to political views.

The missionary's calling is the most exalted of any, for to few men are vouchsafed the opportunities of doing good that fall to his lot; but the misfortune is, that the majority of missionaries busy themselves more in worldly intrigues

than in the amelioration of the human race, and that, instead of inculcating charity, union, and toleration, they excite their followers by their preachings to hate, contemn,
and, if possible, to persecute every sect but their own. I
can only refer my readers to what I have written on this
subject in my former works, particularly concerning the
English and American missionaries.

So the missionary from England came to Tananariva
bearing the sword instead of the olive-branch. He not
only unfolded Mr. Lambert's alarming schemes to the queen,
but gave Prince Rakoto a long lecture on the exceeding
turpitude of his conduct toward his royal mother in medi-
tating revolt, declaring, moreover, that the English court
had been so shocked by the news as verily to have *put on
mourning!*

The prince condescended to excuse himself by asserting,
in reply, that, had he meditated removing his mother from
the throne to place himself upon it, he should have merited
the reproach; but that such was not the case, as he merely
wished to deprive the queen of the power of perpetrating
cruelties; every other privilege he wished her to retain, and
for himself he had asked nothing at all.

At Tananariva, and also in the Mauritius, a report was
circulated that Mr. Lambert had obtained the prince's sig-
nature to the contract by fraud; that the prince had not
been at all inclined to enter into a private treaty with Mr.
Lambert, but that the latter had invited him to a banquet,
intoxicated him, and prevailed on him to sign while in that
condition. It was farther stated that when, on the following day, Prince Rakoto heard what he had done, he was so
incensed against Mr. Lambert that he had banished him
from his presence forever. Mr. Lambert was therefore very
considerately advised never to return to Madagascar, as he
might fear the worst from the hatred and contempt alike of
the queen and of Prince Rakoto.

At Tananariva the prince himself told me the story of the signing of the treaty. He let me read the document, and assured me that the tale of the intoxication was a fiction; that he had perfectly understood what he was doing, and that he never repented this step at all. I much wish the author of this scandalous report could have seen with what contemptuous anger he was spoken of on this occasion.

I must also contradict a statement that the English missionary spread abroad in the Mauritius on his return from Madagascar. He boasted every where of the favorable reception he had met with at Tananariva, and of the great favor he enjoyed at the hands of the queen and of Prince Rakoto. This favor was so great, in fact, that after a stay of scarcely four weeks at Tananariva he received a peremptory order to depart. He applied for permission to remain longer, alleging as a reason that the fever season was not yet past, and disease was still rife in the lowlands. He begged the queen to take this into consideration, and not to expose him to mortal danger. But all was in vain; he was compelled to quit Tananariva. The queen was highly exasperated against him because he had distributed some Bibles, while Prince Rakoto resented his behavior toward Mr. Lambert.

CHAPTER XIII.

Introduction at Court.—The Monosina.—The Royal Palace.—The Hovas.
—Scenes of Horror under the Queen's Rule.—Executions.—The Tan-
guin.—Persecution of the Christians.—One of the Queen's Journeys.—
Her Hatred of Europeans.—Bull-fights.—Taurine Mausoleum.

OUR introduction at court took place on the 2d of June.
Toward four o'clock in the afternoon our bearers carried
us to the palace. Over the door is fixed a great gilt eagle
with extended wings. According to the rule laid down
here by etiquette, we stepped over the threshold first with
the right foot, and observed the same ceremony on coming
to a second gate leading to a great court-yard in front of
the palace. Here we saw the queen sitting on a balcony
on the first story, and were directed to stand in a row in
the court-yard opposite to her. Under the balcony stood
some soldiers, who went through sundry evolutions, concluding with a very comic point of drill, which consisted in
suddenly poking up the right foot as if it had been stung
by a tarantula.

The queen was wrapped, according to the custom of the
country, in a wide silk simbu, and wore on her head a big
golden crown. Though she sat in the shade, a very large
umbrella of crimson silk was held up over her head; this
being, it appears, a point of regal state.

The queen is of rather dark complexion, strong and
sturdily built, and, though already seventy-five years of
age, she is, to the misfortune of her poor country, still hale
and of active mind. At one time she is said to have been
a great drunkard, but she has given up that fatal propensity some years ago.

To the right of the queen stood her son, Prince Rakoto, and on the left her adopted son, Prince Ramboasalama; behind her sat and stood sundry nephews and nieces, and other relatives, male and female, and several grandees of the empire.

The minister who had conducted us to the palace made a short speech to the queen, after which we had to **bow** three times, and to repeat the words "Esaratsara tombokoe," equivalent to "We salute you cordially;" to which she replied, "Esaratsara," which means "Well—good!" Then we turned to the left to salute the tomb of King Radama, lying a **few** paces on one side, with three similar bows, whereupon we returned to our former place in front of the balcony and made three more. **Mr.** Lambert, on this occasion, held up a gold piece **of** fifty francs' value, and put it in the hands of the minister who accompanied **us**. This gift, which every stranger has to offer when he **is presented** for the first time at court, is called "Monosina." **It is not** necessary that it should consist of a fifty-franc piece; **the** queen contents herself with a Spanish dollar or a five-franc piece. Mr. Lambert had, however, already given fifty francs on the occasion of the "sambas-sambas."

After the delivery of the gold piece, the queen asked **Mr.** Lambert if he wished to put any question to her, or if **he stood** in need of any thing; to which he answered "No." She was also condescending enough to turn to me, and ask **if I was** well, and if I had escaped the fever.[*] After I had answered this question, we staid a few minutes longer looking at each other, when the bowings and greetings began anew. We had to take leave of Radama's monument, and **on** retiring were again reminded not on any account to put the left foot first over the threshold.

[*] Even in the favorable season of the year, very few strangers escape the intermittent fever. Mr. Lambert had a slight attack of it on the second day of our arrival at Tananariva, and afterward both he and I suffered terribly from it.

Such is the way in which the proud Queen of Madagascar
grants audiences to strangers. She considers herself far too
high and exalted to let them come near her at the first interview. Those who have the great good fortune to win
her especial favor may afterward be introduced into the
palace itself; but this is never achieved at a first audience.

The royal palace is a very large wooden building, consisting of a ground floor and two stories, surmounted by a
peculiarly high roof. The stories are surrounded by broad
galleries. Around the building are pillars also of wood,
eighty feet high, supporting the roof, which rises to a height
of forty feet above them, resting in the centre on a pillar
no less than a hundred and twenty feet high. All these
columns, the one in the centre not excepted, consist of a
single trunk; and when it is considered that the woods
which contain trees of a sufficient size to furnish these
colums are fifty or sixty English miles from the capital,
that the roads are nowhere paved, and in some places quite
impassable, and that all the pillars are dragged hither without the help of a single beast of burden, or any kind of
machine, and are afterward prepared and set up by means
of the simplest tools, the building of this palace may with
truth be called a gigantic undertaking, and the place itself
be ranked among the wonders of the world. In bringing
home the chief pillar alone, five thousand persons were employed, and twelve days were occupied in its erection.

All these labors were performed by the people as compulsory service, for which they received neither wages nor
food. I was told that during the progress of the work fifteen thousand people fell victims to the hard toil and the
want of proper nourishment. But the queen is very little disturbed by such a circumstance; half the population
might perish, if only her high behests are fulfilled.

In front of the principal building a handsome spacious
court-yard has been left; around this space stand several

pretty houses, all of wood. The chief building is, in fact, uninhabited, and contains only great halls of state and banqueting-rooms; the dwelling-rooms and sleeping-rooms of the queen are in one of the side buildings, communicating by a gallery with the palace.

On the left, the "silver palace" adjoins the larger one. It takes its name from the fact that all the Vandyked ends with which the roof is decorated, and the window and door frames, are hung with innumerable little silver bells. This palace is the residence of Prince Rakoto, who, however, makes very little use of it, generally living at his house in the city.

Beside the silver palace stands the monument of King Radama, a tiny wooden house without windows; to this fact, however, and to the farther circumstance of its being built upon a pedestal, it owes its sole resemblance to a monument.

The singular custom prevails in Madagascar, that when a king dies, all his treasures in gold and silver ware and other valuables are laid with him in the grave. In case of need, the heir can dig up the treasure, and, so far as I could ascertain, this had been done in every instance.

Radama's treasure is only estimated at 50,000 piastres, but his father's was valued at a million. The treasure or property of the present reigning queen is computed, according to the account I received, at between 500,000 and 600,000 dollars, and her yearly income at 30,000 to 40,000 dollars. The latter sum she is able to add annually, almost without deduction, to her fund, for she incurs no expense in her government or for her personal wants. As to the first, the whole burden falls upon the people, who have to work without pay; and with respect to the latter, the queen is the owner of the land, and possesses a great number of slaves, who have to provide every necessary for her household. Even the very clothes she wears are mostly made

of materials produced in the country, and woven and prepared by male and female slaves.

Among the natives at Tananariva there are said to be
some who have property to the amount of several hundred
thousand dollars; but they make a secret of their wealth,
for if the queen should obtain intelligence of the where-
abouts of such a treasure, the wish to seize it and carry it
off might very probably enter her royal mind.

The whole wealth of the island in ready money is estimated at one million dollars at most.

I do not grudge the queen the treasure she has accumulated; but it would be a fortunate thing for the population
of the island if it were to be buried very soon, in company
—of course—with its gracious possessor. She **is** certainly
one of the proudest and most cruel women on the face of
the earth, and her whole history **is a record of** bloodshed
and deeds of horror. **At a moderate computation, it is**
reckoned that from twenty to thirty thousand **people per-**
ish annually in Madagascar, some through the continual **ex-**
ecutions and poisonings, others through grievous labor purposely inflicted, and from warfare. If this woman's rule
lasts much longer, the beautiful island will be quite depop-
ulated; the population is said to have already shrunk to
half the number that it comprised in King Radama's time,
and a vast number of villages have disappeared from the
face of the land.

Executions and massacres are often conducted in whole-
sale fashion, and fall chiefly upon the Seklaves, whom the
queen seems to look upon with peculiar hatred; but the
Malagaseys and the other nations are not much less distaste-
ful to her; and the only tribe that finds any favor **at all in**
her eyes is, as I have already said, the Hovas, from whom
she herself is descended.

These Hovas were once the most scorned and hated of all
the races in Madagascar; they were regarded as the Pariahs

are regarded in India. Under King Radama, however, and especially under the present queen, this race has distinguished itself, and attained the first place by dint of intelligence, bravery, and ambition. But, unhappily, the race has not been improved by prosperity, and the good qualities of the Hovas are more than overbalanced by their evil propensities: Mr. Laborde even declares that the Hova embodies in himself the vices of all the tribes in the island. Mendacity, cunning, and hypocrisy are not only habitual, but cherished vices with him, and he tries to initiate his offspring therein at the earliest possible age. The Hovas dwell among themselves in a continual state of suspicion, and friendship is with them an impossibility. Their cunning and slyness are said to be incredible: the most practiced diplomatists of Europe would be no match for them in these qualities.

Of Malay origin, the Hovas are undoubtedly less ugly than the other races in Madagascar. Their features have less of the negro type, and are even better shaped than those of the Malays in Java and the Indian Archipelago, whose superiors they are also in stature and bodily strength. Their complexion varies through every shade from olive-yellow to dark reddish-brown. Some are very light; but, on the other hand, I noticed many, especially among the soldiers, whose color approximated so much to the red tint that I should have taken them for more genuine "red-skins" than even the North American Indians, to whom that name is applied from the ruddy tinge in their skin. Their eyes and hair are black; they wear the hair long, and this is of a frizzly woolly texture.

Even the Hovas, the favorites of the queen, are ruled with a ruthless iron hand; and though they may not be put to death by hundreds and thousands like the other nations, they are still punished with death for very trifling offenses.

Blood—and always blood—is the maxim of Queen Ra-navola, and every day seems lost to this wicked woman on which she can not sign at least half a dozen death-war-rants.

That my readers may become better acquainted with this queen, whose cause the English missionary society, in its philanthropy, has so warmly espoused, whose defense their agent has dared to undertake, and whom he has sought to maintain on the throne, I will cite a few of the deeds of horror which have been perpetrated on the unhappy land at her command, and of which the first alone would be suf-ficient to brand with infamy the name of Ranavola forever.

In the year 1831, when the army was still well trained, and the discipline introduced by King Radama had not yet been quite forgotten, the queen conquered a great por-tion of the eastern part of the coast, whose chief population consisted of Seklaves. She ordered all the men of the con-quered country to come to an appointed place to do homage to her. When the men, twenty-five thousand in number, were assembled, they were commanded to lay down their arms, and they were then led out into a large open space quite surrounded by soldiers. Here they were told to kneel down in token of submission; but scarcely had they done this, when the soldiers fell upon the unhappy wretch-es, and massacred them every one. Their wives and chil-dren were afterward sold as slaves.

Such is the lot of the conquered nations; but the queen's own subjects are not much better off.

In the year 1837, for instance, the queen received a re-port from her ministers to the effect that there were many magicians, thieves, violators of graves, and other evil-doers among the people. The queen immediately convened a kabar, or judicial meeting, for seven weeks, and at the same time caused it to be proclaimed to the people that all evil-doers who delivered themselves up should have their lives granted to them, but that those who failed so to do should suffer the punishment of death. A body of nearly sixteen hundred men gave themselves up accordingly. About fifteen hundred had voluntarily surrendered themselves to justice, and ninety-six had been denounced. Of these ninety-six, fourteen were burnt; and of the remaining eighty-two, some were hurled over a high rock, in the district of Tananariva, which has been the death-place of thousands; others were put into pits, and scalded to death with boiling water; others, again, were executed with the spear, or poisoned; a few were beheaded, and several had their limbs separately hacked off. The most painful death of all, perhaps, was inflicted on a portion of the victims, who were sewn up in mats in such a way that the head only protruded, and who were then left alive to rot.

Those who had been their own accusers were spared from execution, in accordance with the royal promise; but their fate was far worse than that of the men condemned to death. The queen declared that it would be dangerous to set such a number of criminals at liberty, and that they must, at any rate, be made harmless. So she had heavy irons fastened round their necks and wrists, and the unhappy victims were fastened together in gangs of four and five by very thick iron bars, about eighteen inches long. After this operation had been performed on them, they were set free—that is to say, they were at liberty to go where they would, only that guards were appointed in all directions, whose office it was to give strict heed that none of the irons were filed off. If one of a group died, it was necessary to cut off his head to extricate the corpse from the iron neckring, and the dead man's fetters were left to weigh upon the survivors, so that at last they could hardly drag themselves from place to place, and perished miserably at last under the heavy weight.

In the year 1855 certain people in the province of Voni-

zonga unfortunately took it into their heads to assert that
they had discovered a means of catching a thief by invisi-
ble agency; that when he stretched out his hand with felo-
nious intent, they could charm his arm so as to prevent him
from drawing it back or moving from the spot. When the
queen heard of this, she commanded that the people **in ques-**
tion should be severely punished, for she fancied she herself might one day come into that district, and be killed by
similar witchcraft. Two hundred persons were taken prisoners, and condemned to the *tanguin*, of whom a hundred
and eighty perished.

The tanguin, or poisoning test, is often applied to persons
of all grades—to the high nobles as well as the slaves; for
the mere accusation of any crime is sufficient to bring it
upon the victim. Any man may start up as accuser. He
need not bring forward any proofs, for the only condition
he has to fulfill is to deposit a sum of twenty-eight and a
half dollars. The accused persons are not allowed to make
any defense, for they must submit to the poisoning **ordeal**
under all circumstances. When any one gets **through**
without perishing, a third part of the deposited money is
given to him, a second third belongs to the queen, and the
remainder is given back to the accuser. If the accused
dies, the accuser receives all his money back, for then the
accusation is looked upon as well founded.

The poisoning process in managed in the following man-
ner: The poison employed is taken from the kernel of a
fruit as large as a peach, growing upon trees called *Tan-
guinca Veneniflora*. The lampi-tanguini, or person who ad-
ministers the poison, announces to the accused the day on
which he is to take it. For forty-eight hours before the
appointed time he is allowed to eat very little, and for the
last twenty-four hours before the trial nothing at all. His
friends accompany him to the poisoner's house; here he
has to undress himself, and make oath that he has not had

recourse to any kind of magic. The lampi-tanguini **then** scrapes away as much powder from the kernel with a knife as he judges necessary for the trial. Before administering the dose to the accused, he asks **him if he** confesses his crime; but the culprit never does this, as he would have to take the poison notwithstanding. The lampi-tanguini spreads the poison on three little pieces of skin, about an inch in size, cut from the back of a fat fowl; these he rolls together, and bids the accused swallow them.

In former days, almost every one who was subjected to this ordeal died in great agony; but for the last ten years every one who has not been condemned by the queen her-self to the tanguin is permitted to make use of the follow-**ing antidote.** As soon as he has **taken the** poison, his friends make him drink rice-water in such quantities that his whole body sometimes swells visibly, and quick and vi-olent vomiting is generally brought on. If the poisoned man is fortunate enough to get rid not only of the poison, but of the three little skins (which latter must be returned uninjured), he is declared innocent, and his relations carry him home in triumph with songs and rejoicings. But if one of the pieces of skin should fail to reappear, or if it be at all injured, his life is forfeited, and he is executed with the spear or by some other means.

One of the nobles who frequently visited our house had been **condemned several years ago to** take the tanguin. Happily for him, he threw up **the poison** and the three pieces of skin **in perfect** condition. His brother ran **in** great haste to **the wife** of the accused to announce this joy-ful event to her, and the poor woman was so moved by it that she sank fainting to the ground. I was astonished at hearing of such a display of feeling from one of the women of Madagascar, and could not at first believe the account true. I heard, however, that if the husband had died, she would have been called a witch, and probably condemned to the tanguin likewise, so that the violent emotion was probably caused more by joy at her own deliverance than the good fortune of her husband.

During my stay in Tananariva a woman suddenly lost several of her children by death. The mother was accused of causing the fate of the poor little ones by magic arts, and was condemned to the tanguin. The poor creature threw up the poison and two of the skins, but as the third did not make its appearance, she was killed without mercy.

As I have already said, the queen, immediately on her accession, had strictly forbidden the profession of the Christian faith, which had been introduced under King Radama. Notwithstanding this, there are said to be a considerable number of Christians still in the island, who, of course, keep their belief as secret as possible. In spite of all their caution, however, about six years ago all the members of a little congregation were denounced and captured. One of their number was burnt by the queen's orders. This punishment is generally inflicted only on nobles, officers, and soldiers; fourteen were thrown over the rock, and many others beaten to death. Of the remainder, the nobles were deprived of their titles and honors, and the commoners sold as slaves. All the Bibles discovered were publicly burnt in the great market-place.

The punishment of being sold as a slave is one of the lightest to which the queen condemns her subjects. The following facts will show on what slight grounds such sales are effected.

Once the queen had caused some Spanish dollars to be melted down for silver dishes. When these dishes were brought to her, she found fault with the workmanship, summoned the goldsmiths and silversmiths to the palace, and exhorted them to furnish better work. The good people did their very best, and, to their own misfortune, turned out better dishes than they had at first produced. The queen was satisfied, praised the workmen, and, as a reward for their exertions, had the whole guild sold as slaves, on the ground that they had not at first delivered such good dishes as they had since proved themselves able to make.

At another time many persons lost their freedom in consequence of a death in the royal family. When a nobleman of any caste dies, the duty of wrapping him in the dead-cloth and placing him in the grave devolves upon the fourth caste. The deceased in this case had fallen into disgrace, and been banished from the capital, and mourning was not put on for him at court; under these circumstances, the nobles of the fourth class feared to offend the queen by paying the last honors to the dead man, and left this duty to men from among the people. As soon as this came to the queen's ears, she laid a fine of four hundred dollars upon the whole caste, and had one hundred and twenty-six persons selected from it and sold as slaves; among these were many women and children.

The entire population of a village sometimes fall into slavery merely for eating the flesh of a stolen ox. Stealing an ox is a crime punished with death; but if the stolen beast belonged to the queen, not only is the thief executed, but all who have partaken of the ox's flesh are sold into slavery; and as no one takes the trouble to ascertain who has been implicated and who not, the punishment falls upon the whole village in which the ox was sold and slaughtered. None are spared but unweaned children, who are graciously supposed not to have eaten any of the meat.

To have attained to wealth and independence is too great a crime in a subject not to draw down all kinds of persecution on the luckless delinquent. If the queen gets to know that any village is rich in cattle, rice, and other produce—money, of course, is out of the question among the villagers—she imposes a task upon the people which they can not execute; for instance, she requires them to deposit a cer-

K

tain amount **of wood, or a** certain number of stones, at a
given place on an appointed day. The quantity of materials to be delivered is made so large, and the time allowed
for their delivery so short, that, even with the greatest exertion, and every anxiety to fulfill the conditions, the **com-**
pletion becomes impossible. ·The people are then condemned to **pay** a fine of some hundreds of dollars; and **as**
they have no money, they are obliged to sell their cattle,
their rice, their slaves, and not unfrequently themselves.

Separate wealthy persons are plundered in the following
way: An Ysitralenga—that is to say, **a** man who does not
tell lies—proceeds to the house of the selected victim, accompanied by some soldiers; here, sticking a lance in the
ground, he accuses the head of the family of **some** offense
against the government—of having spoken disrespectfully
of the queen, or committed some other crime, and takes
him prisoner, and leads him **before the judge. If the ac-**
cused loses the suit, his whole property is confiscated; if
he wins it, half his wealth will have gone in bribes **and**
other expenses; for, although Madagascar is a half **savage**
country, the judges understand their business just as well
as in the most civilized states in Europe.

But executions, poisonings, slavery, plunderings, and other punishments do not exhaust the people's catalogue of
woes. In devising plans of malignity and cruelty, Queen
Ranavola's penetration is wonderful; and she has invented
farther means for ruining **the unhappy** population, and
plunging it still deeper into misery. One device for carrying out this end, often adopted by the queen, is a royal
journey. Thus, in the year 1845, Queen Ranavola made a
progress to the province of Mancrinerina, ostensibly to enjoy the sport of buffalo-hunting. On this journey she was
accompanied by more than 50,000 persons. She had invited all the officers, all the nobles, far and near, around
Tananariva; and that the procession should appear as splen-

did as possible, every one had **to bring** with **him all** his
servants and slaves. **Of** soldiers alone, 10,000 marched
with them, and almost as many bearers, and 12,000 **men**
always kept a day's journey in advance, to make the **roads**
broader and repair them. Nor were the inhabitants **of the**
villages spared through which the queen passed. A certain number, at least, had to follow the train with **their**
wives **and** children. **Many** of the people were sent forward, **like** the road-menders, **to** prepare the night's lodging
for the queen; no trifling task, **as** the houses or tents prepared for the royal family had to be surrounded **by a** high
rampart of earth, lest her gracious majesty **should** be attacked by enemies during the night, and torn forcibly away
from her beloved people.

Inasmuch as this philanthropic potentate is accustomed,
on a journey of this kind, only to make **provision for** her
own support, and gives her companions nothing **but the**
permission to live on the stores they have brought for **them-**
selves (provided, of course, they have been able to procure
any), famine very soon makes its appearance among the
mass of soldiers, people, and slaves. This was the case in
the journey of which I speak; and in the four months of
its duration, nearly 10,000 people, and among them a great
proportion of women and children, are said to have perished. Even the **majority of the nobles had to** suffer the
greatest privations; for, wherever a little **rice was left**, it
was sold at such a high **price** that only **the richest** and noblest were able to purchase it.

In the first **years** of **Queen Ranavola's** rule, before **she**
found herself seated securely enough on the throne to **grat-**
ify her bloodthirsty propensities on her own subjects, her
hatred **was** chiefly directed toward the descendants of King
Radama and toward the Europeans. Regarding the latter,
she frequently held councils with her ministers and other
grandees concerning the measures to be taken to keep the

detested race away from her territories. Mr. Laborde informed me that on these occasions the most absurd and extravagant propositions were brought forward. Thus, for instance, one of the wise councilors urged the expediency of building a very high, strong wall in the sea round about Madagascar, so that no ship should be able to approach any of the harbors. A second wiseacre proposed to the queen to have four gigantic pairs of shears manufactured, and fixed on the roads leading from the various harbors to the capital. Whenever a European came along, the shears were to be clapped-to the moment he stepped between them, and thus the daring intruder would be cut in two. A third councilor, as wise as his companions, advised the queen to have a machine prepared with a great iron plate, against which the cannon balls fired from hostile ships would rebound, and sink the aggressive vessels by being hurled back upon them.

All these suggestions were received by her majesty with much approbation, and formed matter for deliberation in the exalted council for days and weeks; but, unfortunately, none of them were found practicable.

I must mention another touching trait, which the English missionary society will not fail to interpret greatly to the advantage of Queen Ranavola, should it not have done so already.

The queen is particularly fond of witnessing fights between bulls, and this noble sport is frequently carried on in the fine large court-yard in front of the palace. Among the horned combatants, some are her favorites: she asks after their health every day, and is as anxious about them as a European lady might be about her lapdogs; and, to carry out the simile, she often takes more interest in their well-being than in the comforts of her servants and friends.

In one of these contests, one of her favorite bulls—in fact, the chief of them—was slain: the poor queen was inconsolable at her loss. Until **now, no** one had ever seen her weep. But **then,** she had never before met with so heavy a misfortune. She had certainly lost her parents, her husband, a few children, and some brothers and **sisters;** but what were all these in comparison to the favorite **bull?** She wept much and bitterly, and it was long before **she** would take comfort. The animal was buried with all the honors accorded to a grandee of the state. It was wrapped in a number of simbus, and covered with a great white cloth, and the marshals had to lay it in the grave. The marshals showed on this occasion that **the** race of courtiers flourishes in Madagascar; they were so proud of the distinction that they boast of it to the present day. Two great stones are placed upon the grave, in memory of the dear departed; and the queen is said to think of him still with gentle sorrow.

The bull's monument is in the inner town. **I saw it my-**self, and thought, also with sorrow, not of **the bull,** but of the unhappy people languishing under the cruel oppression of this barbarous queen; and with sorrow, too, I thought of the equally unhappy sectarian spirit that can induce any section of a Christian community to become the champions of such a woman!

CHAPTER XIV.

Dinner at Mr. Laborde's.—Foot-boxing.—Ladies of Madagascar and Parisian Fashions.—The Conspiracy.—A Dream.—A Fancy-dress Ball.—An unquiet Night.—Concert at Court.—The Silver Palace.—An Excursion the Queen.

On the 3d, 4th, and 5th of June I was very unwell, with premonitory symptoms announcing a coming attack of the malignant fever of Madagascar. It luckily happened that, during these days, nothing of any interest occurred.

On the 6th of June Mr. Laborde gave a grand dinner in honor of Prince Rakoto, in his garden-house, situate at the foot of the hill.

Although the dinner was announced for six o'clock, we were carried to the house as early as three o'clock. On the way we passed a place in the upper town on which nineteen heavy guns (eighteen-pounders) were planted, the muzzles pointing toward the lower town, the suburbs, and the valley. They were placed there by King Radama, who had received them as a present from the English. They were not landed at Tamatavé, but at Bombetok, on the eastern coast. The distance from this place to the capital is greater than from Tamatavé, but the roads are better, and river conveyance can be made available for several days' journey.

On our arrival at Mr. Laborde's garden-house, all kinds of efforts were made to shorten the interval before dinner: several native sports were exhibited, the most popular of which was a kind of "foot-boxing." The combatants kicked each other all over, and with such hearty good-will that I expected every moment broken legs or ribs would be the result. This delicate sport is in particular favor among the people in winter, as it effectually warms those engaged in

it. The coldest season here is between the month of May
till the end of July, when the thermometer often falls **to**
four, three, or even to one degree (Réaumur). **Neverthe-**
less, every thing remains green; the trees do not lose **their**
leaves, and the landscape looks as pretty and blooming as
in Europe in the middle of spring. The inhabitants **of**
Tananariva are fond of the summer heat, and as they **have**
no means of procuring wood, and of thus artificially sup-
plying the want of animal heat, they resort to the aforesaid
pastime of foot-boxing.

The rich make their slaves bring wood from the distant
forests to kindle fires. In Mr. **Laborde's** house, a coal fire
was kept up in **a** great brazier from early in the morning
till late at night, but, of course, the door or the windows re-
mained always open. This piece of luxury costs a dollar
per day—a very high price compared with the cheapness
of all other necessaries.

The foot-boxing was followed by dancing and gymnastic
exercises; nor was music wanting, for a band had been **pro-**
vided, which executed some pieces skillfully enough. **I was**
not so well pleased with the songs of a number of native
girls, who had been taught by a missionary residing with
Mr. Laborde. They knew a number of songs by heart, and
did not scream in such shrill fashion as those whom we had
before heard; on the contrary, their performance was toler-
ably correct; but it was a dreary entertainment, and I was
devoutly thankful when they **came to the** last bar.

A little before six o'clock came the prince, accompanied
by his little son, his beloved Mary, and a female friend of
hers. Mary made even a less favorable impression upon
me than when I first saw her. The fault was in her dress,
for she was attired completely in the European **style.**
Whatever other people may say, the stiff, exaggerated fashions diffused by Paris over the world do not charm me,
even when worn by our own countrywomen, and only look

well on those whom nothing can disfigure; but where there
is a complete lack of natural beauty and grace, they become
whimsical and ridiculous, and particularly so in conjunction with clumsy figures and monkey faces. Madame Mary
may be a very good creature, and I should not like to offend her in any way; but that did not prevent me from
being obliged to bite my lips till the blood almost came in
the effort to avoid laughing aloud at her appearance. Over
half a dozen stiff-hooped petticoats she wore a woolen dress
with a number of great flounces, and great bows of ribbon,
the latter fastened, not in front, but at the back. She had
thrown a French shawl over her shoulders, and could never
arrange it to her satisfaction; and on the top of her head,
woolly as a curled poodle's, was perched a quizzical little
bonnet of reeds.

Her friend wore a muslin dress, and a cap of such anti-
quated form that, sexagenarian as I am, I could never remember having seen one of similar fashion; but afterward
I remembered having seen a similar one on a portrait of
my grandmother, who lived about the middle of the last
century. This woman, who was of a more clumsy figure
and had uglier features than Mary, positively frightened
me every time I looked at her; she always gave me the
idea of a cannibal chief in disguise.

The dinner-party was very cheerful. I had never seen
Mr. Lambert in such excellent spirits; as for the prince, he
seems always in good-humor. After dinner, Mr. Lambert
and Mr. Laborde held a short political discussion with the
prince in another room. I was admitted to take part in
this conversation, and shall have to recur to it. The evening was unfortunately somewhat spoiled for me by the singing chorus. The plentiful repast seemed to have inspired
the ladies with peculiar powers, for they screamed much
worse than before dinner, and, to increase the noise, clapped
their hands as an accompaniment. A few also performed

the dreary dance of Madagascar to the sound of the *maro-vane*, the only instrument yet invented by Malagasey musical genius. It consists of a bamboo, as thick as a man's arm, and four feet long. Shreds of the bark are fastened all around it, supported by little bridges of wood. The tone is very like that of a bad, worn-out cithern.

As a conclusion, the guests themselves danced, and between the dances Mr. Lambert gave us some very pretty songs.

About ten o'clock Mr. Laborde whispered to me that I should allege the weakness that still remained from my late indisposition as a pretext for breaking up the party. I replied that this was not my province, but that of Prince Rakoto; but he urged me to do it, adding that he had a particular reason for his request, which he would explain to me later; and, accordingly, I broke up the party.

Favored by the brightest of moonlight, we marched up the hill toward our dwellings to the sound of merry music.

Prince Rakoto and Mr. Lambert then called me into a side-chamber, and the prince declared to me once more that the private contract between himself and Mr. Lambert had been drawn up with his full concurrence, and that he, the prince, had been grossly calumniated when he was represented as intoxicated at the time of his signing it. He told me farther that Mr. Lambert had come to Madagascar by his wish, and with the intention, in conjunction with himself and a portion of the nobility and soldiers, to remove Queen Ranavola from the throne, but without depriving her of her freedom, her wealth, or the honors which were her due.

Mr. Lambert, on his part, informed me that we had dined in Mr. Laborde's garden-house because every thing could be more quietly discussed there, and that I had been requested to break up the party that the little feast might seem to have been given in my honor; finally, that we had gone through the town with the noisy music as a sign that the object of our meeting had been social amusement.

He then showed me in the house a complete little arsenal of sabres, daggers, pistols, and guns, wherewith to **arm** the conspirators, and leather shirts of mail for resisting lance-thrusts; and told me, in conclusion, that all preparations **bad** been made, and the time for action had almost **come**— in fact, I might expect it every hour.

I confess that a strange feeling **came** over me when I found myself thus suddenly involved in a political move-ment of grave importance, and at the first moment a crowd of conflicting thoughts rushed through my brain. I could **not conceal** from myself the fact **that** if the affair failed, my life would be in the same danger as Mr. Lambert's; for, in a country like Madagascar, where every thing depends on the despotic will of the ruler, no trouble is taken to de-termine the question of guilty or not guilty. I had come to Tananariva in the company of one of the chief **conspir-**ators; I had also been present at several meetings; more was not required **to** make me an accomplice in the **plot,** and therefore just as worthy of punishment as the active members themselves.

My friends in the Mauritius had certainly warned me **previously** against undertaking the journey in Mr. Lam-**bert's** company, and, from what had been reported there, **and** likewise from some scattered words which Mr. Lam-bert had let fall from time to time, I was able to form an idea of what was going on; but my wish to obtain a knowl-edge of Madagascar was so great that it stifled all fear. Now, indeed, there was **no** drawing back; and the best I could do was to put a good face **upon a** bad matter, and trust in that Providence which **had** already helped me in many and great dangers.

I gave Prince Rakoto and **Mr.** Lambert my most heart-**felt** wishes for the success of their undertaking, and then retired to my **room**. It was **already past midnight**. I went to bed, and, exhausted **as I was, soon fell asleep**; but **all** night long I had disturbed dreams, and, among others, the following very singular one: I dreamed that the plot **had been** discovered, and that the queen had summoned **Mr. Lambert** and myself to the palace. We were brought into a large room, and had to wait there a long, long time. At **length the queen** appeared with all her court; Prince Rakoto was there **too**, but he stood aside in a window, and dared not look **at us**.

One of the ministers—the **same** who had taken us to **court on our** first reception—made a long speech, the purport **of which** I understood, **in spite of my** ignorance of the Malagasey languages, **and in which he** reproached Mr. Lambert for his ingratitude and treachery. Another minister then took up the harangue, and announced **that we were** condemned to the tanguin.

Hereupon we were led into another room, and a tall **ne**gro, wrapped in a full white garment, came toward us with the little skins of poison. Mr. Lambert was obliged to take them first; but, at the moment when I was about to follow **his** example, there arose suddenly **a** loud din of music and rejoicing shouts, and—I awoke, and really heard music and shouting in the streets. It was broad day; I hastily wrap-**ped** myself in **my clothes, and** hurried **to the** gate to see **what** was going **on; and lo! two** men who had been condemned to the tanguin had fortunately got rid of the poison and the three **little** pieces of skin, and were being led home in triumph **by** their friends.

If I were of a superstitious nature, who knows what importance I might have attached to this dream, which was partly verified by subsequent events; but, fortunately, my temperament is not of that kind, and dreams never trouble me but during my sleeping hours.

June 8th. To-day the prince **held a** grand kabar in our

house, at which many **nobles and** officers were present.
From this period not **a** day passed in which greater or
smaller kabars were **not** held at **our house,** which was, in
fact, the head-quarters **of** the conspiracy.

June 9th. A great fancy-ball has been **given at court to-**
day in honor of Mr. Lambert.

What strange contrasts! On one side a conspiracy hatch-
ing—on the other, festivals are the order of the day!

Does the queen really doubt the existence of the treaty
between Prince Rakoto **and Mr.** Lambert, and has she no
suspicion of its intended accomplishment? or does she wish
to let the conspirators commit some **overt** act, that she may
afterward satiate her revenge with apparent justice? Events
will show.

Although both **Mr. Lambert and** myself were still very
unwell, we made up our minds **to be** present **at this** feast.

The ball began soon after **one** o'clock **in the** day, and
was not held in the apartments of the palace, **but in front**
of the building, in the great fore-court in which **we had**
been admitted to our audience. As on that former occasion, the queen sat on the balcony under the shade of her
great parasol, and we were obliged to make the usual obeisances to her and to the tomb of King Radama. This time,
however, we were not made **to** stand; comfortable arm-
chairs were assigned to **us.** Gradually the ball company
began to assemble; **the** guests comprised nobles of both
sexes, officers and their wives, **and** the queen's female singers and dancers. The nobles wore various costumes, and
the officers appeared in European **dress;** all **were** obliged
to make numerous obeisances. Those who appeared in
costume had seats like ours given them; the **rest** squatted
about as they liked, in groups **on** the ground.

The queen's female dancers opened **the ball** with the
dreary Malagasey dance. These charming creatures were
wrapped from top to toe in white simbus, and wore on their

heads artificial, or, I should say, very inartificial flowers, standing up stiffly like little flagstaffs; they crowded into a group in such a way that they seemed all tied together. As often as they staggered past the queen's balcony or the monument of King Radama, they repeated their salutes, and likewise at the end of every separate dance. After the female dancers had retired, the officers executed a very similar dance, only that they kept somewhat quicker time, and their gestures were more animated—that is to say, they lifted their feet rather higher than the performers of the other sex. Those who had hats and caps waved them in the air from time to time, and set up a sharp howling, intended to represent cries of joy.

After the officers followed six couples of children in fancy dresses. The boys wore the old Spanish costume, or were attired as pages, and looked tolerably well; but the girls were perfect scarecrows. They wore old-fashioned French costumes—large, stiff petticoats, with short bodices —and their heads were quite loaded with ostrich feathers, flowers, and ribbons. After this little monkey community had performed certain Polonaises, Schottisches, and contredanses, acquitting themselves, contrary to my expectation, with considerable skill, they bowed low and retired, making way for a larger company, the males likewise clad in the old Spanish, the females in the old French garb.

All these various costumes are commanded by the queen, who generally gets her ideas from pictures or engravings that come in her way. The ladies add to the costume prescribed by royalty whatever their own taste and invention may suggest, generally showing great boldness and originality in the combination of colors. I will give my readers an idea of what these costumes are like by describing one of them.

The dress was of blue satin, with a border of orange color, above which ran a broad stripe of bright cherry-colored

satin. The body, also **of satin, with long** skirt, shone with
a brimstone hue, and a light sea-green silk shawl was draped
above it. The head was **covered in such** style with stiff,
clumsily-made artificial flowers, with ostrich feathers, silk
ribbons, glass beads, and all kinds of millinery, that the hair
was entirely hidden; not that the fair one lost much thereby, but that **I** pitied her for the burden she had to carry.

The costumes of the other ladies showed similar contrasts
in color, and some of these tasteful dresses had been im-
proved by a farther stroke of ingenuity, **being** surmounted
by high conical hats, **very like those worn by the** Tyrolese
peasants.

The company, consisting exclusively of the higher aris-
tocracy, executed various European dances, and also performed the Sega, which **the** Malagaseys assert to be a native dance, though it is really derived from the Moors. The
figures, steps, and music of the Sega are all so pleasing that,
if it were once introduced in Europe, **it** could not fail **to**
become universally **fashionable.**

This beautiful dance was far from concluding the ball.
After a short pause, during which no refreshments were offered, the *élite* of the company, consisting of six couples,
stepped into the court-yards. The gentlemen were Prince
Rakoto, the two Labordes, father **and son, two** ministers,
and a general—all the ladies were princesses **or** countesses.
The gentlemen were dressed in old Spanish costume except
Prince Rakoto, **who wore a** fancy dress so tastefully chosen
that he might have appeared with distinction in any European court ball. He wore trowsers of dark blue cloth, with
a stripe down the side, a kind of loose jerkin of maroon-col-
ored velvet, ornamented with gold stripes and the most delicate embroidery, and a velvet cap of the same color, with
two ostrich feathers, fastened by a golden brooch. The
whole dress fitted so well, and the embroidery was so good,
that I thought Mr. Lambert must have taken the prince's

measure with him to Paris, and that the clothes **had been** made there; but this was not the case. **Every thing, with** the exception of the material, had been prepared at Tana-nariva—a proof that, if the people **of** Madagascar are **defi**-cient in invention, they are exceedingly clever in imitating models set before them.

This **group of dancers** appeared with much more effect than **their** predecessors, for all the ladies and gentlemen were **much** more tastefully attired than the rest of the company. **They only** performed European dances.

The ball was concluded, as it had been begun, by the female court dancers.

The whole of these festivities, which occupied three **hours,** had not put the queen to the slightest expense. The court-yard was the dancing-floor, the sun provided the illumination, and every guest was at liberty to take what refreshment he chose—*when he got home.* **Happy queen!** how sincerely many of our European ball-givers **might** envy her!

June 10. Again there was noise and singing in the streets. I hurried to the gate, and saw long files of men carrying earth and stones in baskets. The labor of these people, **eight** hundred in number, had been granted by the queen **to the** commander-in-chief of the army to build him a house. **They** received neither wages nor food, and were obliged to **sing and shout, to** prove to the queen that they were hap-**py, and** contented with their lot.

A few days **before I had seen** similar processions still more numerous, consisting of fifteen hundred men; they were carrying fuel to the royal forge, in which a thousand workmen are employed in manufacturing all kinds of weapons, under **the** superintendence of Mr. Laborde. **Like** the coal-bearers, the smiths receive nothing at all for their la-**bor;** and not only does the queen require all kinds of work from her subjects without paying them, but when there is any government expense to be incurred they have to find the money. Thus, in the year 1845, when the queen imported 30,000 muskets from France at a cost of 145,000 dollars, the whole sum was raised among the people. A few of the richest had to give as much as 500 dollars each; but even the poorest had to contribute, and not even the slaves were excepted.

June 11. Last night I heard a slight noise and muffled footsteps in our house. I knew that the conspirators were to go from here during the night to the palace. I listened for many hours—all was silent as the grave; but suddenly there resounded a loud barking of dogs, followed by quick footsteps of men. I started involuntarily. I thought that the attempt must have failed, and that the hurrying steps were those of fugitives, and I felt how much more trying it is to be obliged to remain in passive suspense amid threatened danger than boldly to oppose and combat the peril.

I would not leave my room, lest I should betray my weakness if it proved to be a false alarm; so I avoided waking my companions, and awaited patiently what Heaven should send. But nothing farther occurred; the remainder of the night passed quietly, and next morning I learned that nothing had been undertaken, and that the favorable moment was not yet come.

I begin to fear that every thing will be spoiled by this long delay; the more so, as the meetings are not very cautiously conducted, and a traitor might easily be found among the nobles and officers apparently devoted to the prince. A good deal of the fault may lie with the prince himself. He is, as I have observed, a man of many good and noble qualities, but he wants decision and firmness of purpose; and his affection for the queen is, moreover, so great, that he might lack courage at the decisive moment to undertake any thing against her. It behooves him, however, to consider that there is no intention of robbing the queen of her titles, her freedom, or her wealth; the sole object of the movement being to take from her the power of perpetrating the cruelties and deeds of blood which have brought her subjects to misery and despair. The prince, who loves his mother above every thing, and only seeks to prevent her from being the scourge of a whole country, can not certainly be considered guilty of a crime. God strengthen him, and give him courage to be the deliverer of his people!

June 12. Mr. Lambert had so severe an attack of fever that for several days his life was in the greatest danger. But he terribly neglected all dietary precautions. As soon as he felt himself at all better, he ate all kind of things one after another, just as the whim took him—cold Strasburg pie, meat, and fruit, and drank Champagne and other wines. The other Europeans do just the same thing, so that I should not at all wonder if all who caught the fever fell victims to it. While I was in the Mauritius in the month of March, a stout gentleman from Tamatavé arrived there, and remained a few days in Mr. Lambert's house, waiting for an opportunity to get to Bourbon. This gentleman asserted that he had the Madagascar fever, and when he appeared at breakfast complained that he had been suffering from it all night. Accordingly, some strong meat broth was prepared for him, which he enjoyed exceedingly; but it did not nearly satisfy him, for he ate in addition a mighty slice of sweet melon, partook of the other dishes to an extent which would have served me for a week, and finished his repast with a mango. He did equal justice to the various beverages; and at the evening meal he returned to the attack with renewed vigor, eating as if he had fasted the whole day.

In Tananariva I had frequent opportunities of noticing similar imprudences in diet; and when I made any remark, I was met with the profound reply, "What would you have? It is the custom of the country; the people say that the fever is very weakening, and that one must try to get up one's strength by taking nourishing things."

This belief really prevails among the people; the worse a man is, the more he is urged to eat. When a Malagasey is at the last gasp, they stuff rice into his mouth; and when he dies, they cry out in astonishment, "How wonderful! only just now he was eating!"

And because the stupid, uncultivated natives do this, the sensible and educated Europeans think it right to do like-wise!

June 18. To-day I had the great honor of displaying my skill, or rather my want of skill, on the piano in the presence of the queen. Mr. Lambert had made her a present of a piano from the manufactory of Mr. Debain, in Paris, on his first visit to Tananariva. These pianos are not only made for playing upon with the hands, but can also be played in the manner of a barrel-organ by turning a handle or "manivelle."

Mr. Lambert had told me of this when we were in the Mauritius, and added that the queen had never seen any one play the piano with their hands, and that it would be a great surprise to her. In my youth I had been a tolerably accomplished pianist, but that is a long time ago; for more than thirty years I had given up music, and had nearly forgotten all I once knew. Who would ever have thought that I should have to give a concert, under royal patronage, in my sixtieth year, when I strummed worse than many children at home who have only learned for a few months! But so it is when people go out in quest of adventure, and roam through the wide world; one never knows what may happen, and must be prepared for every thing.

With great difficulty I forced my stiff old fingers through a few scales and exercises, and contrived to remember a few easy, melodious waltzes and dance tunes; and, thus prepared, I ventured to risk the criticism of the strict royal connoisseur of Madagascar.

The invitation, however, was very welcome to me; for I hoped to be introduced into the inner apartments of the palace, and to have the high felicity of obtaining a near view of her majesty.

As Mr. Lambert was ill of the fever, the two clerical gentlemen accompanied me to the palace. When we got to the court-yard—oh, sad disenchantment!—there sat the queen on the eternal balcony, and away fled all my hopes of seeing the interior of the palace. Besides, what a shock to my artistic pride! It seemed that I was to be treated like a street musician, and made to play here in the court-yard.

But it was not quite so bad as that, though enough was done to make me duly sensible of the enormous difference between my insignificant person and the mighty queen. This overbearing, puffed-up woman seems really to believe herself a sacred being, raised above all the rest of the human race, and appears to think it would derogate from her dignity to permit a stranger to come close to her. It was only with Mr. Lambert, when he first came to Tananariva, three years ago, that she made an exception, admitting him not merely into the interior of the palace, but even allowing him the honor of accompanying her on a short excursion.

We were conducted to the gallery on the ground floor of the Silver Palace, where chairs had been already placed for us. The broad door leading to the court-yard was thrown quite open, the piano brought forward, and placed just in the doorway, in such a manner that the queen could look down from her balcony upon the key-board.

While these preparations were being made, I had an opportunity of examining the reception-room of the Silver

Palace, which, as my readers will remember, belongs to
Prince Rakoto. **It is spacious and** lofty, and furnished
quite in European style. The furniture seemed rich, but
not overladen with ornament, and had been arranged with
taste. True to the custom of Madagascar, there stood a bed
in the **room—a** right royal bed, certainly, with **no lack of**
gold ornament or of silken hangings, and in which I was
assured no mortal had ever slept; but still it was a bed, and
that particular piece of furniture in a reception-room always
disturbs the idea of fitness in the eyes of a European.

Far more, however, was my taste **offended** by the drawings and paintings that decorated **the** walls of the hall—
productions of native genius—representing officers in red
uniforms, and female figures in European costumes. I hard-
ly knew which to admire most in these sketches, the coloring or the drawing. The latter was more wooden and stiff
in character than the worst Chinese work of the kind, and
the coloring was a wonderful chaos of the most glaring hues
daubed together without any attempt **at** light and **shade.**
I had never in my life seen such works of Art. The landscape backgrounds had the most comical effect of all. The
figures stood with little trees on each side of them. They
were only half-length portraits; but as the genial artist
wished, nevertheless, to indicate the fact that the trees grew
out of the earth, he had drawn a green stripe from the gir-
dle of each person to that of his neighbor, intending thereby
to represent the earth, thus unintentionally giving his he-
roes **the** unusual appearance of being buried up to the
waist; out of the green stripe rose a brown line, the stem
of the tree, straight as an arrow, as high as the shoulders
of the figures, and a few green patches were added to represent the leafy crown.

I was still absorbed in the contemplation of these masterpieces when one of the missionaries came to inform me that
the piano was ready, and that I could begin my perform-

ance. Before doing this I had to present the usual "monosina" to the queen, and deliver it into the hands of an officer; this tribute is demanded of every stranger, not only at his first introduction at court, but every time he sets foot in a building belonging to royalty. This was my case in the Silver Palace; but I considered it unnecessary to give a fifty-franc piece, as Mr. Lambert had done, and therefore confined my liberality to the offer of a dollar.

I took my seat at the piano, and played a few preliminary chords to test the qualities of the instrument; but what was my horror on finding it so woefully out of tune that not a single note produced any thing like harmony with the rest; many of the keys, moreover, were so obstinate as to refuse to emit any sound whatever. I had to loosen them, lift them, press them down, and resort to all sorts of expedients to bring them into working order; and upon such an instrument as this I was to give my grand concert! But true artistic greatness rises superior to all adverse circumstances; and, inspired by the thought of exhibiting my talents to such an appreciating audience, I perpetrated the most wonderful runs over the whole key-board, thumped with all my might on the stubborn keys, and, without any attempt at selection or sequence, played the first part of a waltz and the second of a march, in short, any thing and every thing that came into my head. But I had the great satisfaction to find that my talents were fully appreciated by the whole audience, and I was rewarded with her majesty's especial thanks. Prince Rakoto even gave me the flattering assurance that every thing I had done had met with the queen's approbation, especially the waltzes, and that in a short time she would do me the honor of letting me play before her in the interior of the palace. Who knows, if the unhappy conspiracy had not occurred, if I might not have enjoyed the distinction of becoming pianiste to her majesty the Queen of Madagascar!

On the same day she sent me, as a proof of favor and condescension, a large quantity of fat poultry and a great basket of eggs.

On the 17th of June the exalted lady made an excursion to one of her pleasure palaces, situate at the foot of the hill on an island in the middle of a large pond. Whenever the queen makes such excursions, all the officers and nobles, and the European residents in Tananariva, have to accompany her. I would gladly have taken part in this expedition, but as the queen knew that Mr. Lambert was still lying very ill, and did not wish to deprive him of any of his nurses, none of us were invited. The procession passed close by our house, and we were all, with the exception of Mr. Lambert, made to stand at the gate to salute her majesty as she passed.

Every festival in this country bears on its face a peculiar stamp of whim and folly: in these excursions, for instance, the notables who accompany the queen are ordered to appear in Turkish or Arab costume, with turbans on their heads. These dresses, however, suit the natives much better than the Spanish costume, although here, too, their peculiar taste is brought into play, to spoil the effect of what would be handsome enough if left alone.

Women seldom take part in these expeditions, and when they do they are wrapped in simbus. The queen herself wore a large simbu of silk, but had her great crown on her head. Without this regal ornament she never shows herself to her subjects; and I should really not be surprised to hear that she usually wears a small crown when she goes to sleep at night.

She remained all day in her little palace, and did not return to the city till just before sunset. The people take part in these excursions to some extent, being obliged to crowd into the streets through which the procession passes, and many who wish to show peculiar loyalty join the train.

CHAPTER XV.

Failure of the *Coup d'État*.—Prince Ramboasalama.—The *Pas de Deux*.—
Discovery of the Plot.—Death of Prince Razakaratrino.—Freedom of
Manners.—Irreligion.—Beginning of our Captivity.—A Kabar.—Perse-
cution of the Christians.—The Delivery of the Presents.

JUNE 20. This was at length to be the great and decisive
day. Mr. Lambert was nearly recovered from the fever;
so there was to be no more delay, and to-night the long-
contemplated *coup d'état* was to be carried out.

The two missionaries, who were not to appear to bear
any part in these political disturbances, went in the morning to one of the possessions of Mr. Laborde, distant thirty
miles from the capital. It was proposed to send me there
too; but I preferred remaining at Tananariva; for I thought,
if the attempt should fail, it would not be difficult to find
my head, even if I were a hundred miles from the capital.

The following plan had been devised by the conspirators.
The prince was to dine at eight o'clock in the evening with
Mr. Lambert, Marius, Laborde, and his son, in the garden-
house belonging to the latter, and thither all reports from
the other conspirators were to be carried, that it might be
known if every thing was progressing favorably, and that
every man was at his post. At the conclusion of the dinner, at eleven o'clock at night, the gentlemen were to march
home to the upper part of the town, accompanied by music,
as if they came from a feast; and each man was to remain
quiet in his own house until two o'clock. At the latter
hour all the conspirators were to slip silently into the palace, the gates of which Prince Raharo, the chief of the army,
was to keep open, and guarded by officers devoted to Prince
Rakoto; they were to assemble in the great court-yard, in

front of the apartments inhabited by the queen, and at a
given signal loudly to proclaim Prince Rakoto king. The
new ministers, who had already been nominated by the
prince, were to explain to the queen that this was the will
of the nobles, the military, and the people; and, at the same
time, the thunder of cannon from the royal palace was to
announce to the people the change in the government, and
the deliverance from the sanguinary rule of Queen Ranavola.

Unhappily, this plan was not carried out. It was frus-
trated by the cowardice or treachery of Prince Raharo, the
commander-in-chief of the army. While the gentlemen
were still at table, they received from him the disastrous
news that, in consequence of unforeseen obstacles, he had
found it impossible to fill the palace exclusively with officers devoted to the prince's interest, that he would consequently be unable to keep the gates open to-night, and that
the attempt must be deferred for a more favorable opportunity. In vain did the prince send messenger after messenger to him. He could not be induced to risk any thing.

In the year 1856 Prince Rakoto had placed himself at
the head of a similar conspiracy against the queen. Then
also the night and the hour had been fixed upon for the attempt, and, as in the present instance, every thing failed
through the sudden defection of the commander-in-chief.
It may be that this occurred partly through that personage
losing courage at the decisive moment; but I am more inclined to think that his participation in the plot must be a
feigned one, and that he is in reality a creature of the queen
and her prime minister, Rainizahoro; and, I fear most of
all, that he is a partisan of Prince Ramboasalama.

This prince, a son of a sister of Queen Ranavola, was
adopted by the queen many years ago, when she had no
son of her own, and, owing to her time of life, could scarcely hope to have any offspring. So she looked upon the

prince as her natural successor, and declared him her heir with all the usual formalities. Soon afterward she had hopes of becoming a mother, and Prince Rakoto was born. It is asserted by many that though, in consequence of this event, she removed Ramboasalama from the succession, and declared her own son to be the heir-apparent, this was not done with the usual ceremonies, and it is much to be feared that upon the queen's decease great and bloody dissensions may arise between the parties of the rival princes, and the faction of Ramboasalama may obtain the mastery. This prince, several years older than Rakoto, is naturally far more experienced than the latter; he has also the reputation of being very astute and enterprising; and, though not so good-natured and philanthropic as the queen's son, he is far less cruel and bloodthirsty than Ranavola.

So far as I could judge from what was told me, he appears to have formed a powerful party for himself, and to have secured the greater portion of the nobility, chiefly through great concessions, and from the fact that he is entirely averse to the abolition of slavery, while, on the other hand, Prince Rakoto means to carry out this measure, and wishes in general to curtail the privileges of the higher classes.

These reasons ought in themselves to be sufficient to induce one of the European powers to take Prince Rakoto's part; but European governments only take up cases in which they have the prospect of some immediate and material advantage—to act from mere philanthropy forms no part of their plans.

The plot has unfortunately become what may be called a "well-known secret." Every body knows of it, and even among the people reports of the contemplated change in the government have become rife; and it is only the queen, we have been assured, who is in profound ignorance of what is going on around her. I can not believe this. We are

L

certainly told that no one would venture to accuse the
prince to his mother, for in such a case the queen would
surely at once summon her son and make him acquainted
with the charges against him, when it might be anticipated
that he would deny every thing, and the denouncer would
be considered as a traitor, and executed accordingly. I can
not believe that the adherents and favorites of the queen
have entirely left out the prince's name, and merely have
denounced Mr. Lambert, Mr. Laborde, and a few of the other conspirators. Of adherents and favorites the queen has
plenty, in spite of her cruelty and egotism; and she knows
how to attach the most influential men in the land to her
person, though they do not receive the smallest salary from
her; but she gratifies them with estates and slaves, or gives
them a still more valuable reward, by assigning to them,
under the name of aids-de-camp, a number of people who
are obliged to do them service like slaves, receiving neither
provisions nor wages in return. Thus Raharo, the present
commander-in-chief of the army, has eight hundred of these
aids-de-camp continually under his command; his father,
who preceded him as commander-in-chief, had fifteen hundred.

June 21. To-day Prince Rakoto told us that his mother
would receive Mr. Lambert as soon as his health was restored, and me too, in the inner palace, and that she wished
very much to see us dance together. He added that it
would give her great pleasure to see us exhibit some new
dance, and that, as Europeans, we were doubtless acquainted with several. A strange idea this! First I had to give
a concert, and now I am to turn ballet-dancer, and perhaps
afterward dancing-mistress—I who, even in my youth,
cared very little for dancing, and always had the greatest
difficulty in remembering the various steps and figures.
And Mr. Lambert! What a thing to expect from a man
who is still young, that he should execute a *pas de deux*

with a woman nearly sixty years old! Neither of us had the slightest intention to gratify this ridiculous whim; and as Mr. Lambert suffered much again this morning from the fever, and I also had a renewed attack of that insidious disease, we made our illness serve as an excuse for the present.

June 22. To-day we received very bad news: the queen has received information of the plot. Our friends told us, however, that efforts were being made to divert her suspicions from the right direction, and to make her believe that the people wished for a change in the government. It is said that no names have been denounced to her, but that the wish is represented as having been generally expressed among the people.

Our friends may try to screen us, but our enemies, of whom Mr. Lambert, as I have already remarked, has several, will not be so considerate; and it is unfortunately certain that the queen has for some time looked upon Mr. Lambert with suspicion, for to-day she told her son that when Mr. Lambert lay dangerously ill of the fever, she had consulted the oracle upon the question whether he had any evil design against her, and if so, whether he would die of the fever. The reply of the Sikidy was, that "if Mr. Lambert had any such evil design, the fever would assuredly carry him off:" as this had not been the case—as he had not died, she thought he could not be plotting any evil against her.

Is this the truth, or does the cunning woman only say it in the hope of worming something out of the prince himself? Even if it is the truth, can she not consult the Sikidy over and over again, until, some fine day, it may give a different answer?

At any rate, I consider our cause is lost; and Heaven knows what the queen may intend to do to us. These are the consequences of the prince's delays and irresolution.

But who knows? Several times the thought has arisen in my mind, chiefly from the demeanor of Prince Raharo, that the prince is surrounded by traitors, who pretend to acquiesce in his projects, but only do so to obtain a knowledge of them, and afterward carry intelligence to the queen. Perhaps in this view they treat him like a child, and let him have his hobby, always, however, taking the necessary precautions to be able to stop his highness's sport before things go too far.

June 27. Last night died Marshal Prince Razakaratrino, the queen's brother-in-law. The death of this grand lord will give me an opportunity of seeing a new and interesting sight, for the funeral of such an exalted personage is conducted in Madagascar with **the greatest** solemnity. After the body has been washed, it is wrapped in simbus of red silk, often to the number of several hundred, and none of which must cost less than ten piastres, though they generally cost much more. Thus enshrouded, the corpse is placed in a kind of coffin, and lies in state in the **principal** apartment in the house, under a canopy of red silk. **Slaves** crouch around it, crowded together as closely as possible, with their hair hanging loose, and their heads bent down in token of mourning; each of them is furnished with a kind of fan to keep off the flies and musquitoes from the deceased. This strange occupation is continued day and night; and as high personages are frequently kept unburied for several weeks, the slaves have to be continually relieved by others.

During the time the corpse is lying under the canopy, envoys come from every caste of the nobility and from every district of the country, accompanied by long trains of servants and slaves, to present tokens of condolence for themselves, and in the names of those by whom they are sent. Each of the envoys brings an offering of money, varying according to his own fortune, and the amount of popularity enjoyed by the deceased, from half a **dollar to** fifty or more. These presents are **received** by the nearest relation of the dead man, and are devoted to defraying the expenses of the burial, which often come to a great sum; for, besides the large number **of** simbus to be purchased, a great many oxen must be killed. All visitors and envoys stay until the day of the funeral, and are entertained, as well **as their** servants and slaves, at the expense of the heirs. When the funeral ceremonies extend over several weeks, and the number of the guests is large, it may be **easily** imagined that a goodly stock of provisions is con**sumed,** especially as the people of Madagascar, masters and servants, **are** valiant trenchermen **when** they feed at the cost of another. Thus, at the death of the last commander **of the** army, **the** father of Prince Raharo, no fewer than 1500 oxen were slaughtered and eaten. But then this man had stood very high in the queen's favor, and his funeral is recorded as the most splendid in the memory **of man:** he lay in state for three weeks, and young and old streamed in from the farthest corners of the kingdom to pay him the last honors.

With regard to the performances of the people of Madagascar as trenchermen, I have been told that four natives **can** eat up an ox in a space of twenty-four hours, and that **after such a** meal they go away as comfortable and light as **if they** had barely satisfied their **hunger. I should be** sorry, however, to vouch **for the** authenticity of this report to **my readers. I have never** witnessed such a feat; and, looking at the size of the **oxen** that are sacrificed upon such occasions, I should say that the estimate was undoubtedly exaggerated.

Voracious as the natives are (I can use no milder epithet) when an opportunity for gluttony occurs, they have, on the other hand, like the wild Indians, the power of enduring great privation with consummate patience, and will support themselves for weeks together on a little rice and a few thin slices of dried meat.

When the corpse is carried out of the house, a few slaughtered oxen must be laid at the door, and the bearers have to step over their bodies.

The period of lying in state, and of mourning generally, is fixed by the queen herself; for this marshal the former ceremony was fixed for four days, the latter for ten. If he had been a near relation of the queen—a brother or uncle —or one of her particular favorites, he could not have been buried under from ten to fourteen days, and the period of mourning would have extended to twenty or thirty days at least.

The body is prevented from becoming offensive by the number of simbus in which it is wrapped.

We did not follow the funeral procession, but saw it pass from Mr. Laborde's house; its extent was very great, and it consisted of nobles, officers, women, mourning women, and slaves, in large numbers. From the highest to the lowest, all wore their hair loose as a token of mourning; and with this loosened hair they looked so particularly hideous —so horribly ugly—that I had never seen any thing like them among the ugliest races of India and America. The women especially, who let their hair grow longer than the men wear it, might indeed have passed for scarecrows or furies.

In the midst of the procession came the catafalque, borne by more than thirty men. Like the costumes at the court balls, so this catafalque had evidently been copied from some engraving, for its ornamentation was quite European in character, with this one difference, that the machine was hung with red and variegated silk stuffs instead of the customary black cloth. The marshal's hat, with other insignia of rank and honor, were placed upon it, and on both sides marched slaves, with clappers to scare away the flies from the catafalque.

The corpse was conveyed thirty miles away to an estate of the deceased, to be burned there; the greater number of nobles and officers only escorted it for the first few miles, but many carried their politeness so far as to go the whole distance.

In all Madagascar there is no place exclusively set apart for the burial of the dead. Those who possess land are buried on their own estates; the poor are carried to some place that belongs to nobody, and are there frequently thrown under a bush, or put into any hollow, no one taking the trouble even to throw a little earth upon them.

When I saw this funeral conducted in such truly European style, I thought, as I had frequently done before, what a strange country this Madagascar was, and what striking contrasts were found among these people—cultivation and savagery, imitation of European manners and customs and the rudest barbarism go here hand in hand. One finds here, as in Europe, all the titles of rank and nobility, from the prince down to the lieutenant: many of the nobles often go about in European garb; many speak and write English or French, and the rich dine off plate, and possess handsome, well-furnished houses. Farther imitations of our European customs are seen in the etiquette with which the queen surrounds her own person, the ceremonious splendor she seeks to impart to her court, the solemn excursions to her pleasure palaces, the fancy balls, the great dinners, the funerals of high personages, and other occasions of the kind.

The industrial education of the people has also made great progress in certain districts; and it is easy to see that, if properly cultivated and directed, industrial arts would soon attain a higher development. Thus, as already stated, the goldsmiths and silversmiths furnish specimens that excite my unqualified admiration; the women silk-weavers make very pretty pieces from native silk; and Mr. Laborde turns out from his various factories of native workmen all kinds of weapons, even to small cannon, and powder, as well as glass, soap, wax-lights, rum, and the most delicious liqueurs.

With respect to the cultivation of the mind and heart, the inhabitants of Madagascar have not sought to imitate the Europeans. In this particular, indeed, many of the wildest tribes, who have scarcely come into communication with Europeans at all—for instance, the Dyaks of Borneo; the Afoxes, in the island of Celebes; the Anthropophagi, in the interior of Sumatra, and others—stand far above the Hovas and Malagaseys. Incredible as it may appear, the latter have no religion at all—not the slightest idea of a God, of the immortality of the soul, or even of its existence. The queen, I was told, certainly worships a few household idols, but she places far less reliance on these than on the verdicts of the Sikidy; and when a missionary once spoke to her of the immortality of the soul, she is said to have considered him mad, and to have laughed aloud in his face. The people are allowed to worship any thing they like—a tree, a river, or a rock—but belief in Christ is strictly forbidden. With the exception of the few who have become converted to the Christian faith in spite of the queen's prohibition, the bulk of the people believe in nothing at all, at which I wondered the more when I considered that some of the races living in Madagascar are descended from the Arabs and Malays, nations who in the earliest times had some ideas of God and of religion.

Oh, how much it is to be wished that the government should pass into Prince Rakoto's hands! I am certain that this beautiful country would then make the most rapid strides in intellectual progress and in material wealth.

June 30. When I was traveling in the United States, I thought I had found the country where women had the greatest freedom, and the greatest independence of thought and action. What an error! Here, in Madagascar, they lead a much more independent, unrestrained life. I do not speak of Queen Ranavola, whose rank gives her a kind of right to follow only the dictates of her will, but of the other women, who are not subjected to the laws of propriety which trammel us poor European females. Thus, for instance, Mary, the favorite of Prince Rakoto, came very frequently, with his full knowledge, quite alone to our house, not only to pay a visit to Mr. Lambert while he was ill with the fever, but when he was in perfect health. She had often partaken of our evening repast, and to-day she joined us again. While we were sitting at table they brought her little son. I had never seen her in a domestic circle with her child, and was anxious to see how her feelings would be displayed, so I noticed the mother and child during the whole evening. Each treated the other as coldly as if they had never known, much less belonged to, each other. When the child came into the room he did not even greet his mother, but went at once toward the table, where room was made for him at Mr. Lambert's side; during the whole of supper-time, mother and child never exchanged a word or a glance, although they were only separated from each other by Mr. Lambert.

In vain do Mr. Laborde and other Europeans in Madagascar assure me that strong affection exists here among the natives between parents and children, but that it is not customary to display that affection. I can not believe it, with such a display of indifference before my eyes. A mother who felt real affection toward her child would certainly not be able to conform to custom so completely as to prevent herself from giving the little one a loving glance from time to time. And the observations I made this evening were not the only ones of the same kind; during the whole period of my stay in Madagascar I did not see a mother show any affection, or child that seemed to love its parents.

L 2

July 2. What will become **of us!** The carrying out of
the design seems to have become impracticable, **for** from
the day when the commander refused to **open the** doors of
the palace, one after another of the conspirators has fallen
away, and traitors and spies surround us on all sides. Ever
since the 20th **of June** hardly any one associates **with us;**
we are looked upon partly as state prisoners, and we **are**
compelled **to** remain the whole day long in our houses, and
dare **not so much as set** foot across **the** threshold.

The best proof that the queen is perfectly well informed
of the conspiracy, and only pretends **to know** nothing about
it for the sake of her son, of whom she is very fond, appears
in the fact of her having, a few days since, forbidden every
one, on pain of death, to make **any** accusation whatever
against the prince, or to impart any surmise of his guilt to
her.

This trait is worthy of the cunning characteristic of **her**
race. Having taken all necessary measures, and **convinced**
herself that the power of the conspirators is broken, **and**
that she has nothing to fear, she seeks to hide her **son's**
fault from the people.

July **3.** To-day sorrow and fear have been spread over
all the city. Early in the morning the people were called
together, and ordered to betake themselves at a certain hour
to the bazar, to be present at a great kabar to be held there.
Such an announcement always spreads terror and apprehension among the people, for they know from sad experience that a kabar signifies, for them, persecution, and torture, and sentences of death. There was a general howling
and wailing, a rushing and running through the streets,
as if the town had been attacked by a hostile army, and, as
if to strengthen that belief, all entrances to the town were
occupied by troops, and the poor people were torn forcibly
from their houses by the soldiers, and driven to the market-
place.

We Europeans, shut up in our house, **saw** very little of these scenes, with the exception of Mr. Laborde, who, thanks to his great popularity, could **still** venture abroad to pursue his usual avocations.   Full of anxious expectation, **we** awaited his return; **he** came home pale and excited, **and** told us that the present kabar was the most cruel and **disastrous** that had been held since his arrival at Tananariva. The majority of the inhabitants—men, women, and children —had been assembled in the great square, and there waited in trembling fear **to hear** the royal will, which one of the officials announced **in a loud** voice.

The kabar was as follows: **The queen** had long suspected **that** there were many Christians **among her** people. **Within** the last few days she **had become** certain of the **fact, and had heard with** horror that **several** thousands of this sect dwelt **in and** around Tananariva.   Every one knew how much she hated and detested this sect, and **how** strictly she had forbidden the practice of their religion. As her commands were so little regarded, she should **use** every effort to discover the guilty, and should punish them with the greatest severity.   The duration of the kabar was fixed for fifteen **days**, and it was announced to the people, in conclusion, that **those** who gave themselves up during that period should have their lives spared, but that all who were denounced **by** others **might be prepared** to die a terrible **death.**

I can hardly believe that, **after** the experience the people **had had** this very year, any of them will voluntarily surrender.   My readers will recollect a similar case I mentioned among the cruelties of the queen, in which the unhappy culprits who confessed their crime had their lives spared, according to the letter of the promise, but were fettered heavily and perished miserably; and then the accusation was only one of sorcery, theft, violation of graves, and other **crimes, which are in** the queen's eyes of far less consequence than that of conversion **to the** Christian faith. The followers of the Christian religion might expect to have far worse tortures practiced on **them.**

Who would believe that the traitor, the denouncer of the Christians, was a Christian himself, and half a priest into the bargain, **whom** the English missionaries had honored with the title "Reverendissimus!" The name of this miserable creature is Ratsimandisa. He belongs to the race of the Hovas, and is a native of Tananariva, and has had a semi-European education, which unfortunately had no effect in ennobling **his mind** or his heart. In order to win the favor of the queen, **and** hoping to obtain **a** great reward, **he declared that he** only pretended **to** adopt the Christian religion with the **view** of getting a knowledge of all the Christians, and thus giving the queen an opportunity of annihilating them **at one** blow. He had really made out a complete register of the names of Christians residing in Tananariva. Fortunately, it did not occur to him to request an audience of the queen, and to give this register into **her** own hands. He gave it to one of the ministers who **belonged** to Prince Rakoto's party, and was one of the prince's most faithful followers. This man would not deliver a document of such importance to the queen without first telling the prince of the circumstance. No sooner had the latter read the document than he tore it in pieces, and announced **that** any one who dared **to** make **out a** second list, or even to accept one with the intention of laying it before the government, should **be** immediately put to death. This action certainly saved the lives of some thousands of Christians; they gained time, and had an opportunity of escaping, of which the majority have availed themselves. But in the wild, inhospitable forests, where alone they can hide themselves, without a roof to shelter them, without food to eat, how many of these poor people must fall victims to hunger **and** misery!

To increase their misfortune, an English missionary, Mr. Lebrun, had come from the Mauritius to Tamatavé for a few days, shortly before Ratsimandisa's treason, and **had** written letters from Tamatavé to several Christians in Tananariva, exhorting them to be firm in their faith, and seeking to strengthen their courage with the assurance that the day of persecution would not last much longer, and that better times would soon come for them. The poorer among them also received promises of aid, and some money was, it is said, distributed among them. Unhappily, a few of these letters fell into the hands of the government, and others were found during the search instituted in the houses of those suspected of Christianity; and as the names of several Christians were mentioned in these letters, to whom the missionary sent messages or greeting through the recipients, these at least could be seized. The unhappy people were tortured in all kinds of ways, like the Protestants of Spain in the days of the Inquisition, to induce them **to** give up the names of the Christians they **knew, and the** government succeeded in capturing a tolerable number **in** the first few days.

July 4. Mr. Lambert had a relapse of the fever, and, in-deed, such a severe one that we are very anxious about his life. My health, too, is not satisfactory. I have not such **violent attacks of** the fever **as those** from which Mr. Lambert suffers, **but I can not get rid of** the disease, and my **strength becomes less from day to** day.

July 6. More than **two** hundred Christians are said to have been either denounced or discovered in the few days that have elapsed since the kabar was announced. They are being sought for every where. Every house is entered —every one suspected of Christianity, be **it man, woman,** or child, is seized by the soldiers, and dragged **to one of** the prisons.

Unless the fall of the government be speedily brought

about, and this Megæra deprived of her power before the expiration of the fifteen days fixed as the duration of the kabar, there will be horrible deeds and executions here. In spite of all the untoward events that have happened, Messrs. Lambert and Laborde do not appear to have given up all hope, and consider the contemplated *coup d'état* as still practicable. I hope with all my heart it may be so— less, I can solemnly assert, because my own life is involved in the question, than for the sake of my numerous brethren in the faith, and for the whole people, who would awake to a new life under the mild rule of Prince Rakoto. But, alas! I can not participate in the hopes of my companions. As things now stand, I can not see the slightest prospect of success. The commander-in-chief of the army is not to be induced to act; and it is probable that he never intended to fulfill his promise of opening the gates of the palace to the conspirators. The party against Prince Rakoto gains strength every day, and there is not the slightest chance of a popular revolution. The poor natives of Madagascar have been too much oppressed, and are too submissive for that. They have such a wholesome terror of the power of the queen, and the influence of the nobles and the military, that it would be useless to try to persuade them to undertake any thing against the existing powers.

July 7. The queen has been told that Mr. Lambert has had a dangerous relapse of the fever, and she sends confidential officers five or six times in the day—different envoys each time—to ask after his health. The officers always ask to be taken into his room, and to see him; probably they have been commissioned to find out if his illness is real or simulated. How the queen would rejoice at Mr. Lambert's death!

For the last three days Prince Rakoto has not been to see us; for his mother, the queen, treats him almost as a prisoner. She will not let him quit her side, alleging that she is in great danger and needs his protection. Through this really politic course of action she gains the twofold object of making her son appear, on the one hand, as a non-participator in the conspiracy, and of taking from him, on the other, all opportunity of entering into communication with his confederates, who might, perhaps, induce him to strike a decisive blow. She has taken farther precautions. The palace has been surrounded with treble the usual number of guards. No one is allowed to pass near it, and only those are admitted into the interior of whose fidelity and loyalty the queen feels quite assured.

July 8. Our prison is closing more straitly around us, and our position really begins to be very critical. We have just learned that, since yesterday evening, every one has been prohibited, on pain of death, from entering our house. Mr. Laborde now no longer ventures to appear in the streets. I marvel much that our slaves are still allowed to go to the bazar, and make the necessary purchases; but doubtless this will soon be stopped; and I am much mistaken if the moment is not at hand when the queen will throw off the mask, and, openly denouncing us as traitors, cause our house to be surrounded by soldiers, and thus completely isolate us. Nobody can tell what this woman purposes to do to us, and her character gives us no reason to expect any thing good. If we are once made prisoners, she can easily get rid of us by means of poisoned food or by some other method.

Our slaves tell us that more than eight hundred soldiers are employed in searching for Christians; they not only search the whole town, but scour the country within a circuit of between twenty and thirty miles; but, happily, it is said they do not take many prisoners. All flee to the mountains and forests, and in such numbers that small detachments of soldiers, who pursue the fugitives and seek to capture them, are put to flight.

July 9. To-day we received fresh news of the persecution against the Christians. The queen has heard that until
now very few prisoners, comparatively, have been brought
in; she is stated to be extremely enraged **at** this, and to
have exclaimed in great anger that the bowels of the earth
must be searched, and the rivers and lakes dragged with
nets, so that **not one** of the traitors may escape his just punishment. These inflated expressions, and the new and strict
orders she has issued to the officers and soldiers charged
with **the duty** of pursuing the Christians, have, however, I
am thankful to say, had no great result. Her majesty will
doubtless be enraged when she hears **that** the inhabitants
of whole villages have succeeded in escaping **from** her
vengeance by flight. Thus it happened, a few days ago, in
the village of Ambohitra-Biby, nine miles from Tananariva,
that when **the soldiers** arrived they **found nothing but the**
empty huts.

To-day at noon another great kabár was held in the market-place; the **queen** caused it to be announced that **all**
who helped the Christians in their flight, who did **not** stop
them, or sought to conceal them, should suffer the punishment of death; but that those, on the contrary, who brought
them in, or hindered them in their flight, would gain the
especial favor of the queen, and in future, if they committed
any offense, should either be pardoned or subjected to a
very mitigated punishment.

A corps **of** soldiers **one thousand five** hundred strong
was also dispatched to-day to a large district, situate on the
eastern coast. This extended region is inhabited by Seklaves, and is only partly subject to the sway of Queen Ranavola. In a village in the independent portion, five Catholic missionaries have been living for the last three or four
years, and have established a little congregation. The
queen is naturally much enraged at this, the more so as,
boasting that she was queen of the whole island, she issued

an edict some years ago to the effect **that all white** men
should be killed who landed in Madagascar, **or** made any
stay in a place where none of her Hova soldiers **are** station-
ed. In pursuance of this law, she intends to **have these**
missionaries captured and executed.

I hardly believe that the attachment of the Seklaves **to-**
ward the missionaries will be sufficiently strong to make
them **refuse** to surrender the latter, and expose themselves
to **a war** against such a powerful enemy as Queen Rana-
vola, and even **if** they risked it there would not be the
slightest prospect of a good result. Yet we cherish the
hope that before the troops can reach the spot the missionaries may have got off safely, for Prince Rakoto has some
time since sent a reliable messenger to them to warn them
of the impending danger.

Though Prince Rakoto is **to all intents and** purposes **a**
prisoner, and unable to visit us, **a** day seldom passes without our receiving news from him, and he informs **us of all**
the schemes of the queen and her ministers **against us.**
Like Mr. Laborde, the prince has confidential slaves. **These**
trusty servants on either side meet, apparently by chance,
in the bazar or elsewhere, and exchange intelligence. Thus
he let us know to-day that the queen had given orders to
have our house searched on the morrow, upon the pretext
that it was generally asserted **there** were Christians concealed therein, **but** in reality **to** obtain possession of our
papers and writings. Of course **we** immediately concealed
these **as well as** we could.

We have **also learned** that the queen has in the last few
days occupied herself much about us, and has held long
sittings with **her** ministers, in which the question of **our**
fate **was** discussed. If she had consulted only her **own**
fury, **she** would long ago have dispatched us into **the next**
world; but **to** kill six Europeans at once seems almost too
bold a stroke; and she is said to have told her prime min-

ister, who voted for our death from the first, that the only reason which deterred her from the measure was the probability that such severity against persons of our importance might induce the Europeans to wage war against her. Two fortunate mistakes for us! The first, in her considering us to be important personages; the second, that she should suppose the European powers would take so much trouble in a matter involving only a few human lives instead of more weighty interests. But, be this as it may, our lives are certainly in great peril, for they are in the hands of a woman so governed by her passions that she may at any moment cast aside all considerations of prudence or policy. Even if our lives are spared, I fear we shall undergo a long imprisonment; merely to banish us from the country will not satisfy the queen, or she would have done it long ago.

July 10. To-day our gates were suddenly opened, and about a dozen officers of high rank, with a large train, came into the court-yard. We thought they were coming to make the search of which the prince had warned us; but, to our great astonishment, they explained to Mr. Lambert that they had been sent by the queen to receive the costly presents which he had brought with him for her and her court.

Mr. Lambert at once had the chests brought out and unpacked; the contents were placed, according to their various destinations, in great baskets, which the slaves who accompanied the officers at once carried off to the palace. A few of the officers went away with the bearers; the others walked into our reception-room, conversed for a few moments with Mr. Laborde and Mr. Lambert, and then very politely took their leave.

This was the first opportunity I had had of examining the splendid presents Mr. Lambert had brought.

The dresses, of which he had provided a considerable number for the queen, her sisters, and other female relatives, were really very handsome. Mr. Lambert had pro-

cured them in Paris from the dress-maker of the Empress
of the French, and they were made according to the empress's own patterns. Some of these dresses had cost more
than three hundred dollars. To each were added the appropriate sash, ribbons, and head-dress—in a word, every
thing necessary to make the toilette complete.

Thus bedizened, the fortunate ladies for whom these
splendid garments are intended will doubtless look still
more ridiculous than those who took part in the costume
ball. I fancy I see them, with their clumsy figures and
duck-like walk, in these splendid low-necked dresses, with
long trains and short sleeves; and the delicate head-dresses
—how *piquant* and charming!—stuck at the back of their
woolly polls. Truly, if Mr. Lambert had made up his mind
thoroughly to expose the ugliness of the female world of
Madagascar, he could not have found any thing more suited
to his purpose than these handsome costumes.

Not less numerous and splendid were the presents brought
for Prince Rakoto. There were uniforms splendidly made,
and as elaborately ornamented with gold embroidery as
those of the Emperor of the French himself; private suits
of the most various fabrics, forms, and colors; embroidered
cambric shirts, pocket-handkerchiefs, shoes of all kinds, and
every conceivable article of the toilet. A great deal of admiration, and perhaps a little jealousy too, was excited
among the officers by a rich saddle-cloth, saddle, and bridle.
The good people could not admire it sufficiently; and in
the reception-room one of them asked me if in France the
emperor was the only man who had such a saddle, or if the
officers had them too. I was wicked enough to reply that
only the emperor used such a handsome saddle, but that,
when it became shabby, he gave it to one of his favorites,
and ordered a new one for himself. Perhaps my querist
may attach himself to the party of the prince in the hope
of gaining the confidence of his chief, and with it the re-
version of the saddle-cloth.

CHAPTER XVI.

JULY 11. Yesterday evening an old woman was denounced to the authorities as a Christian. She was seized immediately, and this morning—my pen almost refuses to record the cruel torture to which the unhappy creature was subjected—they dragged her to the market-place, and her backbone was sawn asunder.

But a thousand horrors like these will not move the powers of Europe to come to the rescue of this unhappy people. In one respect, civilized and uncivilized governments are strangely alike; both are swayed only by political considerations, and humanity does not enter into their calculations.

July 12. This morning, I am sorry to say, six Christians were seized in a hut at a village not far from the city. The soldiers had already searched the hut, and were ready to depart, when one of them heard a cough. A new search was at once begun, and in a great hole dug in the earth, and covered over with straw, the poor victims were discovered. What astonished me most in this episode was, that the other inhabitants of the village, who were not Christians, did not betray the concealed ones, although they must have had intelligence of the last kabar, threatening death to all who kept Christians concealed, favored their flight, or neglected to assist in their capture. I should not have thought so much generosity existed among this people. Unfortunately, it met **with** a bad reward. The **commanding** officer cared nothing for the magnanimity **of** the action; he kept strictly to his instructions, **and** caused **not only** the six Christians, but the whole population of the village—men, women, and children—to be bound and dragged to **the capital.**

I fear there will be horrible scenes of blood. The poor people may all be executed, for it will be presumed that they were aware of their neighbors' hiding-place. From the queen they have certainly no mercy to expect, for she has death-sentences carried out with the utmost rigor; indeed, no instance is known in which she has pardoned any one condemned to lose his life.

Prince Rakoto sent us word to-day that the queen intended giving a great banquet to Mr. Lambert, **to** which all the other Europeans would of course be invited. What is the meaning of this? For more than a week we have been treated like state prisoners, and now **all at once we are to** have this distinction! Are our prospects brightening, or is it a trap? I fear the latter.

We were no ways rejoiced at this news, for even if the invitation does not conceal some treacherous design, we have a drearily irksome ordeal to go through. The more the queen wishes to honor the guest whom she invites to a banquet, the more tremendous is the banquet placed before him, and the greater is the number of hours he is compelled to pass at table; for the duration of time is considered an element in the distinction. When Mr. Lambert came to Tananariva for the first time, the queen gave a banquet in honor of him. It consisted of several hundreds of dishes, materials for which had been collected from every part of the island. The rarest dainties (of course for Madagascar palates) were served up, including land- and water-beetles, the latter being considered particularly delicious; locusts, silk-worms, and other insects. The banquet lasted more than twenty-four hours, during the greater part of which period the assembled guests were employed in consuming the various dainties. Of course Mr. Lambert could not remain so long at table, and, with the queen's permission, rose from time to time; but he was obliged to remain present till all was over.

Even while we were on the best terms with the queen we had looked forward to such an invitation with great apprehension; how much more dismayed ought we not to feel under present circumstances, when this banquet may prove our death-meal! But, if the queen chooses to show us this honor, we must accept it, for if it has been settled that we are to die, we have no chance of escaping our fate.

July 13. This woman is said never to have been seen in such continued ill-humor, in such fits of rage, as she has exhibited for the last eight or ten days. That augurs ill for us, but is far more unfortunate for the poor Christians, whom she causes to be pursued with a more furious zeal than she has shown since her accession. Almost every day kabars are held in the bazars of the city and in those of the neighboring villages, in which the people are exhorted to denounce the Christians; and they are told the queen is certain that, all the misfortunes which have befallen the country are solely attributable to this sect, and that she shall not rest until the last Christian has been exterminated.

What an inestimable mercy was it for those poor persecuted people that the register of their names fell into the hands of Prince Rakoto, who destroyed it! had this not been the case, there would have been executions without number. It is now hoped that, in spite of the queen's rage, and of all her commands and exhortations, not more than perhaps forty or fifty victims will be sacrificed. Many of the great men of the kingdom and many of the royal officials are Christians in secret, and try to assist the escape of their brethren in every possible way. We have been assured that, of the two hundred Christians **who** were captured some **days** ago, and also **among the villagers** who were brought yesterday to the city **in a body, by far** the greater number have escaped.

July 16. We have just received intelligence **of a very** great kabar held yesterday in the queen's palace. **It lasted** six hours, and the discussion is reported to have been very stormy. This kabar concerned us Europeans, and the question of our fate was debated. According to the usual way of the **world**, nearly all **our** friends began to fall away from **us from** the moment when they saw **that** our cause was **lost**; and, in order to divert suspicion from themselves, the majority insisted more vehemently **on our** condemnation than even our enemies. That we deserved **to be** punished **with** death was soon unanimously resolved, but the method by which we were to be dispatched to **the next** world gave rise to much discussion and debate. Some **voted for a** public execution in the market-place, others for **a nocturnal attack** on our house, and others, again, for an invitation to **the** before-mentioned banquet, at which we were to be poisoned, or murdered at a given signal.

The queen was undecided between these various proposals, but would certainly have accepted one of them had **not** Prince Rakoto been our protecting spirit. He spoke **with the** greatest energy against the **sentence of** death, warned the queen not to let her anger lead her astray, and expressed his conviction that the European powers would certainly not allow the execution of six such important (?) persons as we were to pass unpunished. **The** prince is said never to have spoken with such **warmth** and energy to the queen as on this occasion.

We received all this intelligence partly, as I have **stated**, through confidential slaves of the prince, partly from the few friends who, contrary to expectation, have remained true to us.

July 17. Our captivity had already lasted thirteen long
days—for thirteen long days we had lived in the most trying suspense as to our impending fate, expecting every moment to hear some fatal news, and alarmed day and night
at every slight noise. It was a terrible time.

This morning I was sitting at my writing-table; I had
just put down my pen, and was thinking that, after the
last kabar, the queen must at least have come to some decision, when suddenly I heard an unusual stir in the court-
yard. I was hastily quitting my room, the windows of
which were in the opposite direction, to see what was the
matter, when Mr. Laborde came to meet me with the announcement that a great kabar was being held in the court-
yard, and that we Europeans were summoned to be present
thereat.

We went accordingly, and found more than a hundred
persons—judges, nobles, and officers—sitting in a large half
circle on benches and chairs, and some on the **ground**; behind them stood a number of soldiers. One of the **officers**
received us, and made us sit down opposite the judges.
These judges were shrouded in long simbus; their glances
rested gloomily and gravely upon us, and for a considerable
time **there** was deep silence. I confess to having felt some-
what alarmed, and whispered to Mr. Laborde, "I think our
last hour has come!" His reply was, "I am prepared for
every thing."

At length one of the ministers or judges rose, and in se-
pulchral tones, embellished with a multitude of high-sound-
ing epithets, he spoke somewhat to the following effect,
telling us:

"The people had heard that we were Republicans, and
that we had come to Madagascar with the intention of in-
troducing a similar form of government here; that we intended to overturn the throne **of** their beloved ruler, to give
the people equal rights with the nobility, and to abolish

slavery; also, that we had had several interviews with the Christians, a sect equally obnoxious to the queen and the people, and had exhorted them to hold fast to their faith, and to expect speedy succor. These treasonable proceedings," he continued, "had so greatly exasperated the natives against us, that the queen had been compelled to treat us as prisoners as a protection against the popular indignation. The whole population of Tananariva was clamoring for our death; but as the queen had never yet deprived a white person of life, she would abstain in this instance also, though the crimes we had committed could fully have justified her in such a course; in her magnanimity and mercy she had accordingly decided to limit our punishment to perpetual banishment from her territories.

"Mr. Lambert, Mr. Marius, the two other Europeans who lived at Mr. Laborde's, and myself, were accordingly to depart from the city within an hour. Mr. Laborde might remain twenty-four hours longer; and, in consideration of his former services, he was to be allowed to take away all his property that was not fixed, with the exception of his slaves. These, with his houses, estates, etc., were to revert to the queen, by whose bounty they had been bestowed on him. With regard to his son, inasmuch as the youth was a native by the mother's side, and might be supposed, on account of his tender years, to have taken no part in the conspiracy, it should be optional with him either to remain in the island or to quit it with us.

"The **queen would allow us,** and Mr. Laborde also, as many bearers as we required to carry us and our property, and, as a measure of precaution, she would cause us to be escorted by a company of soldiers, consisting of fifty **pri**vates, twenty officers, and a commandant. Mr. Laborde would have a similar escort, and was commanded to keep at least one day's journey in our rear."

In spite of our critical position, we could hardly refrain

M

from laughing at this oration. All at once the people were made out to be important—the poor people who were groaning in bondage like Russian serfs or the slaves of the United States; now all at once **we found the poor people** influencing the royal will, and invested with **the** right, not only of expressing a wish, but even of uttering threats! The orator, however, did not seem at all familiar with the word people, frequently substituting for it that of "queen," **by** mistake, **in the course** of his speech.

Of course we were **not allowed** to say a single word in **our own** defense or justification, nor, indeed, did we think of such a thing; for we were very glad to escape so easily, and could hardly understand this unexpected magnanimity **on her** majesty's part. Alas! we neither knew nor suspected **what** sufferings lay before us.

At the close of the kabar Mr. Lambert received back the presents which had been carried away a few days before; but not all of them, as we could see at the first glance. I fancy, however, that the missing articles had not **been detained** by the queen, but by the officers and grandees. Prince Rakoto kept nearly the whole of his share, sending **back** only a few trifles, as it seemed, in nominal acquiescence to the queen's wishes.

All the officers and nobles among whom Mr. Lambert had distributed presents were ordered to bring them back; but the considerable sums of money they had received from **the visitor, and of** which the queen knew nothing, remained in their **possession.**

Within an hour we were not only to get our baggage in order, and make the necessary preparations for our journey in the **way** of laying in provisions, but likewise to pack up all the valuable articles returned to Mr. Lambert. How to do this was the question. Most of the chests had been broken to pieces; for, after the queen had so solemnly fetched away the presents, who would have thought of their **being sent back?**

We were really in a very serious dilemma; but there was no help for it. So Mr. Lambert looked out the costliest articles in all haste, and we threw pell-mell into our traveling trunks whatever we could cram in, and pressed a few of the least battered of the chests into the service; thus in a few hours we were ready to start. Fortunately for us, the officers, soldiers, and bearers did not interpret the queen's commands so literally as we should have done. They set about their preparations deliberately enough, and the rest of the day passed without our seeing any thing more of them. We did not set out on our journey till the next morning; and this delay gave Mr. Lambert an opportunity of packing up many more of the returned presents.

July 18. With a truly heartfelt joy I turned my back upon a place where I had suffered so much, and in which I heard of nothing all day long but of poisonings and executions. This very morning, for example, a few hours before our departure, ten Christians were put to death, with the most frightful tortures. During their passage from the prison to the market-place, the soldiers continually thrust at them with their spears; and when they arrived at the place of execution, they were almost stoned to death before their tormentors mercifully cut off the victims' heads. I am told that the poor creatures behaved with great fortitude, and continued to sing hymns till they died.

On our way through the city we had to pass the market-place, and encountered this terrible spectacle as a parting scene. Involuntarily the thought arose within me that the magnanimity of so cruel and cunning a woman could not be greatly depended on, and that perhaps the people might have received secret orders to fall upon us and stone us to death. But such was not the case. The natives came flocking round in crowds to see us, and many even accompanied us a long distance from curiosity, but no one offered to molest or insult us in any way.

Our progress from the capital to Tamatavé was one of the most disagreeable and toilsome journeys I had ever made; never, in all my various wanderings, had I endured any thing like such suffering. The queen had not dared to have us publicly executed, but we soon discovered her object to be that we should perish on our journey from the capital. Mr. Lambert and I were suffering severely from fever. It was very dangerous for us to stay long in the low-lying lands, where we were inhaling deleterious gases, and highly important that we should travel to Tamatavé as quickly as possible, and embark without delay for the Mauritius, in quest of a better climate, proper nursing, and, above all, of medical assistance; for there is no physician to be found at Tananariva, or elsewhere in Madagascar, where every person doctors himself as best he can. But we were not allowed to proceed as we wished. The queen had issued her orders in a very different spirit; and, instead of accomplishing the journey in eight days, the time usually occupied, we were made to linger fifty-three days, nearly eight weeks, on the road. In the most pestiferous regions we were left in wretched huts for one or two weeks at a time; and frequently, when we suffered from violent attacks of fever, our escort dragged us from our miserable couches, and we had to continue our journey whether the day was fine or rainy.

At Befora, one of the most unhealthy places on the whole line of march—a squalid little village, so entirely surrounded by morasses that it was impossible to advance fifty paces on firm ground—we were detained eighteen entire days. Mr. Lambert endeavored by all conceivable means to induce the commandant to accelerate our progress, and even, I believe, offered him a considerable sum of money, but all his efforts were vain. The queen's orders had probably been so distinct and peremptory that the officer dared not evade them in any way.

The huts in which we were lodged were generally in such a wretched condition that they **scarcely** afforded shelter from the weather. Wind and rain came rushing in every direction through the broken roofs and the three half-decayed walls. To increase my sufferings, I had **not** even the necessary bedding; and my warm clothes, in which I might have wrapped myself at night, were stolen during our first day's march. I had not, like my companions, two or three servants, who could take care of my things; unfortunately, I was master and servant both in **one, and** in my weak state I found it impossible to attend to any thing. Whenever we came to our resting-places I threw myself on my couch, and was often unable to rise for days together. And what a couch it was! a thin mat, a hard pillow, with my traveling cloak for a coverlet. One of the missionaries afterward gave me one of his own pillows. During the whole fifty-three days I did not change my clothes once, for my most earnest entreaties **were powerless** to move the commandant to assign me a separate place where I might dress and undress. We were thrust all together into the same hut, however small it might be. My sufferings were beyond description during the last three weeks, when I was unable even to raise myself from my **bed** and totter a few paces.

Every illness is trying; but the Madagascar fever is, perhaps, **one** of the most malignant of all diseases, and in my opinion it is far more formidable than the yellow fever or the cholera. In the two last-named diseases the patient's sufferings are certainly more violent, but a few days decide the question of death or recovery, while, on the other hand, this horrible fever hangs about those it attacks month after month. Violent **pains** are felt in the lower parts of the body, frequent vomitings ensue, with total loss of appetite, and such weakness that the sufferer can hardly move hand or foot. At last a feeling of entire apathy supervenes, from which the sick person is unable to rouse himself by even the strongest exertion of his will. I, who had been accustomed from my earliest childhood to employment and activity, was now best pleased when I could lie stretched for days on my couch, sunk in a kind of trance, and wholly indifferent to what was going on around me. This apathy, moreover, is not peculiar to persons of my age when attacked by this illness, but is felt by the strongest men in the prime of life; and it continues to plague the patient, as do also the pains in the body, long after the fever itself has left him.

In the village of Eranomaro we met a French physician from the island of Bourbon who had made an agreement with the queen and some of the nobles to come to Tananariva for a few months every two years, bringing with him some necessary medicaments. Mr. Lambert and I wished to consult this gentleman on the subject of our fever, and to procure some medicine from him. I specially stood in need of his help, for I was in far worse health than Mr. Lambert, who only had attacks of fever once a fortnight, while in my case they recurred every third or fourth day. The commandant refused to allow us to go and see the physician, or to request him to visit us, declaring that he had been imperatively commanded by the queen herself not to let us hold communication with any one on our way, and least of all with a European. This strictness, as we afterward learned, was confined to ourselves, and was purposely intended to cut us off from any assistance. Mr. Laborde, who traveled a few days' journey in the rear of our party, was much more leniently treated, and was allowed, on meeting the physician, to spend a whole evening in his company.

Though the journey from Tananariva to Tamatavé lasted long enough in all conscience, I had scant opportunity of seeing any thing of the manners and customs of the people,

being hampered as much by my illness as by the strict sur-
veillance under which we were placed. What cursory observations I could make showed me that the natives possess
some very bad qualities. They are excessively idle, very
frequently intoxicate themselves, chatter continually, and
seem to be entirely destitute of natural modesty.

Thus our soldiers, who received neither provisions nor
pay, and who often suffered the greatest privations, would,
I think, have died of hunger rather than endeavor to earn
any thing by any slight service. At first I pitied the poor
fellows, and bought rice and sweet potatoes for them now
and then, or made them a little present of money. When
we came to the forest region, where beautiful insects and
snails were to be found in abundance, I requested the men
to procure me some specimens, offering to pay for them in
rice or money. My promises were unheeded; not one of
these people could I induce to comply. They would rather
crouch in any corner and suffer hunger than subject themselves to the least exertion. This was not only the case
among the soldiers; the natives generally—men, women,
and children—were all alike lazy. During my first stay
at Tamatavé, before visiting the capital, I had wished to take
three or four persons into monthly pay, and send them out
into the woods to collect specimens of insects, and offered
four times the wages they usually receive, promising a farther reward whenever they brought me any thing really
fine; but not a soul responded to my appeal. Just as vainly did I display to the women and children my store of
handsome large glass beads, rings, bracelets, and similar
treasures. They were delighted with the articles, and would
have been glad to possess them, but only if I would give
them away unconditionally. Never have I met with such
thoroughly indolent people. In nearly every country I
visited during my travels, and even among the quite uncivilized inhabitants of Borneo and Sumatra, the natives

often helped me, of their own accord, when they saw me searching for shells and insects, or snails; and if I rewarded them with a trifling gift, they brought me more than I could carry away. I thus often made valuable collections; and here, in this unexplored country, where there must be an abundance of insect life, I unfortunately found it impossible to obtain any thing like a respectable show. The few specimens I possess I have been obliged, almost without exception, to collect for myself.

Drunkenness prevails throughout every district of Madagascar, with the exception of the Emir territory, where some of the severe laws of Dianampoiene, the founder of the Malagasey monarchy, are still observed; among which there is one prohibiting the sale of ardent spirits, under pain of death, and commanding the summary execution of every drunkard. In this last-named district the people seem much more steady, orderly, and respectable than in the others, where intemperance goes unpunished. The favorite drink of the natives is the before-mentioned *besa-besa*, prepared from the juice of the sugar-cane. In almost every village drunkards of both sexes are seen reeling about even in the daytime; and late at night we often heard music and singing, loud voices and laughter, and not unfrequently quarreling and fighting.

Judged by this apparently continual state of hilarity, the people here would seem to be the happiest on earth; but the condition of the poor creatures is that of slaves and bondmen, and, like true serfs, they seek in the pleasures of intoxication forgetfulness of their bondage and misery.

Greatly as the Hovas and Malagaseys are addicted to drink, they are, I think, still more fond of chattering. They seem unable to hold their peace for two minutes together; and instead of saying their say quietly and peaceably, they talk with such haste and eagerness, that it would seem they thought the day too short for the interchange of their ideas.

Those who are not speaking keep up an almost continual laugh, so that I often asked to be informed of the subject of their conversation, thinking that something very witty and amusing was going on. But every time I was assured that I was mistaken; their talking was of the most trivial and sometimes of the most untranslatable kind, and they repeated the same things a dozen times within the hour.

An instance of the peculiar garrulousness of these people came under my own notice. Once, at Tananariva, I sent a messenger upon some errand, and noticed that he immediately sought for a companion. On my announcing that I would pay one messenger, but not two, my Mercury assured me I need not give his comrade any thing, but added that he could not think of accomplishing his journey on a long and solitary road without having some one to converse with, and that he should therefore give his companion a share of the fee.

Our bearers were no exception to the general rule. They chattered and laughed without a moment's pause, so that my poor sick head sometimes fairly reeled. At first I fondly fancied, when we came to a steep hill, that the exertion would make them pause. Vain hope! they panted and groaned, but they never left off talking.

I have spoken of the impudence and shamelessness of these people; but my pen refuses to record the scenes I witnessed on this doleful journey. We were looked upon as state prisoners, and accordingly treated with less respect and consideration than we had received during our progress to the capital; and the natives who escorted us showed themselves without disguise in all their natural viciousness. Frequently I did not know which way to look; and my companions often pronounced me fortunate in my ignorance of the native language.

At length, on the 12th of September, we arrived at Tamatavé; and we two fever-patients, Mr. Lambert and I, had

M 2

274 IDA PFEIFFER'S LAST TRAVELS.

not done **Queen** Ranavola **the favor of** dying, after all. It **was** really almost a miracle that we escaped with **our** lives, and I, for my part, **never** expected **that my weak,** exhausted frame could have endured the compulsory long **delays** in unwholesome regions, the cruel usage, and **the continual** succession of various hardships to which we had **been subjected.**

Neither Mr. Lambert nor I could obtain permission **to stay in Mademoiselle Julie's house.** We were taken to a **little hut, and** were there **guarded** with the same strictness **that had** been exhibited **on the whole route.** The commander of the escort announced **to us that we were to** quit **the** island by **the first** ship **that sailed for the** Mauritius, **and** that he had **received** orders to prevent us from holding communication **with** any person **in Tamatavé, and to** accompany **us** with **his** soldiers till **we had fairly** embarked.

I must say for the commandant and his officers that they fulfilled to the **very** letter the orders **the queen** had **given** them; **and if her majesty of** Madagascar should ever **think** of establishing an order **of** knighthood, as she may prob**ably some day do,** they **deserve** to be Grand Crosses, every one.

Queen Ranavola will **probably take another** view of the **case,** and these zealous **servants will,** I fancy, be very un**graciously** received when they return with **the** unwelcome **news that Mr.** Lambert and I have quitted Madagascar alive. I am sorry **for** her disappointment, but am selfish enough **to** think it is better that it has happened so, after **all.**

We were fortunate enough to be **detained** only **three** days at Tamatavé. On the 16th of **September a** ship was ready to sail **for the** Mauritius, and **we** were then obliged **to** tear ourselves from **our** amiable escort and this hospitable country. I shed no parting tear on the occasion—my heart felt light as I stepped on board; and it was with in-

tense satisfaction that I saw the boat **containing the** commandant and his men paddling **back to the shore.** Nevertheless, I do not regret having undertaken this journey,
and shall do so the less if I am fortunate enough to regain
my health.

In Madagascar **I saw** and heard more marvelous **things**
than had come under my notice in any other country; **and**
if little can be said to the advantage of the people, it **must**
be remembered that, under the cruel, insensate rule of Queen
Ranavola, and in the entire absence of instruction in religion
and morality, no great expectations can reasonably be form-
ed. If Madagascar should once obtain a well-ordered, civil-
ized government, and should be visited by missionaries who,
instead of busying themselves with political intrigues, would
devote **their** energies to imparting the Christian religion, in
its true sense, to the people, a happy and flourishing kingdom may be founded in this beautiful **land**: the materials
of prosperity are certainly not wanting.

Of our return journey to the Mauritius I have little **to**
tell. Our vessel, the brig "Castro," Captain Schneider, **was**
about as slow a sailer as the *quondam* man-of-war which
had borne us from the Mauritius to Tamatavé about five
months ago; and as the wind was not very favorable to us,
six days were consumed in the passage; but, in the enjoy-
ment of our newly-attained freedom, they fled blithely
away.

At nine o'clock in the evening of the 22d of September
we arrived in the Mauritian waters, when an accident of a
highly dangerous character occurred, which might have cost
us all our lives, to the great satisfaction, no doubt, in such
an event, of Queen Ranavola. The night being dark **and**
cloudy, the captain determined to cast anchor, and to have
the ship taken into harbor next morning by a steam-tug.
Every preparation had been made, and they were just
about to let go the anchor, when the rudder struck with

such violence against a rock that it was shattered into atoms. The crash of the broken beams and planks was so great that it seemed as though the whole vessel were going to pieces. I was already in bed, and started up in alarm to see what could be the matter, when I heard the shout of the second officer, "Come up this moment, Madame Pfeiffer, if you want to be saved; the ship is broken in two, and sinking."

I threw my cloak round me and hurried on deck. The kind officer, Mr. St. Ange, helped me into one of the boats, and told me to sit still, and I should be quite safe. On a closer inspection, it happily turned out that the ship had not even sprung a leak, and that the whole damage was limited to the loss of the rudder and the fright we had endured.

The anchors were lowered, and we went quietly to bed. Next morning the bright sunshine woke us, signals were hoisted, and a steam-tug came puffing out to tow us into the welcome harbor of the Mauritius.

My friends here were very much surprised to see me again. It appeared that the most exaggerated reports had been received from Tamatavé of the unfortunate issue of our undertaking. Some people gave out that Queen Ranavola had caused all the Europeans in Tananariva to be executed; others declared that the sentence of death had only been carried out on Mr. Lambert, and that the rest, including myself, had been sold as slaves; while another party maintained that we had been banished from the country, and murdered on the journey by command of the queen.

I was happily enabled to give a very practical denial to these reports; but the danger was not yet quite past. A few days after my arrival, the moral and physical sufferings I had undergone, added to the peculiar effects of the fever, brought on such a severe illness that the doctors were long doubtful about my recovery, and I should certainly have died but for the kind and active sympathy of the Moon family.

Mr. Moon, a medical man and apothecary, lives in a very retired manner, with his amiable wife, on a sugar-plantation in Vacoa. I had, my readers will remember, spent a few very happy days with this family before my departure for Madagascar. As soon as Mr. Moon heard that I had returned from my journey, and was very ill, he came to the capital to take me to his house, where I arrived almost in a dying state. To his, and to Dr. A. Perrot's scientific skill, and to the unceasing care bestowed upon me in his house, I have to ascribe my recovery; and it chanced that exactly on my sixtieth birthday, the 9th of October, 1860, I was pronounced out of danger.

May God reward Dr. Moon and his wife, and Dr. Perrot, for all they did for me, a total stranger as I was to them!

Here the diary of Madame Ida Pfeiffer ends. Unhappily, the hopes expressed in its last lines were delusive. The danger was not past; and though the attacks of the fever left her for longer or shorter periods, they always returned, and she never entirely recovered her health and strength. Her stay in the Mauritius was prolonged through several months; and the letters written by her during this period to her sons show that she had made various plans for new voyages, none of which were destined to be carried into effect.

Thus, in a letter dated the 16th of December, 1857, she wrote:

"My sufferings from fever, and especially from its effects, have been great, and are not yet quite past; but I hope that a sea-voyage will completely set me up. I can not go to Europe at this season of the year. I should have to contend against cold and bad weather, and am not sure if I could do so in my present state of health. To wait here for better weather would not do, as the air of this island does not agree with me, so I shall probably proceed to Australia."

In another letter, of the 13th of January, she says:

"I hope this is the last letter I shall date from the Mauritius. I shall really be very glad to bid farewell to this island; but the parting from the Moon and Kerr families will be very, very bitter. If these excellent people had not taken care of me as they did, I should certainly have perished here. No daughter could tend her mother with greater solicitude than Mrs. Moon evinced toward me; and, indeed, all the members of both families have vied with each other in doing me all kinds of service. My dear sons, store up these names in your memory; and if chance should ever bring you together with any one belonging to either of these households, look upon them as brothers, and esteem yourselves happy if you can do any thing for them.

"For the last three weeks my health has been improving day by day; the fever seems at last about to quit me entirely; I can sleep now, and my appetite is returning.

"A few days ago I made the acquaintance of a young German botanist here, Mr. Herbst. He resides at Rio de Janeiro, and has been sent by the Brazilian government to the Mauritius and the Ile de Bourbon to collect sugar-cane plants, to improve the species cultivated in the Brazils. He is to take a whole cargo home with him, and hopes to arrive in Rio de Janeiro in May. I almost intended to accompany him; but, as I do not know if you will be there at that date, it will perhaps be better to make the voyage to Australia first. I have met with a very good opportunity of going to Sydney, and shall start in a few days; the sea-voyage, and the bracing air in Australia, where I shall arrive at the best season of the year, late in autumn, will, I hope, set the seal on my recovery, and entirely re-establish my health."

Only two days later, in a letter dated the 1st of March, she thus wrote:

"I was compelled suddenly to give up my project on account of the detestable Madagascar fever, which persists in returning, and weakens me very much. I was ready to embark for Australia, and had sent the greater part of my effects on board, when I was seized with a fresh attack. I had my chest landed from the ship, and intend to start on the 8th with the packet for London, where I shall, however, only stay a short time, for it is my wish to get to my own home as fast as possible."

At length she quitted the Mauritius. During the tedious passage she experienced no attack of fever, and at the beginning of the month of June arrived in London, where she, however, only remained a few weeks. From London she betook herself to Hamburg; but there, too, she could not find rest; and in the month of July she went to Berlin, on the invitation of her friend, the wife of Privy Councilor Weisz, in whose house she was nursed with the tenderest care.

Her brothers sent urgent letters, begging her to come home to her native Vienna, and Madame Maria Reyer, the wife of her brother, Cæsar Reyer, wished to proceed to Berlin for the express purpose of fetching her. But she positively declined this proposal. Although her strength was waning from day to day, she seems to have considered her illness as only temporary, and in this belief she wrote to her brother, expressing a hope that she should soon recover, or at least be in a better condition for traveling, and promised them to come to Vienna.

Still she seemed to yearn secretly for home; and when week after week elapsed without bringing any improvement in her health, she had herself conveyed to the residence of a friend, Baroness Stem, who lived on an estate in the neighborhood of Cracow.

Her illness unhappily increased, and at last, abandoning the hope of a speedy recovery, she consented to be removed to Vienna. Her sister-in-law came for her; and sad indeed was the meeting with her affectionate friend and relative, who found her in such a weak condition as to despair of the possibility of proceeding to Vienna. But as the physician declared that she might undertake the journey, and the sick lady herself showed the greatest anxiety to behold her home once more, she was taken with the greatest care, in a separate railway carriage, to Vienna, to the house of her brother, Charles Reyer, where she arrived in September.

Here several medical consultations were held upon her case, to which her brother summoned the most distinguished physicians of the capital. One and all pronounced that she was suffering from cancer in the liver—a consequence probably of the Madagascar fever; that the disease had deranged and was destroying the internal organs, and that her malady was incurable.

Her native air seemed to do her good; for a few weeks she suffered but little pain, and new hope awoke within her; she even spoke of undertaking short journeys, and visiting her friends in Grätz, Trieste, and other places. But this restlessness was probably only a symptom of her disease, for her strength gave way more and more; violent pains came on, which continued almost without intermission during the last four weeks of her life, and frequently she sank into delirium.

She was most affectionately tended and nursed in her brother's house, under the especial supervision of her sister-in-law, whose affection for her was so great as to keep her continually by the sufferer's bedside; and a few days before her death she had the happiness to embrace her eldest son, who lived in Steyermark, and hastened to Vienna upon the first intelligence of his mother's serious illness.

During the last days of her life opiates were administered to lessen her sufferings, and in the night between the 27th and 28th of October she expired peacefully, and apparently without pain.

Her funeral took place on the 30th of the same month. Besides a very numerous gathering of relations and personal friends, many scientific notabilities and other distinguished inhabitants of Vienna followed her to the grave. Peace be to her ashes!

Let me be permitted herewith to offer my warmest, my most heartfelt thanks to you, dear Aunt Maria Reyer, and to you, dear Uncle Charles Reyer, for all you did for my mother. Unhappily, I was not privileged to hear her last words or to receive her parting glance, for I was far away when the sad news was brought me. Through you both, I at least enjoy the consolation of knowing that my poor mother had every care and attention shown to her, and that she heard friendly and beloved voices around her bed to the last.

To our other relations, and the numerous friends who showed her such true, such delicate kindness, and particularly to Mr. and Mrs. Moon, in the Mauritius, I return my most hearty thanks. Let them be assured that their names will ever live in my memory with the remembrance of my beloved mother.

OSCAR PFEIFFER.

THE END.